Finding Los Angeles
by Foot

The author may be contacted at **LAStairways@pacbell.net** and welcomes comments, additions and corrections.

All photographs by the author unless noted otherwise.
Some material in this book has appeared in
A Guide to the Public Stairways of Los Angeles by Bob Inman
Published through Blurb Books, 2008, 2010

Safety notice: The author has made every attempt to ensure that the information in this book is accurate as of date of publication. He is not responsible of any loss, damage, injury, or inconvenience that may occur to anyone while using this book. You are responsible for your own safety and health while conducting yourself at any location or on any walk described in this book. You should always check local conditions, know your own limitations and be aware of your surroundings. You should use the maps and descriptions in this book in conjunction with information you gain independently from maps and mapping devices.

ISBN 0-9797955-4-0

Finding
Los Angeles
by Foot

Stairstreet, bridge, pathway and lane

By

Bob Inman

CONTENTS

CONTENTS

This book is about locating and enjoying the pedestrian assets of Los Angeles: the stairways, paths, walk streets, foot bridges and tunnels and the most walkable streets that they connect.

This book is about finding what is notable, historical, quizzical and beautiful in this great city while walking.

This book is about making the world's 13th most populous metropolitan area seem smaller and more approachable on foot. It is about perforating the barriers within communities that the car culture creates. Use of this book should assist a foot traveler find bridges between neighborhoods while promoting an understanding of what makes those neighborhoods unique.

People DO walk in LA for both their everyday needs and for exercise and pleasure. This book describes how contemporary pedestrianism is a pastime with social value and how it is enthusiastically pursued individually and in groups. An idea of a local hike once meant a trip to the mountains. This book describes local "hikes" on the lanes, stairstreets and pathways within the city itself.

In 2008 I published "The Guide to the Public Stairways of Los Angeles" and expected it to be filed away as a preservation resource. Instead it's become a user tool for an audience that I had not known was there. The goal of this book is further illustrate the stairways and other walking resources and to suggest journeys by foot that are great city experiences.

In the past 4 years I have joined many community walks and led hundreds of participants on 7 dozen walks of my own. This book is the product of what I have learned preparing for those enthusiasts and what they have taught me.

Bob Inman
Eagle Rock 2013

Sunnynook Bridge - Atwater Village   Carl Encke photo

Walkability is a term that has come into use in the past half-decade as a measurement of how pedestrian friendly a city, a neighborhood or a specific address is. One definition (from the Victoria Transport Policy Institute) is "Walkability reflects overall walking conditions in an area. Walkability takes into account the quality of pedestrian facilities, roadway conditions, land use patterns, community support, security and comfort for walking." A popular website, walkscore.com, operates under the slogan, "Drive less, live more" and computes a grade for each city, for each neighborhood and, when asked, for any location. They use an algorithm that measures how far an address to be graded is from various amenities like shops, transit stops, and restaurants. Smaller blocks and more narrow streets contribute to a higher score. Los Angeles scored 15th of the 50 largest US cities. Downtown earned the highest neighborhood grade in LA. It has bee shown that property values benefit from high walkability. Walkability is relevant to this book because these maps and guides provide a more accurate "boots on the ground" evaluation of where you can actually walk and how that can shorten the distance to the amenities that add up to create a walkscore. A website like Walkscore is going to have to rely on a lot of blind digital content that may not truly calculate the shortest walking distance between two points or how amenable the digitally selected amenities really are.

Two signs observed in Cornwall, England that portray the type of walking routes in Los Angeles that this book describes.

Using the maps in this book

The 29 neighborhood maps define the "chapters" of the book. The maps are custom drawn to illustrate the walkable assets of the LA area. This means that the maps are subjective. The city of Los Angeles is 470 square miles; only 80 square miles of that is mapped in this book. Parts of the city with no network of stairstreets and other pedestrian zones are not covered, including much of the city's vast flatlands. One such part of the city that has been woefully disregarded by my coverage is the San Fernando Valley. The valley has no public stairways but miles of trails, numerous pedestrian bridges and a beautiful soft bottom stretch of the LA River. All of that lies outside of the scope of this book. That also applies to much of the Westside: from Cheviot Hills to Brentwood, from Beverly Crest to South Carthay. As well appointed as these areas may be, they do not possess the network of stairways and paths to gain a section in this book. The information on the maps is also selective: automotive "no-go" zones are emphasized while many streets are not shown. Curious motorists trying to find listings in this book by car may encounter impediments.

Stairways or stairstreets: These represent a high point of pedestrian accommodation and have become the darlings of much civic enthusiasm. They are illustrated on the maps showing the uphill direction and those that have been gated. They are indexed on the facing page with the address at each end, a description, the step count and a "grade" A-C.

Stairway definitions and the idea of a list. I define public stairways as being extensions of city streets. I exclude "park" stairs and dead-end stairs from "the list". I have marked some "non-qualifying" stairways on the maps with a question mark because they are too obvious or well-used for me to pretend that they are not there. This book strives to list comprehensively each public stairway that we are aware of at the time of publication for all of Los Angeles and the communities it borders. A complete list addresses the desire by many to "walk them all", perhaps even on the same extended excursion. It also helps relate our city with other cities and their stairways. "PublicStairs.com" (facebook: Friends of Public Stairs) serves as a national clearing house to inventory the stairways of America's cities and towns. Putting a filter on the subject, Public Stairs limits consideration to stairs of 100 steps or more. A 10 step minimum applies here. This book is not a legal document but I believe that all the "public access stairways" indexed are truly public property.

"Walk streets" and elevated sidewalks: Mapped are the walk streets of Venice and many dedicated pedestrian-ways

Pedestrian overpasses and subways: These are foot-portals that reconnect highway-severed areas and are illustrated and listed. Those underpasses that are adjacent to schools and open specific to school hours are not in the listings. I regard those as the province of the students.

Bridges, ghost railways and waterways, murals, parks, historic and cultural attractions: Each "chapter" pinpoints and describes many aspects of the city that may not be a traditional Michelin/AAA type destination. These are facets of the city's character that can be particularly appreciated at walk speed and pedestrian scale.

Notable architecture in homes, commercial buildings and churches: Walking the city is a fabulous means to discover the distinctive and/or significant works of architecture that add to or affect our urban experience. Dozens of these sites are listed in this book indicating the general or specific location. In almost all cases, the intention is to direct the walker's eyes and mind towards them for appreciation before he or she keeps walking. Unless this book discusses visiting information, the reader MUST understand that these are mostly private locations where the walker is not to intrude. Do not bother the occupants. Some rare cases a resident of a significant home will appreciate that they are being appreciated but you may not presume that will be the case. When entry into a commercial building or place of worship is permissible, please be discreet. Hushed voices, non-use or limited use of cameras, silenced phones, removal of packs and sometimes even shoes: all of these will help create a satisfactory visit and help insure that future walkers can visit just as you have done.

Footpaths and undeveloped roads: The foot paths mapped in this guide are selected if they fit in the network of means to link streets and fuse neighborhoods. There is a wealth of literature available about hiking the trails of the parks within and around our city. This book is interested in the paths that join the populated parts of the city to itself within parks, along undeveloped "paper streets" and in seams between lots. My hand drawn maps lack the precision of a topo map and locations and lengths are provided as accurately as is possible. Many roads and paths outside of parks or unmarked with trail signs might be undeveloped private property; access is not guaranteed. I avoid listing those paths characterized as "slip through a hole in the fence, hang on to tree roots and slide down on your rear end" although those exist. My listings are easily walkable trails that are popularly used.

Sometimes the best idea is to just get out and walk!

Creating your own walk: I hope that illustrations of pedestrian shortcuts and the tips about what to appreciate will be just enough to inspire a reader to make their own personal route. *The Gentle Art of Wandering* by David Ryan (2012-New Mountain Books) suggests how much a walker can discover on his or her own by being curious, by being comfortable with where they are and by allowing themselves to become connected to their surroundings. That is guidance this book aims to give. Pick out an approximate route that you want to follow and fine tune it with selections as you go.

Why even draw these maps?

The usefulness of this book would be limited if complete, accurate up-to date information on the pedestrian assets was already available on smartphones, guidebooks and internet maps. What is offered on these pages is a walker's atlas based mainly on "boots on the ground" verification with additional detail combed from many sources.

If you use your I-phone with a map program like Google you will get visibility of one-third of the public stairways indexed in this book. For the most part, they would be displayed as an unnamed channel by two parallel lines. If you ask Google to select the shortest walking route for you, it often succeeds in selecting a stairway or pedway but only IF it knows it is there.

Walk #	Walk	Page	miles	elevation gain
1	Allesandro Valley Fellowship park loop	44	4.5	++
2	Big Parade Echo Park loop	50	5.3	++
3	South of Sunset to Westlake	65	12	+
4	Tomato Pie: Franklin Hills circuit	73	2.9	++
5	Glassell Park-Atwater Village-LA River	87	8.7	+
6	Mount Washington west	95	7.6	+++
7	Mount Washington east	102	7.8	+++
8	Highland Park, York Valley, Hermon	117	8.4	++
9	South Pasadena to Arroyo Terrace	131	6.2	+
10	South Pasadena to Montecito Heights	141	9.5	+
11	Lincoln Park - El Sereno	150	10.4	+++
12	Arts District - Boyle Heights	158	9.7	+
13	Chinatown, Elysian, Frogtown,Cypress Pk	170	10.5	++
14	Little Tokyo to Watts Towers	176	12.2	none
15	Los Feliz, Observatory to Franklin Village	187	6.7	+++
16	Hollywood&Vine to Beachwood Canyon	195	7.1	+
17	Whitley Heights and Hollywood Heights	204	5.2	+
18	Santa Monica Rustic Canyon	215	8.5	+
19	Venice and Mar Vista west	223	8.25	+
20	Culver City, Baldwin Hills	233	5.5	+
21	Palos Verdes - Malaga Cove	242	4.4	+
22	Palos Verdes - Lunada Bay-Wallace Ranch	244	11.5	+++
23	San Pedro	252	11.4	+

elevation gain:

+ : *less than 800 feet of ascent*

++: *800 to 1200 feet ascent*

+++: *more than 1200 feet of ascent*

All the walks in this book are designed from a culture that believes retracing your steps is very poor form. Of the 186 miles on these walks, there is but 2 miles total backtracking.

Walking the walks in this book

Described in this book are 23 neighborhood walks. Each of these routes is among the LA walks that I have designed through trial and error and led during the past four years.

What "style" of walks are these? My walks aim to be a hybrid. Start with an energetic 4 to 12 mile up and down effort along paved lanes, public stairways, pathways, walk streets, pedestrian bridges and tunnels. Season that route with interesting historic, social and artistic background material. I'd like to think they come to some happy medium of the level of effort of a Sierra Club hike with the cultural exposure of an LA Conservancy shuffle around the block. These typically are three to seven hour excursions in one or several neighborhoods. These are longer than the walks you find in the excellent books by Erin Mahoney-Harris or Charles Fleming. Two to three mile walks are what many prefer; included here are treks for those who want something a tad longer.

About the walk descriptions: I provide turn by turn directions but, compared to the authors just mentioned, my narrative descriptions are sparse. The neighborhood's notes are written and maps drawn to try to suggest many walks, not just the single route that I picked to describe. So, when following my walk, typically you need to read the "turn by turn" page and also flip back a couple of pages in the guide book to read the descriptive content and follow the route along the chapter map. Each walk is written to help enjoy that particular "chapter" but many of the walks bridge into an adjoining chapter. The walk descriptions will advise which page number contains the map, stairway description or background info for where you are at.

A primer for the urban hiker in Los Angeles

How did the conversation turn from walks to urban hikes?

This guide describes 17 walks longer than 6 miles or 10km. The idea of this book is to suggest the pedestrian means and points of interest to keep a walker out all day or perhaps all week! Single day 1000-3000' elevation gains are very possible. "Hiking" is an appropriate term, even in the city. It is the point of view here that transporting yourself to set out on a foot adventure on Mt. Washington (LA) will fall in the same broad category as one on Mt. Wilson or Mt. Whitney.

Doesn't "hiking" mean that you are on a trail out in nature?

Our pedestrian stairways, bridges, urban trails and the sometimes very hilly lanes that connect them take the form of trails. A short drive or transit journey to a kick off spot in an LA neighborhood will maximize the time you have available for your adventure and be more "green" than a long drive to a distant trailhead. Yes, nature will all be in an adapted state but enjoyment of the trees, gardens, birdlife in their eco-structure will be a key benefit of your urban hike.

Is Los Angeles urban hiking safe?

Safe from "bad people"? The more interesting areas to walk are the older parts of the city. That often equates to poorer neighborhoods and unfortunate presumptions about crime. I am comfortable walking alone or with friends in daylight in any of the areas this book describes and in nighttime in most. This is an urban environment with sore spots as well as treasures and users of this book are advised to always be aware of their surroundings and to think about their safety.

Safe from bad drivers? I walk with greater concern for the car that will roll through a stop sign without looking; for drivers too distracted by the street layout or their devices – care needs to be taken.

Safe from what is underfoot? An LA urban hiker particularly needs to be careful walking on uneven surfaces; that ultimately will be the cause of the most personal injuries.

Carl Encke photo

Is solitude and peace available on an urban hike?
No, it is not like the woods or a mountain ridgeline but you might be surprised at how often you have the streets, trails and stairways to yourself when walking and how long you can walk in the hills without encountering a traffic signal.

How should you equip yourself for an LA urban hike?
"Proper footwear" is a loaded topic that would incite pages of comment. We even see the occasional barefoot walker in our groups. Consider though that a long day on hard pavement is very different than soft trails and we see expert traditional trail walkers who lean to heavier, not lighter, shoes when hitting the stairways. **Water** is of course key and it is essential to carry water and stay hydrated in our arid climate. Finding water refills when deep in the residential hills and canyons needs to be anticipated in advance. Similarly, the availability of bathrooms becomes a major consideration. Park facilities have become notoriously unreliable in these tight budget times. Don't be shy about using an available construction toilet. "Andy Gump" can save a day – carry hand sanitizer.
Sun protection is another big deal; sunscreen, big brim hats, perhaps even umbrellas should be on the checklist. **Light gloves** can save your hands if you rely on stairway handrails.
Trekking poles? – don't laugh. If you've used to them on dirt trails, you might miss them on a street with 32% grade.
Backpacks, bivy sacks, sleeping pads? Read about "The 300" and endeavors like that of Liz Thomas at the end of this book.

A more pedestrian friendly city?

There is something of a walking revolution in LA. Dozens turn out for a half dozen monthly walking events promoted independent of each other through social media and blogs. Dan Koeppel's Big Parade returned for its 5th annual rendition in May 2013 leading 400+ walkers through the stairways between downtown and Griffith Park. Dan leads another ten "epic" or theme walks throughout the year. Michael Schneider's Great Los Angeles Walk is 8 years in, gathering a few hundred people to walk from LA's central core to the ocean before Thanksgiving. Charles Fleming's *Secret Stairs* has been a huge success since its 2010 release and enthusiasts can be found around the stairs clutching the familiar green/gold paperback. Dave Ptach's LA Stairstreet Advocates hosts the "Tomato Pie" walk every Tuesday night in Franklin Hills to rigorously tackle that set of stairs and the pizza afterwards. "Meet up" groups often adopt urban walks as their focus activity. Additions to the LA scene like CicLAvia, Ballona Creek and the LA River bike paths, though designed for bike riders, have a walking component. Broadcast and social media both are loaded with features about how cool it is to walk to get to know our city.

A population who once always gave thumbs up to motorist related proposals like "smart streets", crosswalk elimination and street widening now rumbles with a backdraft of challenge asking how these modifications are going to impact those on foot. An organization called Los Angeles Walks has had meetings around town to discuss taking back the streets from motorist mania. These aren't blue hairs waving their AARP cards; they might be 20-30 something professionals that chose foot travel and public transit as the way to go. They discuss both cultivating an urban walking culture as well as the enforcement and expansion of laws that would give walkers more satisfactory use of their streets.

"WalkLAvia": Los Angeles Walks group joins in with CicLAvia - April 2013

LA hired their first two pedestrian coordinators in 2012. The city cited a focus on pedestrian safety and the walking experience in a job announcement that stated, "Walking is a critical component of a world-class transportation system we envision for Los Angeles..." The challenges are large. A recent study showed that pedestrian deaths amounted to a third of LA's traffic fatalities, three times the national average. The city calculated in 2012 that they might be looking at $1.5 billion of sidewalk repairs, and then suggested spending $10 million on a three year survey to learn how bad the situation is. Walking in Los Angeles just has a hard time being taken seriously although a 2009 survey of urban planners figured that 17% of all Los Angeles County trips are done on foot! It is hard to get out from under the old "Nobody walks in LA" punch line. Any media frame of reference on the Los Angeles stairways has been packaged for a laugh. We've seen the stairs as a comic venue for Laurel and Hardy's struggle to move a piano, for The 3 Stooges sledding them on ice blocks in "An Ache in Every Stake", as a path for cow out of the Tyrolean Alps in "Echo Park" and as a commuter shortcut in "LA Story". When I see a believable TV or movie character simply walk up or down a Los Angeles stairway for exercise or enjoyment I will know that reality is perhaps sinking in; the stairways are a commonplace conveyance that people use.

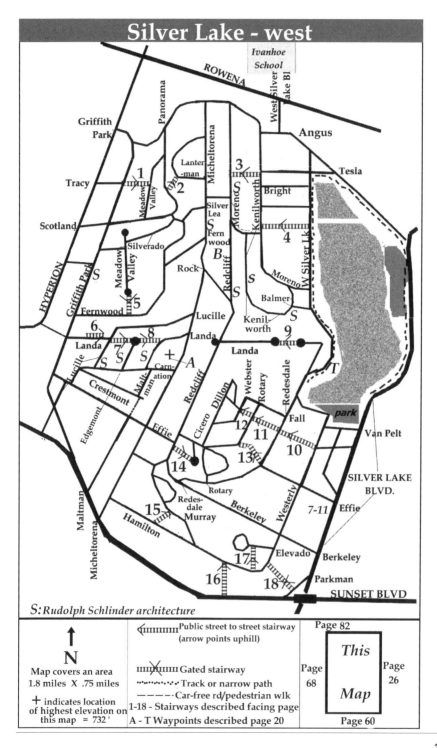

Silver Lake - west

Ivanhoe School

ROWENA

West Silver Lake Bl

Panorama

Griffith Park

Angus

Tracy

Lanter-man

Micheltorena

Tesla

Bright

Scotland

Silverado

Silver Lea

Fernwood

Moreno

Kenilworth

Meadow Valley

Rock

Redcliff

Moreno

Balmer

HYPERION

Griffith Park

Meadow Valley

B

W Silver Lk

Fernwood

Lucille

Kenilworth

Landa

Landa

Landa

Landa

Lucille

Carn-ation

Maltman

Redcliff

Dillon

Webster

Rotary

Redesdale

T

Crestmont

Cicero

Fall

park

Effie

Van Pelt

Edgemont

Rotary

SILVER LAKE BLVD.

Redes-dale

Berkeley

Westerly

7-11 Effie

Maltman

Hamilton

Murray

Micheltorena

Elevado

Berkeley

Parkman

SUNSET BLVD

S: Rudolph Schlinder architecture

N

Map covers an area 1.8 miles X .75 miles

+ indicates location of highest elevation on this map = 732'

⟨ıııııııı Public street to street stairway (arrow points uphill)

ıııııXıııı Gated stairway

········ Track or narrow path

— — — — Car-free rd/pedestrian wlk

1-18 - Stairways described facing page

A - T Waypoints described page 20

Page 82		
Page 68	*This* Map	Page 26
	Page 60	

18

	stairway	location: top / bottom	steps	
1	Tracy Street	2321 Meadow Valley / 2424 Griffith Pk	23	C
	Few steps but a long paved pathway to directly across from Franklin Hills			
2	Lanterman Terr	2423 Lanterman / 2366 Panorama Terr	51	B
	A short slot stairway that is really useful getting through the maze			
3	Tesla Avenue	2358 Moreno Dr / 2421 Kenilworth	111	B
	Has a long paved pathway with good views across the basin & beyond *(pg 24)*			
4	Moreno Drive	2200 Moreno / 2201 W.Silver Lake Blvd	73	B
	The nearest stairs to the lake but have only a narrow slot view of the water			
	Good view of the curved roofline of John Lautner's "Silvertop" house			
5	Meadow Valley	Acr fr 3328 Fernwood / 2009 Meadow Vly	93	B
	Nice stairs with a dog-leg halfway down and a deep canyon feel at bottom			
6	Landa sidewalk	in front of 3729 Landa	19	C
7	Landa-Edgewood	3541 Landa / 3633 Landa	155	A
8	Landa-Lucille	3701 Landa / near 1843 Lucille	92	B
	These pickup serious elevation gain ascending the outer west wall of the			
	Silver Lake basin. The upper stairway is true joy with steps on either end			
	of a long paved pathway and nice stair houses on the uphill side. Recently			
	automobile-oriented homes were built along the stairs on the other side.			
9	Landa-Redesdale	3031 Landa / 2026 Redesdale	84	B
	This stairway has the best lake view of all the stairways- from a bluff top			
	it gives an impression of walking straight for the water before the steps			
	change direction and drop down to Redesdale.			
10	Lower Swan	1760 Redesdale / 2958 Swan	78	B
11	Middle Swan	1784 Rotary / 1760 Redesdale	110	B
12	Upper Swan	1748 Webster / across fr 1784 Rotary	100	B
	No nonsense stair-climbing! These 3 line up in shade-less monotony			
	Favorites of the "up, down & back up again" set.			
13	Effie-Redesdale	1724 Rotary / 1705 Redesdale	82	B
	This one's different-darkly wooded with a 90-degree directional change			
14	Cicero Drive	1637 Cicero Dr / 1632 Redcliff St	90	B
	Delightful 100-yard long cull de sec lane with a 60 yard long stairway at end			
15	Murray Drive	1551 Murray Dr / 3359 Hamilton Way	53	B
16	Hamilton Way	3324 Hamilton Way / 3329 Sunset Blvd	90	C
	Tandem stairs get a walker efficiently high on the ridge east of Sunset			
17	Elevado Street	1435 Elevado St / 3103 Hamilton Way	102	B
	An average stairway but circular Elevado is magical.			
18	Parkman-	1300 Westerly Terr / 1213 Parkman Av	GATED	
	Westerly	Closed by the city in response to neighbor concerns		
	in the 1980's; it has been an active candidate by enthusiasts to reopen.*(pg 23)*			

Silver Lake west

A storied LA neighborhood that conjures up an impression of creative talent, modernist architecture, a diverse population that includes an influential Gay community and a complex web of streets leading to great views. The 2.75 square miles of Silver Lake are so rich with stairways that they are covered in four sections of this book. Silver Lake West, with its Moreno Highlands district, is the wealthiest and most characteristic of the four sections of the "Silver Lake ideal".

Interesting places to walk to in Silver Lake west:
T **Silver Lake Path** Very well used and beloved to the locals, this 2.2 mile loop of the lake is now 100% separated from traffic lanes. Walk this on a weekend or weekday evening and expect to find lots of good company and perhaps even the sight of a blue heron nest on west side.
A **The Paramour** (originally Crestmount) hilltop Villa – built 1922 by oil heiress Daisy Canfield with her husband, Antonio Moreno. Canfield died 1933 racing a car on Mulholland Hwy. Moreno appeared in over 140 silent/sound movies and had an on screen presence as a Latin lover in early film second only to Valentino. The home is now owned and lovingly restored by local restaurateur and designer Diana Hollister.
B **Silvertop** Architect John Lautner's iconic, ridge-hugging home is a masterpiece that has been called "an homage to the curve". Best viewed from across the lake, the home is 7500 square feet.
S **The Schlindler's** A "first generation" modernist architect from Austria, Rudolph Schlindler built nine residences in this area in the 1930's (each indicated by an "S" on the map). Using the then new and liberating materials like plywood, lightweight structural steel and sliding glass windows, Schlindler excelled at imagining the new spaces that those materials could manifest. On the lake side of the ridge, his homes pass almost unnoticed in front while they create exciting downslope terraces of intersecting boxes when viewed from the rear (the Walker House on Redcliff when viewed from Moreno for example). The four Schlindler's on the Griffith Park Bl side of the ridge, while lacking any "wow" factor, are each a study of inventive clustering of dwellings in multiple units. (the Bubeshko Apartments at Griffith Park and Lyric for example).

Rudolph Schindler Bubeshko apartments

Rudolph Schindler's Walker House

This 1953 photograph by Clarence Inman looks north of Silver Lake towards Atwater Village. It shows Ivanhoe School upper left edge and, above that, the Red Car Line crossing the LA River next to the Hyperion Bridge. Upper right, the dark horizontal line above Fletcher is the Red Car trestle.

Landa Street - StairTrek 2011

A "stairway of darkness" - Parkman-Westerly stairs closed by the city since the 1980's

Tesla Stairs   Howard Petersen Photo

Secret Stairs **and Charles Fleming** Published 2010 by Santa Monica Press, this book was an instant success and is a great resource for learning two to four mile introductory stairway based city walks. The descriptions of what you would experience along each walk are wonderfully written with a lot of great information. Charles Fleming also writes a monthly LA Times column on local walks and leads a walk the first Sunday of each month. I'd like to think that my book complements *Secret Stairs* nicely. This list describes how Fleming's walks match up with my area maps in case you want to further explore the area or do a couple of *Secret Stairs* walks consecutively.

"SECRET STAIRS" walk number	Section in this book showing the surrounding area for the "Secret Stairs" walk
1	Garvanza and Southwest Pasadena (page 126)
2	Eagle Rock (page 120)
4	Mt. Washington west (page 90)
3	Mt. Wash west + Verdugo-Atwater (page 82)
5 and 7	Mt. Washington east (page 98)
6 and 8	Highland Park - Hermon (page 106)
9	El Sereno (page 146)
10	Montecito Hts - Lincoln Hts (page 136)
11	Downtown - Elysian slot (page 164)
12 and 13	Echo Park (page 54)
15	Elysian Heights (page 46)
16	Allesandro - Lemoyne (page 40)
14 and 17	Elysian Heights + Allesandro - Lemoyne
18	Silver Lake south to Westlake (page 60)
19,20,21,22, & 25	Silver Lake west (page 18)
24	Silver Lake east (page 26)
27	Glendale - Allesandro (page 34)
23 and 26	Silver Lake east + Glendale - Allesandro
28	Verdugo - Atwater Village (page 82)
29 and 32	Los Feliz (page 182)
30 and 31	Franklin Hills (page 68)
33,34 & 35	Beachwood-Bronson-Hollywood Dell (page 190)
36, 37 & 38	Whitley Heights - Hollywood Heights (page 200)
39 and 40	Rustic Canyon - Santa Monica (page 216)
41	mentioned in Pacific Palisades section (pg 210)

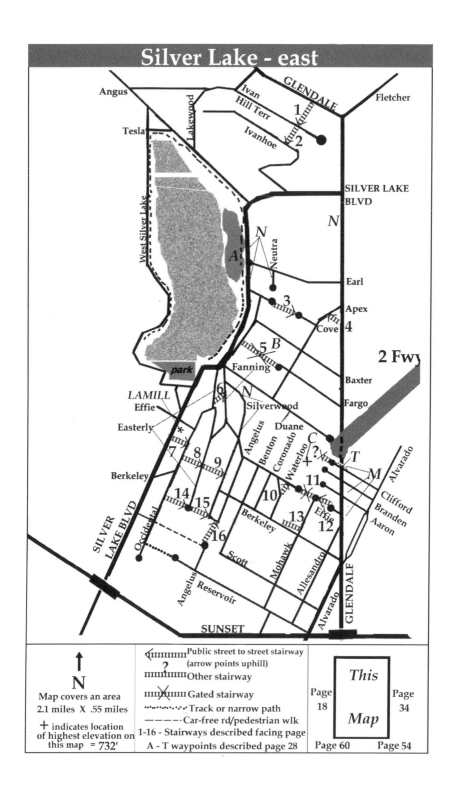

Silver Lake - east

Angus
Fletcher
Ivan
GLENDALE
Lakewood
Hill Terr
1
Tesla
Ivanhoe
2

SILVER LAKE
BLVD

West Silver Lake
N
N
A
Neutra

Earl
Apex
3
Cove 4

2 Fwy
5 B
park
Fanning
Baxter

LAMILL
6
N
Fargo
Effie
Silverwood
Easterly
*
Angelus
Duane
7
Benton
Coronado
Waterloo
C
8
9
?
T
Berkeley
M
Alvarado
14
15
10
11
Clifford
Branden
Aaron
Berkeley
13
Effie
16
12
SILVER LAKE BLVD
Occidental
Scott
Mohawk
Allesandro
Angelus Reservoir
Alvarado
GLENDALE
SUNSET

This
Page
18
Page
34
Map
Page 60   Page 54

	stairway	location: top / bottom	steps	
1	Ivan Hill lower	2615 Ivan Hill Terr / 2617 Glendale Blvd	56	B
2	Ivan Hill upper	2605 Ivanhoe Dr / 2626 Ivan Hill Terr	156	B

Set of two steep stairways passing through a tunnel of vegetation with peekaboo views to Forest Lawn, the Verdugo's and the San Gabriel's. The bottom is hard to spot. Pre-teen Judy Garland lived at the top

3	Mattachine(Cove)	2331 Cove Ave / 2335 Cove Ave	164	A

The loveliest of the Silver Lake basin stairs. Renamed in 2011 to honor the Mattachine Society, an early force in the Gay civil rights movement. Harry Hay was instrumental in founding the group while living at 2328 Cove. *(pg 30)*

4	Apex	2130 Apex / corner Glendale Bl & Apex	19	C

Short stretch of steps makes the third leg of a leafy corner triangle.

5	Fargo	2341 Fargo / across from 1965 Rockford	GATED	

This would be a long, shaded route but has had locked gates for many years. A poster child for the movement to open the "stairs of darkness"

6	Easterly-Fanning	1771 Fanning / across fr 1809 Easterly	108	B

Open-air & straight-up; not as discrete and shaded as others nearby

7	Silverwood N.(L)	near 1623 Occidental / 1618 Silver Lake	22	C
8	Silverwood N.(M)	1601 Easterly / near 1606 Occidental	75	B
9	Silverwood N.(U)	1613 Silverwood / across fr 1601 Easterly	103	B

Silverwood North is a handsome set of three stairways that climb the entire east inner wall of the basin. On the lowest segment, please stay on the public stairs; there is a private passage that is often mistaken for public.

10	Waterloo	2330 Effie Street / 1662 Waterloo	20	C

Tucked away wood stairs inconvenienced by the closure of upper Effie

11	Upper Effie	2305 Effie St / 1661 Mohawk	GATED	
12	Lower Effie	1692 Mohawk / 2219 Effie	101	B

The top is a cull de sec of great views & interesting houses but the gate is always locked. Lower stairs remain a good link to Elysian Heights & Echo Pk

13	Berkeley sidewlk	2321 Berkeley-corner Berkeley+Mohawk	35	C

20 steps up and 15 steps down along an incidental sideway stairway

14	Silverwood S.(L)	1483 Easterly / Across fr 1433 Occidental	82	B
15	Silverwood S.(U)	1525 Silverwood / 1480 Easterly	89	B

Back to back stairways that benefit from passing a dead-end in the middle and topping off at a pretty spot on Silverwood near the Angelus stairs.

16	Angelus Avenue	1482 Angelus / 1456 Angelus	177	A

One of my favorites: wide and colorful with bougainvillea as it passes intriguing gateways. Pairs nicely with the Silverwood south stairs *(pg 31)*

?	Clifford Street	2246 W. Clifford	GATED	

A stairway that never was - related to the Hathaway development (pg 28)

	tunnel			
T	Clifford underpass	open 24/7 gets you under Glendale Blvd near fwy.		

Silver Lake east

The comments about Silver Lake west on page 20 also refer here.
This mapped area includes Edendale and borders Echo Park.

Walkable assets and distinctive destinations to walk to in Silver Lake east
A   The Meadow   Long argued and slow to arrive, this 3 acres of grass opened 2011 as a wonderful addition to the nearby usable open space. As you passed many of the homes in this area in 2006-07, there would be "Save the meadow" signs that might be interpreted to mean, "Keep out the riff raff, save the fences". Eventually the riff raff won the day.*(page 30)*
B   Villa Capistrano   First of the Silver Lake hilltop villas - built 1921 for Julian Eltinge who was a fabulously successful female impersonator in the vaudeville era in London and New York before coming to Los Angeles. Can be seen along Baxter but best viewed from across the lake.
M   Edendale studios   The walker needs to use some imagination to appreciate what this five block stretch of Glendale Blvd (then called Allesandro) was like for just over a decade beginning in 1909. Here were found some of the first studios of the infant Southern California movie industry. Just by the east entrance to the current Clifford St underpass Selig-Polyscope landed first in the area in 1909. In a few years, after Selig moved, William Fox Studios took over the lot featuring stars like Tom Mix and Theda Bara. Within 4 years, the major player in Edendale was Max Sennett Studios who took over the Bison Studios at Glendale & Effie (where the OJ Plumbing is now) and expanded to 5 acres of sets on both sides of the street. Here cinematic slap stick comedy and the chase scene were born and enacted all over these streets. Normand, Swanson and Lombard became stars here. The barn like structure behind Jack in the Box is a remnant from the Keystone Studio days. Just southwest of Glendale and Effie in 1918 you would have found a"cyclorama". A backdrop was painted onto a huge rotating cylinder so the illusion of motion was created for the stationery performers in the foreground. Also about where the Animal Hospital stands, was Norbig Studio, a rental operation that saw use by Hal Roach, Harold Lloyd and Charlie Chaplin.
C   Garbutt House   (and surrounding Hathaway estate) dominate the summit as a locale you CAN'T walk to. The 1923 house is built entirely of concrete by a pyro phobic inventor and is now owned by Dov Charney of American Apparel. The 37 acre property became available in the 1960's and was pushed for conversion to parkland. Instead it was developed in the 1980's into one hundred, banal cookie-cutter homes. Adding a cherry to a nefarious episode of bad city planning, this acropolis-like site was incomprehensibly allowed to become a gated community.

N Neutra Country The legacies of architect Richard Neutra and Silver Lake are intertwined. The lake and the down sloping lots provided a perfect canvas for the master's crisp, modernist designs. Neutra's most famous works are found elsewhere but the special association exists partly because of his continued presence long after his death in 1970. The Neutra offices have been on Glendale Blvd. for six decades and Richard Neutra's son, Dion (a fellow architect) still lives in the neighborhood as a passionate force for the design and for the community. Structure of almost ethereal framing sitting softly on the landscape, creative use of windows, louvers and geometry; and the familiar extended structural "elbow" are signatures of his work. The VDL house, across from the meadow, is owned by Cal Poly and is often open to the public. Each letter "N" on the map indicates where one or several Neutra buildings can be walked past.

Richard Neutra's VDL house (1972 photo)

Silver Lake meadow and path

Mattachine (Cove) stairs

In the historic film studio zone of Edendale: Bedrock Recording Studios

Angelus stairs

Stair Trek 2011 ascends the Silverwood North stairs

Stair Trek: Dan Koeppel is a friend and Los Angeles author who a decade ago began foraging on foot away from his Silver Lake home looking for public stairways. His curiosity had been piqued by the Music Box stairs and he kept doing exploratory walks in ever widening circles to find more. A 2004 *Backpacker* Magazine article Dan wrote described this quest. He came to my attention by a 2007 LA Times piece about his passion and which described a massive loop walk he had designed to link 65 of the stairways in a single extreme sport day of walking. I knew those stairs and, pondering the challenge of that route, thought, "What a kook!" Today that route (with some additions) is called Stair Trek and Dan leads it annually in February. In 2013 it attracted 51 people to start with 21 who finished. The current route is 22.1 miles with a 4800' elevation gain and the group takes a bit over 11 hours to complete. The route has been done in as little as 8.9 hours without the big group. Here is the sequence. Search on Google "Stair Trek 2013" and you should be able to find a map with all the turns.

"STAIR TREK" stairway sequence as mapped in this book
(read top to bottom, left to right)

Page 60
up #5
down #4

Page 18
up #7
up #8
down #5
up #1
up #2
down #9

Page 26
up #7
up #8
up #9
down #16
up #14
up #15
look at gated #11
down #10
up & down #13
down #12

Page 40
down #10
up #11

Page 46
up #11
down #10

Page 54
up # 5
down #6
up #3
up #4

Page 46
up #8
up #7
up #1
down #2
up #3
up #5
down #6
up #4
up #9

Page 40
up #9
dn #8 south side
up #8 north side
up & down #3
up #1
down #2

Page 34
up #9

Page 40
up #4
down #5
up #6

Page 34
up #10
up & down #11
up #12

Page 26
up #4
down #3

Page 34
down #5
down #6
down #7
down #8
up #4
down #3
up #2
up #1

Page 26
up #1
up #2

Page 18
up #3
down #4

Page 26
up #6

Page 18
up #10
up #11
up #12
down #14
down #13
down #17
down #15
down #16

Page 60
up #2
up #3
down #7
down #6

This is the route as of 2013 – Dan might have something up his sleeve, maybe rounding it up to a 26-mile marathon.

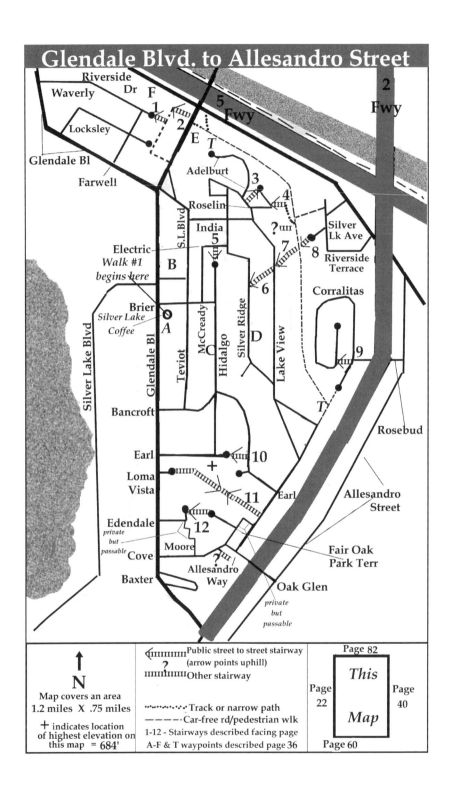

Glendale Blvd. to Allesandro Street

Riverside
Dr F
Waverly
Locksley
Glendale Bl
Farwell

5
Fwy

2
Fwy

Adelburt
Roselin
India
5
Electric
Walk #1
begins here

S.L.Blvd

B

3
4

? llll

7

Silver
Lk Ave

8

Riverside
Terrace

6

Corralitas

Brier
Silver Lake
Coffee

A

McCready
Hidalgo

C

Silver Ridge

D

Lake View

9

Teviot

Glendale Bl

Bancroft

T

Rosebud

Earl
Loma
Vista

10

11

Earl

Allesandro
Street

Edendale
private
but
passable

Cove

Moore

12

Allesandro
Way

Fair Oak
Park Terr

Baxter

Oak Glen
private
but
passable

N

Map covers an area
1.2 miles X .75 miles

+ indicates location
of highest elevation on
this map = 684'

◁ıııııııııı Public street to street stairway
? (arrow points uphill)
ıııııııııı Other stairway

••••••••• Track or narrow path
– – – – – Car-free rd/pedestrian wlk
1-12 - Stairways described facing page
A-F & T waypoints described page 36

Page 82

This
Page
22
Page
40

Map

Page 60

	stairway	location: top / bottom	steps	
1	**Waverly Drive**	2601 Waverly Dr/ Red car path	45	B
2	**Red Car Viaduct**	Red car path / near 2500 Riverside	64	B
	#2 is behind the Home parking lot; (pg 39) Both join to an old paved pathway that runs 700 feet and built for the benefit of the trolley users.			
3	**Adelburt**	across fr 2100 Roselin / 2566 Lake View	35	B
	Top of these cute stairs sits hidden only 100 feet from the top of #4. Some of us still like to call these "Sue's stairs" for the walker who wandered from the pack, noticed them and made them known to the rest of us.			
4	**Roselin**	2104 Roselin / Silver Lake Court	98	C
	To locate bottom follow a diagonal path that starts by the "false" stairway.			
?	**false stairs**	along Red Car roadbed 200' north of Silver Lake Ave strs		
	Official looking but posted as private–they're at start of diagonal path to #4			
5	**Hidalgo**	2470 Hidalgo / 2221 Electric	82	B
	Hidalgo is a fine walking street that once claimed Anais Nin as a resident.			
6	**Silver Lk Av(U)**	2484 Silver Ridge / 2501 Lake View	77	B
7	**Silver Lk Av(M)**	2480 Lake View / Red Car Property	31	B
8	**Silver Lk Av(L)**	Red Car Property / 2112 Silver Lake Ave	30	C
	Three stairs that approach the Red Car roadbed. You can read a street sign where these stairs cross Lakeview. This would cause drivers no end of confusion but a sign reading Silver Lake Ave. is a delightful reminder for walkers that here is an avenue built for them.			
9	**Corralitas**	across fr 2611 Corralitas / 2463 Corralitas	133	B
	Steep steps gain the top of the same dead-end street that they started from			
10	**Earl**	2104 Roselin / Silver Lake Court	218	A
	Blue lake views on top after a switch-backing climb up an open hillside			
11	**Loma Vista Place**	West end: 2384 Loma Vista Place East end:2220 Allesandro	348	A
	Here is perhaps the most unique of this book's stairways. Whether climbing the 182 steps from the west or the 166 steps from the east, the walker expects to find a cross street at the crest of the hill. Instead the walkway continues over the ridge uninterrupted and down other side. Isolated stair-houses line this 1925 vintage walk that gives inspiration to any stair seeker. Dan Koeppel named these the "Mother Stairs". *(page 39)*			
12	**Edendale**	2248 Edendale / 2258 Fair Oak View Terr	147	B
	Find (on YouTube) the 18-minute comedy short made by the Three Stooges in 1941 titled "An Ache in Every Stake". These are the stairs where they repeatedly tried to deliver a block of ice. The block would turn to an ice cube by the time they reached the top. Eventually the boys slide down the steps on ice blocks escaping an angry client at the end of the film. As the film rolls, you see the Red Car passing below on what is now freeway. *(pg 38)*			
?	**Cove Way**	by 2230 Cove Avenue		
	Stairs that were truncated by the construction of the "2" Freeway			

Glendale to Allesandro

This area is the eastern part of Silver Lake; not within the lake basin but along both sides of a steep ridge with a collection of some of the city's best stairways. All of what we now refer to as Silver Lake and some of Los Feliz was first named "Ivanhoe" the late 19th century. The story is that the area reminded a Scotsman named Hugo Reid of his native land and he took many many characters and references from Sir Walter Scott to name the streets of the area. Waverly and Rowena have obvious connection; Teviot, Locksley, Ayr, Bancroft, Brier and Hidalgo in this mapped area all could be related to the Reid/Scott story.

Walkable assets and distinctive destinations to walk to noted on page 34

T	**Red Car Property**	A 4/5's mile long path/dirt road that once was the route of a Red Car interurban line active 1906-1955 and is now a walkable treasure. Starting from the end of Allesandro Way, 500' of sideway joins to the end of Corralitas Drive. Here a path veers left and begins an 800' transit through a deep, hidden valley that is the gem of old rail bed. The path goes through a gate and opens out again to be a rustic dirt road. Walking on, you come to the crossing of the stairways in another 800' and the only car access entering from the right 200 feet after that. In another 1/10 mile the road bed makes the "India Curve" to the left, once a prominent rail feature. Shortly after that there are 2 access paths to Adelburt Ave on left. Soon the road terminates abruptly where the trestle once crossed Fletcher. You can scramble down a trail through the remaining viaduct support footings. This band of land is not publicly owned and has seen a half century of developmental schemes and has heard a half century of promises from the city to preserve a walker's route through here to link Elysian and Griffith Parks. The developments have fizzled and the promises have lacked the courage of civic action. Today another move is afoot to build in the canyon. Stung particularly by the deforestation of the other side of the valley by the Artis development (see page 42) the open space preservationists are rallying their forces.
A	**Red Lion Tavern**	2013 marks the golden anniversary of the serving of traditional gasthaus food and bier at this neighborhood institution.
B	**Mixville**	The king of the Hollywood cowboys in the silent era, Tom Mix built a 12 acre studio about where the Citibank and East-West bank now stand. It was constructed to be a complete frontier town and was a busy movie set in the 1920's when Mix made 160 cowboy films.

The Red Car Property and path leading into the canyon

C Nin - Pole house	At 2335 Hidalgo -The celebrated diarist, eroticist and feminist Anais Nin, having lived parts of her life in Paris, Barcelona, Havana and Manhattan, choose to live her last 15 years with a view of Silver Lake. From the street, not much can be made of the 60 year old Eric Wright design which is a city cultural heritage monument. Photos indicate a lovely natural wood interior with cantilevered ceiling that extends outside large windows which look over a small pool towards the lake. Nin's "second" husband (she never legally ended the marriage to the first one) was Rupert Pole who was Eric Wright's stepbrother. A local connection: Mr Pole was a science teacher at nearby King Middle School.
D How House	This Rudolph Schlindler masterpiece at 2422 Silver Ridge was built for James Eads How, another one (like Barnsdall, like Wilshire) who were millionaires who became prominent leftists. How's passion was for the transient workers and hobos and he tried to organize a union and set up colleges and conventions for the hobo's of America. It is perhaps urban legend, but the story is that the bottom level of this 1925 architectural masterpiece was set up as a dormitory for hobos who came up the hill from the near by railroad tracks to stay a few nights.
E Fletcher viaduct	Imagine here at the end of the Red Car path or at the top of stairway #2 a giant steel trestle that crossed 60 feet above the surface of Fletcher. The support piers are an Historic-Cultural Monument
F "Lost" redcar path	From Fletcher to Glendale Blvd, the trolley tracks once continued their route towards Atwater Village on this terrace for another half mile. The 1972 local general plan proposed to acquire the land to link Elysian and Griffith Parks. A 1984 community plan mapped a non-motor route in this corridor. Neither happened and in 2010 the city council denied an appeal to require developers to maintain the easement.

Edendale stairs (the "3 Stooges stairs")

Red Car stairs - Beacon Hill in Griffith Park in distance

Loma Vista Place stairs

Allesandro Street to Lemoyne Street

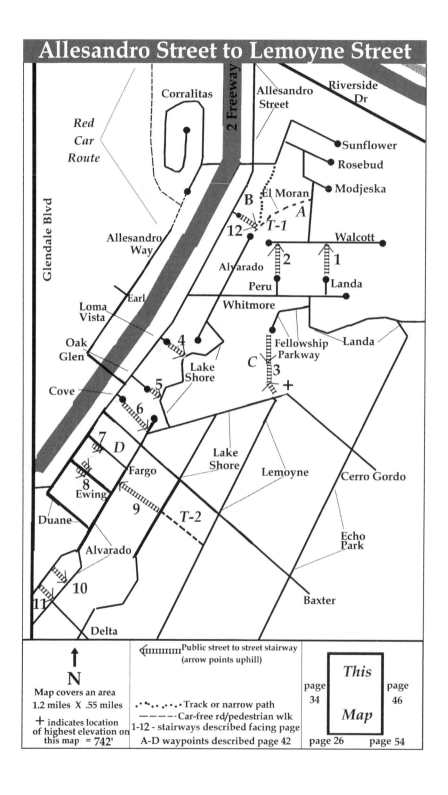

Red Car Route

Corralitas

2 Freeway

Allesandro Street

Riverside Dr

Sunflower

Rosebud

Modjeska

El Moran

B

A

T-1

12

Walcott

Allesandro Way

Glendale Blvd

Alvarado

2

1

Peru

Landa

Earl

Loma Vista

Whitmore

Oak Glen

Fellowship Parkway

Landa

4

Cove

Lake Shore

C

3

5

+

6

7

D

Lake Shore

Lemoyne

Cerro Gordo

Fargo

8

Ewing

9

Duane

T-2

Alvarado

Echo Park

10

Baxter

11

Delta

↑
N

Map covers an area
1.2 miles X .55 miles

+ indicates location
of highest elevation on
this map = 742'

⊲ΙΙΙΙΙΙΙΙΙΙΙΙ Public street to street stairway
(arrow points uphill)

•‧•‧•‧•‧•‧• Track or narrow path

— — — — Car-free rd/pedestrian wlk

1-12 - stairways described facing page

A-D waypoints described page 42

This Map

page 34

page 46

page 26   page 54

	stairway	location: top / bottom	steps	
1	Landa-Wolcott	1926 Walcott / 2359 Landa	146	B
2	Peru	2378 Peru / 2366 Peru	114	B
		A tandem of long stairways climb in parallel just 260 feet from each other to a very remote location. Nice views from each back into Fellowship Park and into Whitmore canyon		
3	Fellowship Park	1831 Cerro Gordo / 2365 Fellowship Pk	162	A
		The secret seems to be out about this stairway and the free form pedestrian community that surrounds it. The author requests that visitors to this quasi-public zone be quiet and respectful. Entering from the Cerro Gordo side, you pass a newer version of the 1906 Edendale tank that was once the highest elevation water storage in the city. A fountain stream, a hammock, century-old cabins, mystery side trails and lonely mailboxes all add to the effect.		
4	Loma Visa - Allesandro	2265 Lake Shore / 2117 Loma Vista	182	A
		On the lower end there are picturesque shallow steps leading between pretty homes; then there is a rustic bit of trail squeezing between agave plants. On top, wooden steps lead to a lonely, shaded lane *(Illustrated back cover)*		
5	Oak Glen	2225 Lake Shore / 2034 Oak Glen	58	B
		Oak Glen is mostly a long, steep block of drivable street then steps on top that are still partially wood		
6	Cove - Allesandro	2265 Lake Shore / 2117 Loma Vista	198	B
		A long stairway that looks straight-forward from the bottom. When the walker reaches the top, he or she has arrived in a tight, cozy corner and is happy to be car-free. On top find a nice sweeping view that ranges from the San Gabriel's on the far right, Silver Lake-Griffith Park in the middle and southwest LA on the left. *(page 43)*		
7	Fargo sidewalk	2142 Fargo / 2146 Fargo	17	C
8	Ewing sidewalk	2137 Ewing / 2161 Ewing	58	C
		Two very steep streets that have stairs built into the sidewalk. At Ewing they are on both sides of the street. Look at Linda Rosa St. in Eagle Rock for a better example of a sidewalk stair.		
9	Ewing west	2004 Alvarado / 2003 Ewing	129	B
		Steep open slope stairway off the high westerly ridge down to a deep valley. Across Lake Shore from the bottom of stairway, Ewing is passable to the walker as a steep dirt track.		
10	Alvarado split	1648 Alvarado / 1645 Alvarado	36	C
11	Delta Alvarado	1678 Alvarado / 1677 Alvarado	30	C
		Two short stairways join the upper and lower levels of Alvarado		
12	El Moran	near 2032 El Moran / 2066 El Moran	93	B
		This is a newly built and highly unusual railroad tie stairway that rises steeply and cleverly up from near Allesandro. It is a gift of the Artis development. The winding stairs with their cable hand rails have a "Tom Sawyer Island" look to them but we can thank Artis for a rare new addition to our city's inventory. *Illustrated page 43*		

Allesandro to Lemoyne

By any definition this section would be considered part of the Echo Park neighborhood. As this neighborhood is so rich with stairways, this sliver is entitled to a chapter of its own. This is a zone of very steep hills and a rusticity that defies anything you would expect from a place three miles distant from the financial district. Hidden in the creases of these hills are very remote lanes and homes, perfectly scaled for exploring on foot.

Walkable assets and distinctive destinations to walk to mapped on pg. 40

T1 El Moran Street Related to A & B below, this is 500 feet of dirt road behind passible barricades off Peru on end and the short paved part of El Moran on other. The Landacre Historical monument sign is found here.

T2 Ewing extension 400 feet of "paper street" that looks like a steep paved driveway on top and an ATV challenge at bottom - good shortcut.

A Landacre cabin Even with much of the soul of the area ripped away by recent development, this spot best represents the spirit of the surrounding community. Paul & Margaret Landacre bought this 1909 cabin in 1932 and they lived there until the 60's. Landacre was the master wood block artistic printer of the day. He beautifully portrayed images of the west by intricately carving nuanced designs. He translated these as white onto black using a Mark Twain era printing press salvaged from Bodie, CA.

B Semi-Tropic tract The Semi Tropic Spiritualists' Association in 1905 laid out a 3 acre tract divided into lots to be used as campsites purposed to hold meetings "devoted to the maintenance and spreading of the religion of Modern Spiritualism". The development Artis@Echo Park has built on that land 15 townhomes. The promise was to maintain most of the three acres as green space. Sadly, the property has been entirely scraped of the century old woodland that was there and the manufactured landscape that grows back will be a woeful replacement.

C Fellowship Park Perhaps the most extraordinary pedestrian zone in the city. This roadless area (which is mostly nominally Lemoyne St) is dotted with small residences along one long stairway and several lateral paths. It includes famous "pavilion" style homes built 1935-42 by modernist Harwell Harris that emulate the "camping lifestyle" at home.

D Fargo and Baxter Fargo Street invariably gets called the steepest in Los Angeles (it is not quite – see page 100F) and between Allesandro and Alvarado, Fargo and Baxter make twin ascents of a 32% grade. Fargo is famed for the LA Wheelman's annual bicycle climb that awards those who finish the climb without stopping. Baxter is a series of steep rises and descents from Silver Lake to the Baxter stairs. An 1880's map shows the intent to run Baxter as a straight line avenue east clear to the LA River.

El Moran stairs

Cove - Allesandro stairs

WALK 1	Allesandro Valley - Fellowship Park		
4 1/2 miles		elevation gain:++	11 stairways
Shorter walk option:		2.7 miles (depart route early)	
start / finish:	Silver Lake Coffee 2388 Glendale Blvd 90039		
Transit:	Metro 92 bus runs 7 days from Civic Center or Glendale-Burbank every 20-40 minutes		
Best time to walk	Anytime that is not too hot. This a great walk for an evening. The Red Car path gets muddy after big rains.		
Highlights	Some of LA's most classic stairways, Fellowship Park, Red Car Path, cool streets with great views		
Break spots	No bathroom or water opportunites on this route		
Please read pg 12-15 for information common to each walk in this book			

This walk overlaps almost a mile of walk #2.

Beginning on map page 34

Start up Brier Street and turn left on McCready- Turn right when it ends at Electric. Go up **stairway #5** on your right. Walk 4/10 mile on lovely Hidalgo passing the **Nin-Pole House ("C",Pg. 37)**. Turn left at Earl and descend **stairway #10**. Turn right at bottom on Earl and follow to its end at Allesandro Way. Turn left. Passing two streets headed left, step over the barrier and follow a sidewalk that parallels the freeway. As the sidewalk approaches Corralitas Dr. bear left on the dirt track of the Red Car right of way. Walk through canyon, through a narrow gate and turn left on **stairway #7**, crossing Lakeview continuing up **stairway #6**. Turn left to follow Silver Ridge for 4/10 mile passing the **How House ("D", Pg. 37)**. Passing Lakeview on the left twice while descending, arrive back at Allesandro Way and turn right. In about 400', pause in front of stairway #11 at 2220. This is the halfway point. If you need to cut the walk short, take these stairs for a half mile walk back to the start. Otherwise walk on. Up ahead turn left on Oak Glen and cross over freeway.

Now on map page 40

Across freeway turn left on Allesandro Street, passing Oak Glen noticing **stairway #5** that we pass.

Turn right at Loma Vista to take **stairway #4 (Pg. 40)**. Having twisted through the vegetation at the top, exit and turn left on Lake Shore. Follow to Alvarado and turn right, then right on Whitmore and left on Peru. Go up **stairway #2**, turn right at top and go down **stairway #1**. From Landa turn right then left at Whitmore to stay on Landa. At the tiles, turn right on Fellowship Park Way. Take that to the end and locate **stairway #3** to the right of 2365. Walking up the non-official looking cinder blocks, pass one pathway on left, then slip quickly right then left on the stairs close to the house on your right. Continue up through a little wood gate; pass some mailboxes and an alluring trail to the right. Keep going straight up the steps passing through a metal gate, crest the hill and walk down steps arriving at Cerro Gordo. This is the far point and the walk is 70% done. Turn right; follow Cerro Gordo one quarter mile until you reach Alvarado. Pause at one of the best view spots in the area before turning right on Alvarado then left down **stairway #6**. At bottom turn right on Allesandro, then left over freeway.

Back on map page 34

Follow Oak Glen straight until it ends at Fair Oak View, turn left and immediately find yourself on Cove. Turn right on Moore and follow it as it curves left, right, left, right. Walk respectfully over the "Private-no through traffic" markings on the pavement to emerge at the top of Edendale Place. Go straight ahead (rather than steeply down to the left) and locate **stairway #12** on your right and go down it. Reaching the bottom of the stairs, continue down the short street and turn left then right. Again, walk respectfully through a short private street. Turn left on Allesandro Way and left up **Stairway #11**. After completing the transit of this 1100' long pedestrian wonderland, come out to Glendale Blvd. Turn right and walk downhill back to the start.

Elysian Heights - Elysian Valley

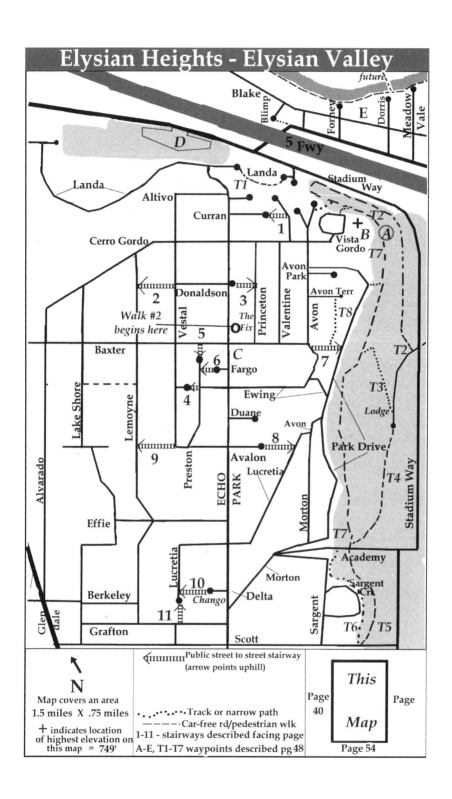

Blake

Blimp

Forney

Dorris

Meadow Vale

E

future

D

5 Fwy

Landa

Landa

T1

Altivo

Curran

1

Stadium Way

T2

Vista Gordo

B

A

T7

Cerro Gordo

Avon Park

2

Donaldson

3

Walk #2 begins here

Vestal

5

The Fix

Princeton

Valentine

Avon

Avon Terr

T8

T2

Baxter

6

C

Fargo

7

T3

4

Ewing

Lodge

Duane

Avon

Lemoyne

9

Preston

8

Avalon

Lucretia

Park Drive

T4

Lake Shore

ECHO PARK

Morton

Stadium Way

Alvarado

Effie

T7

Academy

Lucretia

10

Chango

Delta

Morton

Sargent Cr

Berkeley

11

Sargent

T6

T5

Glendale

Grafton

Scott

N

Map covers an area
1.5 miles X .75 miles

+ indicates location
of highest elevation on
this map = 749'

⊲‖‖‖‖‖‖‖ Public street to street stairway
(arrow points uphill)

•.•‥•‥•• Track or narrow path
– – – –· Car-free rd/pedestrian wlk
1-11 - stairways described facing page
A-E, T1-T7 waypoints described pg 48

Page 40

This

Map

Page

Page 54

	stairway	location: top / bottom	steps	
1	Curran	1540 Curran / 2403 Valentine	130	A

One of my favorite stairways: wide and immaculate with intriguing stair-houses. Curran Street on top is a gem. Valentine Street is great too.

| 2 | Donaldson west | 2200 Lemoyne / 2167 Vestal | 25 | B |

Very few steps, long sloping path. There is a lovely plum tree

| 3 | Donaldson east | across fr 2202 Princeton / 2174 Echo Park | 143 | B |

A long straight up stairway that links an isolated ridge of residences to a pretty part of Echo Park Avenue near the DASH Bus turnaround.

4	Ewing east	1711 Ewing / 1963 Preston	25	B
5	Preston	2051 Preston / across from 1633 Baxter	39	B
6	Little Fargo	2041 Preston / 1630 Fargo	29	B

Within a 600 foot span, three short stairways intersect little Preston Street. The Ewing East stairs are "shoulder wide", making them difficult to notice.

| 7 | Baxter | 2101 Park Drive / near 1501 Baxter Street | 231 | A |

Baxter is one of the three or four "signature" stairways of Los Angeles, notable for its length, its location and its construction. Any long stairway in LA gets its stair count compared to Baxter's 231. Located by itself on an open hillside and not hemmed in by houses, this stairway dominates the slope while being in scale with the broad Echo Park Valley and its collection of other significant stairs. The switchback design invites the tired walker to pause on the climb up and enjoy the view.

| 8 | Avalon east | 1893 Lucretia / 1550 Avalon | 192 | A |

A no-nonsense stairway that to some of us always seems even more exhausting to walk up than nearby Baxter. Very imposing from the bottom and a crossover pathway one third of the way up adds to the experience. The 1990 Bakalinski-Gordon book described rickey wood stairs here that have long since been rebuilt. *(illustrated page 53)*

| 9 | Avalon west | 1902 Lemoyne / 1907 Vestal | 125 | A |

This one is shadier and more discrete than the other top-rated stairs in this neighborhood. The stairs pass by interesting gates and stair houses. One of those stair houses sold in October 2013 for over $700,000, an indication of the allure of the Los Angeles stairs. The house on top at 1902 Lemoyne was not built in the Victorian-Eastlake style it has now but rather was reinvented over the past 5 years

| 10 | Delta | 1600 Lucretia / 1620 Delta | 125 | B |

The coffee house by the bottom of these nice stairs was once Echo Park Drug and you can see this location in the 1935 Three Stooges short "Three Little Beers" when beer barrels came rolling down this block. Stairway aficionados need to look at "sphericalpanoramas.com" for a portrait of this stairway and others by Carel Struycken (think Addams Family). *(pg 10)*

| 11 | Lucretia | 1546 Lucretia / 1701 Grafton | 64 | B |

Nice downtown view on top. These stairs have steeper risers than some These stairs have been site of clean up events twice in past couple of years

Elysian Heights and Elysian Valley

Elysian Heights (including the Allesandro to Lemoyne section covered in the previous chapter) has been for a century the bohemian highlands of not just of greater Echo Park but of all of Los Angeles. An area just less than two-thirds of a square mile is full of deep valleys, tortuously steep streets and acres of undeveloped land. It historically has been good country to stay concealed from the more public avenues down below and to live a life that is more connected to the landscape. The neighborhood fuses into the network of Elysian Park trails and has perhaps the best "package" of stairways in the city.

Red Hill	Beginning with the end of WWI, this area

became a favored choice of residence for the city's socialists and communists and the thicket of cabins along unpaved roads was called by some "Red Hill". Stories told about growing up in this area by their children, the "red diaper babies" have been assembled as a regional oral history. (one survivor has stated that the correct slang was "Red Gulch")

	Pathways:
T1	Landa St. extension – just 800' between the chains that keep out cars on rutted pavement. This woodland resembles what we lost on El Moran St. (see pg 42). Here too, an acre with 7 lots is listed for sale.
T2	North section of the Portero Trail runs 1.1 from Stadium Way to Harlow Grove on a wide dirt track with a fat bend-very pretty- climbs 200 feet
T3	Simons Lodge to trail T7 – 3/10mi start right of the lodge fence
T4	Elysian Pk Dr from lodge to Academy 4/10 mi - pavement closed to autos
T5	Elysian Pk Dr from Academy to Scott 3/10 mi-pavement closed to autos
T6	Scott to Academy narrow dirt path 3/10mi – touches Sargent Pl. & Ct.
T7	Academy to Harlow Grove- 7/10 mi. beloved to the locals - the dog-walkers particularly. Wide, dirt trail that gains more than 200'.
T8	Baxter Stairs to Avon Terrace – 500 feet of narrow track with stellar views Starts at the 11th of 15 flights counting up-comes out at a little parking area across from 1435 Avon Tr-private land passage revocable anytime

Interesting places to walk to in Elysian Heights and Elysian Valley

A	Marion Harlow	(memorial grove) -lovely garden and one of the

best walk-to viewpoints in the city. The Big Parade always stops here.

B	Atwater property	An arrowhead shaped parcel of about 1 ¾ acres

crowns Elysian Heights and does much to define its character. One family has held this land for 4 generations. The patriarch was a 19th century dentist described by his grandson as "a Socialist and a peacenik". Here is a stable, a 1908 home and, in particular, 2 pueblo revival homes facing Avon Park Terrace build 1930 by famous period architect Robert Stacy-Judd.

| C | Room 8 cat | This neighborhood is revered today for its stairs, its |

deep canyons and the cool culture. Elysian Heights gained fame a half century ago by the story of "Room 8", a cat that adopted a classroom of this elementary school. Room 8 eventually attracted a biography that had 6 printings, 100 pieces of fan mail a day, a Look Magazine spread, a TV documentary and, ultimately, a 3 column 1968 obituary in the LA Times.

| D | Elysian Pk addition | In 2010, the city purchased an 18-acre parcel of |

open land. It is lacking in perennial walking paths but the recreation center developed at its base in Elysian Valley is a welcome community addition.

| E | Frogtown | is the historic name for this neighborhood that |

borders the southwest bank of the LA River. The name had been taken up by a local gang but in recent years this interesting community has proudly seized it back. Here you find a blend of small houses and light industry that seem to fit together. Their assets include a Buddhist meditation center and an annual art-walk. Walkers naturally drawn to the riverside bike-path also owe themselves the pleasure of a stroll down Blake Street. Taylor Yard bikeway/pedestrian bridge has been budgeted to be built by 2016 and provide a 400' link from Dorris Place to Cypress Park.

Robert Stacy-Judd's Atwater Bungalows

WALK 2	The Big Parade Echo Park loop		
5.3 miles		elevation gain:++	16 stairways
Shorter walk option:		2-3 miles (leave early or start late)	
start / finish:	Fix Coffee 2100 Echo Park Avenue 90026		
Transit:	Echo Park/Pico-Union DASH bus runs daily about every 15 minutes connecting to the Metro Red Line		
Best time to walk	Just about any time that is not super hot - the views are stellar if you catch a clear winter morning or summer eve.		
Highlights	Best stairway district in LA; lovely, at times funky homes along the way; proximity to open spaces, maze of stairs		
Break spots	pass near the coffee house at the 40% mark of walk		
Please read pg 12-15 for information common to each walk in this book			

Every May, the Big Parade includes this loop on Saturday afternoon and each year this segment draws the biggest assembly of enthusiasts. The snake of walkers stretches long. Come here on your own and have it almost to yourself! This walk overlaps almost a mile of walk #1.

Beginning on map page 46:
From Fix Coffee walk down Echo Park Ave. to the left and turn right on Baxter. Go up **stairway #5** on your left and, almost immediately, down **stairway #6** on the left. Walk down the stub of Fargo to Echo Park Ave. across from the school, once home of the Room 8 cat ("C" page 49) and turn right. Proceed two long blocks down to Avalon St. and turn left. Ascend **stairway #8**, the Avalon East stairs.

Turn left at the top on Lucretia which bends to the right then meets Avon where you turn left. Follow another bend to the right onto Duane and next turn left on Park. Stay on Park only 200' before turning left on little Ewing going back downhill. Bear right at the "T" onto Avon and soon locate the Baxter **Stairs #7**. Zigzag up arriving on Park again to turn left.
Where Park seems to end at a private driveway with another street bending left, take a short park path on right. Turn left on the broader trail and follow to Marion Harlow Grove.
You have come 1 ¼ miles.

View from Marion Harlow Grove on a special day Jan 2011:looking at Cypress Park; behind that Kite Hill of Mount Washington; behind that on right, South Pasadena. Dark hills are San Rafael Hills; snow covered range is San Gabriel Mountains.

Proceed left down the broad trail and, in about 800', take the obvious path on left that connects to Vista Gordo Dr. Out of the park and reaching the street, turn right and do 180 degrees of this loop. Turn right on Cerro Gordo Street. In a couple of blocks, turn right on Valentine then go left **up stairway #1**. Follow Curran to turn left on Echo Park, Turn left on Cerro Gordo, turn right on Princeton. Go **down stairway #3**.

As you cross Echo Park Ave. at bottom, you have covered two miles and The Fix is 700' to the left. The route heads up Donaldson St., entering **stairway #2** after Vestal.

Now on map page 40.
Turn right at top of stairs onto Lemoyne and walk to a 3-way intersection with Cerro Gordo. To the left of the water tank, climb then **descend stairway #3 (read "C", Pg. 42)**.

Exiting onto Fellowship Park Way walk down to the right and turn left when meeting Landa. Jog right then left to **climb stairway #1**. Turn left on Walcott to its end and descend **stairway #2**. At the bottom, follow Peru to Whitmore and turn right. Turn right on Alvarado Street and follow as it becomes El Moran passing a car barrier. Pass the new railroad tie El Moran stairs and come to the Landacre cabin **(read "A", "B" & T-1 on page 42).**This is the three mile point. As the rough road passes a barrier you connect to pavement at Peru St. Turn left. Keep going downhill turning left on Modjeska, left on Rosebud, left on Sunflower.

Now across from the freeway, turn left on Allesandro. Walk about one-third mile on Allesandro to Loma Vista Pl. and turn left to climb **stairway #4**. At the top on Lake Shore turn right at 2225 and go down **stairway #5**. Go down the street at bottom, turn left on Allesandro, walk one block and turn left to climb **stairway #6**. At the top you can only go right passing the junction of Cerro Gordo and Alvarado. Admire the view. **This is the four mile point.**

Carefully cross Baxter **("D" page 42)** and follow Alvarado to turn **down stairway #9,** the Ewing East stairs. At the bottom, go straight across Lake Shore then up the steep rough road.

Now back on map page 46

Turn right at top and follow Lemoyne 600' to find and **descend stairway #9** on your left by the faux Victorian. At the bottom, turn left on Vestal and follow to Ewing and turn right. At the end of this short dead end street, find slender **stairway #4** on the left and walk down. Now at Ewing and Preston, walk steeply straight ahead and turn left on Echo Park. Walk one long block back to Fix Coffee.

Delta stairs   *Howard Petersen photo*

Avalon east stairs   *Howard Petersen photo*

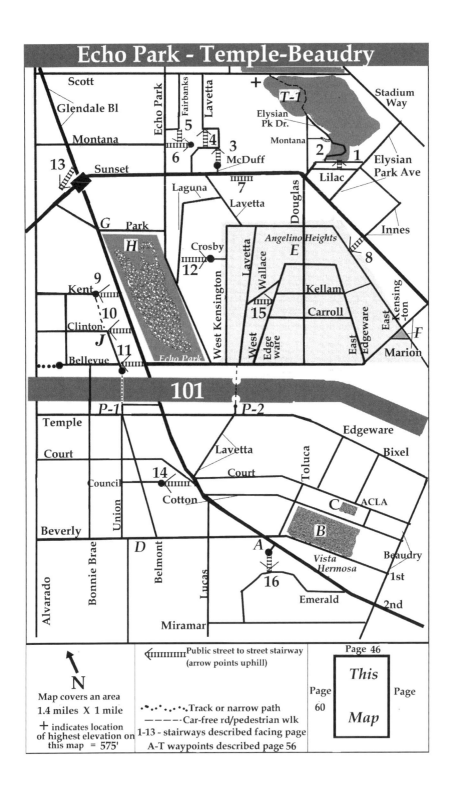

Echo Park - Temple-Beaudry

Scott
Glendale Bl
Echo Park
Fairbanks
Lavetta
+
T-1
Stadium Way
Elysian Pk Dr.
Montana
5
Montana
Elysian Park Ave
13
Sunset
4
3
McDuff
6
2
1
Lilac
7
Laguna
Lavetta
Douglas
G
Park
Innes
H
Crosby
Angelino Heights
E
8
12
Lavetta
Wallace
9
Kent
Kellam
East Kensington
10
West Kensington
Carroll
Clinton
15
East Edgeware
F
J
11
West Edgeware
Marion
Bellevue
Echo Park

101

P-1
P-2

Temple
Edgeware
Court
Lavetta
Bixel
Toluca
14
Court
Council
Cotton
C
ACLA
Union
B
Beverly
Bonnie Brae
D
Belmont
A
Beaudry
Alvarado
Lucas
Vista Hermosa
1st
16
Emerald
2nd
Miramar

N

Map covers an area
1.4 miles X 1 mile
+ indicates location
of highest elevation on
this map = 575'

Public street to street stairway
(arrow points uphill)

·Track or narrow path
- - - - Car-free rd/pedestrian wlk
1-13 - stairways described facing page
A-T waypoints described page 56

Page 46
This
Page 60
Page
Map

	stairway	location: top / bottom	steps	
1	Lilac Terrace	Lilac Terrace / 1266 Lilac Place	24	C
	Wood steps join two one-way segments here on the edge of Elysian Park.			
2	Montana-Elysian Pk Dr.	1331 Elysian Park Dr / 1306 Montana	11	C
	Narrow wood steps, close to the park			
3	McDuff	1332 Laveta / behind 1501 Sunset	74	C
	Very near to the Laveta stairs but has none of the appeal.			
4	Laveta Terrace	1349 Laveta / 1322 Laveta	65	A
	Very wide, formal looking steps look as though they belong at UCLA. They open out to a glorious block of tall palms. From bottom to top, one of LA's great stairway transitions. These stairs are more than a century old. (pg 58)			
5	Fairbanks	Montana Stairs / 1408 Fairbanks	27	C
6	Montana	Fairbank Stairs / 1396 Echo Park	40	C
	Montana is a long dead-end stairway that connects to the short Fairbanks stairs. Look for Anonymous Architect's amazing "Eel's Nest" home. That is the term Japanese use for extremely slender lots. Permission was given to push the project vertically since the site is so horizontally starved.			
7	Sunset sidewalk	west: 1472 Sunset, east: 1428 Sunset	47	B
	A sideway stairway that is pretty ordinary but Big Paraders in 2011-12 will always recall the wonderful hospitality rolled out by residents here			
8	Innis	804 E.Kensington Rd / 1302 Sunset Blvd	100	B
	An entry portal to Angelino Heights from Sunset includes a long walkway			
9	Kent	1728 Kent / 700 block Glendale Blvd	66	B
	Has a mural by the local artist Cache (he of the political chicks), these stairs are a colorful presence viewed from the lake-the path splits on top			
10	Clinton	across fr 617 Belmont / 700 block Glendale	88	B
	A massive double stairway with some nice WPA looking detail on top – has a great view of the refurbished lake. Muralist Ruben Soto painted a mural here for the '84 Olympics that the taggers have not been kind to. The 1986 movie " Echo Park" opened with a dream sequence segue from the Alps to this mural portraying an elderly Tyrolean man leading a cow			
11	Glendale - Bellevue	602 Belmont / corner Bellevue+Glendale	55	C
	Straight up stairs at southwest corner of lake			
12	Crosby	1002 Crosby / 867 Laguna	85	B
	The walker's link between Angelino Heights and Echo Park lake			
13	Glendale - Sunset	across from 1910 Sunset / 1301 Glendale	40	C
	on the north west side corner of overpass			
14	Court Street	236 Lake Shore Terr / Glendale+Court	101	B
	Another stairway that splits – check out interesting Council St on top.			
15	Wallace	1100 West Edgeware / 1484 Wallace	59	C
	In the middle of Angelino Heights			
16	Toluca	across fr 255 Emerald / 244 Toluca	101	B
	Climbs part of "Old Crown Hill" right across from Vista Hermosa Park. The story here is Belmont Station at the bottom - read next page			

Echo Park (and Temple-Beaudry)

This section covers the historic lowland section of Echo Park, home to the city's first suburb, Angelino Heights, and defined largely by the 120 year old park and lake at its center. The LA Times mapping project defines all of Echo Park (including Elysian Heights) as a moderately diverse population of 45,000 living densely in 2.4 square miles.

Pedestrian bridge, tunnel and path

P1 A pedestrian bridge that passes over the 101 Freeway linking the 500 block of Belmont Avenue with the 400 block same street to the south.

P2 A quarter mile southeast of P1, an ominous looking but fairly well used pedestrian tunnel passes under the 101 connecting Laveta Terrace.

T1 Elysian Pk Dr from the end of Douglas St to Scott Ave; the continuation of T4 & T5 on page 40- one quarter mile - pavement closed to autos.

Interesting places to walk to in Echo Park:

A   Belmont Tunnel   Look behind the Belmont Station Apartments from the left side and you find the artfully sealed off portal of the Belmont Tunnel and the remains of the Toluca substation power plant. In 1925-1955 Red Car trains that originated near Pershing Square passed out of a one-mile tunnel here on the way to Hollywood or Glendale. For another 50 years, the tunnel entrance sat open as a gaping hole to be used by filming crews, graffiti artists, impromptu partyers and urban explorers.

B   Vista Hermosa   Only 5 years old, this 10-acre park is the product of Sta Monica Mtns Conservancy on reclaimed land with extraordinary views native plants, pathways, play areas and a little creek.

C   ACLA Park   Spiraling Orchard is a lovely privately developed park on a 50'x140' lot leased from the school district. ACLA stands for art community, land, activism. Enter at 1246 Court St. or from the alley in back.

D   Filipino mural   Located on a building wall inside Unidad Park which was founded by the LA Neighborhood Land Trust. Mural created in the late nineties by local artist Eliseo Art Silva to portray 500   years of history.

E   Angelino Heights   a preserved zone of Victorian homes built in the 1880's in the city's first suburb. This is now a much cherished drive-to destination but walkers should still reward themselves with a visit here as part of a longer walk. Carroll Avenue is darling (perhaps too much so) – be sure to take in surrounding blocks on Kelham, Edgeware and Douglas.

G   Angelus Temple   It would be hard to overstate how popular evangelical Aimee Semple MacPherson was in 1920's Los Angeles and you cannot see this still busy temple and without relating the site to its first decade after opening in 1923. Then it held 5,300 enthusiasts and was topped by two massive radio towers.

H Echo Park and Lake	The lake and park are the historic soul of the

community and the lake is now reopened after a major refurbishment. Once a mid-19th century reservoir, later a private real estate scheme to create waterfront homes, the park was dedicated in the late 1890's. The studios nearby in Edendale often made the lake their filming playground in the 19-teens. The lovely boathouse and enigmatic "Lady of the Lake" sculpture are both products of the Depression era 1930's. The Lake is recently open from several years of restoration. The lotus beds are back and the Lady of the Lake has been returned to the island.

J Inspiration Point	is what mentalist A. Victor Segno named the bluff

at the top of what is now stairway #10 when he built his "School of Success" here in 1904. Subscribers would send him a dollar a day for which "Professor" Segno would send a "success wave" twice daily.

Carroll Avenue Victorians in 1972

The historic block when the homes were not so buffed out, power wires were above ground, vegetation was more unruly and TV antennas were visible.

Echo Park Lake from "Inspiration Point" *(page 57)*

Lavetta Terrace stairs

Cactus courtyard - Angelino Heights

Mural in Temple-Beaudry

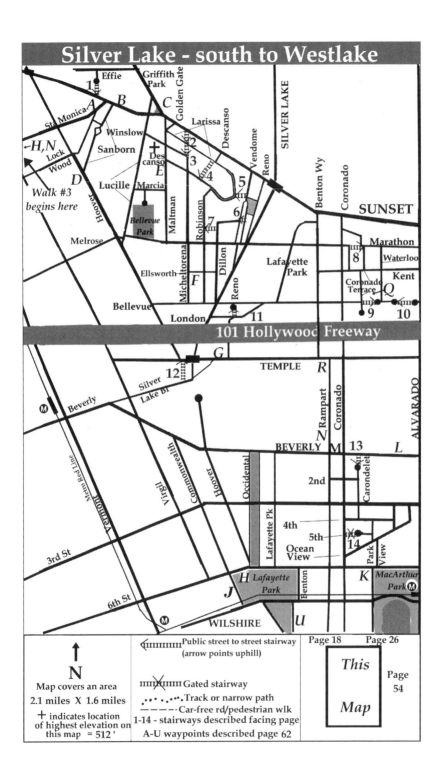

Silver Lake - south to Westlake

Effie

Griffith Park

Golden Gate

SILVER LAKE

1

A   B

C

Sta Monica

Larissa

Descanso

Vendome

Reno

Winslow

H,N

Lock Wood

Sanborn

Des canso

2

Virgil

Benton Wy

Coronado

Walk #3 begins here

D

Lucille

Marcia

E

3

4

5

SUNSET

Melrose

Bellevue Park

Maltman

Robinson

6

7

Marathon

8

Waterloo

Ellsworth

Micheltorena

Dillon

F

Reno

Lafayette Park

Coronado Terrace

Q

Kent

Bellevue

London

11

9

10

101 Hollywood Freeway

G

12

TEMPLE

R

Silver Lake Bl

Rampart

Coronado

ALVARADO

Beverly

N

Metro Red Line

Virgil

Commonwealth

Hoover

Occidental

BEVERLY

M

13

L

2nd

Carondelet

Vermont

Lafayette Pk

4th

5th

Ocean View

14

Park View

3rd St

H

Lafayette Park

Benton

K

MacArthur Park

J

U

6th St

WILSHIRE

	stairway	location: top / bottom	steps	
1	Manzanita St.	4043 Sunset / 1119 Manzanita	40	B
	Close to Sunset Junction, stairs lead to an interesting overlooked hollow			
2	Lwr Micheltorena	3315 Larissa / 3324 Sunset	109	B
3	Upr Micheltorena	1330 Micheltorena / 3316 Larissa	96	B
	A lot of length and height gained by these two stairways as they sweep you from the noise of Sunset to a lovely hilltop.			
4	Descanso	3365 Descanso / 3200 Larissa	139	B
	Look on YouTube for "Hat's off to it's your move" to see an Edgar Kennedy 1945 sketch filmed on these stairs. Derivative but of good historical interest.			
5	Music Box	3278 Descanso / 935 Vendome	133	B
	Home to cinematic history, Laurel & Hardy's "The Music Box" was partially filmed here and released in 1932. It was an Academy Award winner and generations have laughed at and remembered Stan and Ollie's struggle to get that piano up the steps. Five years before that, "Hats Off" by Laurel and Hardy used these same stairs for a sketch where they tried to deliver a washing machine. Eighty years ago this stairway was surrounded by fewer homes and less vegetation but one house seen in the film still sits at the base of the stairs. Travel+Leasure Magazine included this in their March 2012 list of "World's coolest stairways".			
6	Vendome split	on median by 914 Vendome	13	C
	Across from Laurel and Hardy park near base of Music Box stairs			
7	Robinson	832 Robinson / 827 Dillon	66	B
	Hidden away and interesting. Nice downtown views from top.			
8	Marathon	3278 Descanso / 935 Vendome	133	B
	Wide bluff-side stairway with a wonderful view west. It borders the very intriguing Marathon Manor enclave behind the gates. Steve Martin drove his Mercedes down these steps as a rush-hour shortcut in "LA Story". *(pg. 64)*			
9	Bellevue - Coronado	side of 626 Coronado / 2416 Bellevue	92	B
	A double stairway climbs to the old "noirish" Queen of Angels Hospital			
10	Bellevue - Alvarado	2132 Bellevue / 2112 Bellevue	87	B
	I call these the "Blue Stairs" of LA after a recent cleanup and paint job.*(page 63)*			
11	Reno	511 Reno / 3001 London	66	B
	Really out of the way; a nice straight-forward stairway close to the 101.			
12	Hoover Bridge	Hoover+Temple / 200 block Silver Lake	30	B
	Little stairs with a DWP garden. Near the classic Western Exterminator sign			
13	Carondelet	107 Carondelet / faces 2417 Beverly Blvd	36	B
	Double stairway nicely framed on top by trees - has a good view north			
14	West 5th Street	side of 626 Coronado / 2416 Bellevue	GATED	
	This double stairway would be nice without the gates - Westlake District			

Silver Lake south and Westlake

"Silver Lake South" is a neighborhood distinction invented for this book and includes the part of Silver Lake from the hip commercial zone by Sunset Junction through a magical hilly district that ends at the Hollywood Fwy. I have always thought the part of Silver Lake bordered by Sunset, Silver Lake Blvd. the freeway and Hoover was so unique that it deserved a name of its own. Given the property value that "Silver Lake" brings, many who live here will pass on my suggestion. This chapter also includes the Westlake neighborhood which has bounced from the glamour days of the first half of the 20th century to a deservedly bad rap in the 1980-90's for blight and crime that accompanied an explosion of immigrants. Now the beauty of the built environment of Westlake is enhanced by the vitality of that immigrant population and it is a good area to walk.

Interesting places to walk to in Silver Lake south and Westlake:

A	**Sunset Junction**	named for the 1890's inter-urban rail lines that joined here; this zone still has a vibe even as the music festival is long gone.
B	**The Black Cat**	At 3909 Sunset, this bar played a seminal role in the LA gay rights movement. A 1967 New year's eve police action instigated subsequent street protests two years before the Stonewall riots in NYC.
C	**Sunset Triangle**	The polka dot plaza was reclaimed from a busy street in 2012 - a wonderful reversal of car craziness!
D	**Angled streets**	Hoover St runs true north-south; streets to the east are angled 36 degrees per the conventions of the 16th century "Law of the Indies" that Spain drafted for the design of their colonial towns.

The Westlake neighborhood in the mid-1950's   *Clarence Inman photo*

E	**Richard Neutra**	At 1317 Maltman is an 870 sq. ft. redwood home the modernist master built in 1939 for Ceramist Harrison McIntosh
F	**Russian Church**	Holy Virgin Mary Cathedral built 1928, LA's first Russian Orthodox church, founded by refuges of WWI & Revolution
G	**Little Man**	For 60 years (even before the freeway was built) the little man with the hammer and the running neon rats have graced this location. Van Halen used this iconic image for their 1980 world tour
H	**Distinctive Library**	2 masterworks of the LAPL system: the 1929 Felipe De Neve branch by Lafayette Park and the 1916 Carnegie Cahuenga branch just off map at Santa Monica and Virgil
J	**Lafayette Park**	Sort of a 19th century style park trying to relate to 21st century urban needs-beautiful 1st Congregational has famous organ.
K	**Park Plaza**	1923 Claud Beelman Art Deco, once an Elks Lodge
L	**Brooklyn Bagel**	Hearth style baked- a 60 year LA institution
M	**Tommy's**	Original corner burger shack here since 1946
N	**Streetlights**	Classic original street lights on Rampart (in situ as in contrast to the staged art project of street lights at LACMA) The service yard just off map on Santa Monica Blvd is also a great display.
Q	**Queen of Angels**	built 1926-"noirish" - home to decades of filming before being taken over by Four Square Gospel's Dream Center
R	**Rampart Station**	decommissioned precinct station best known for the 1990's officer misconduct scandal - planned to be the Swat Team HQ
U	**Granada Building**	Classic studio-shop complex of 4 linked buildings that occupy the entire block - Mediterranean-Spanish-Moorish revival

Bellevue - Alvarado stairs (The Blue Stairs)

Marathon stairs   Jinjer Hundley photo

WALK 3	South of Sunset to Westlake		
12 miles		elevation gain: +	11 stairways
Shorter walk option:		2 segments: 5 1/2 mile or 6 1/2 mile	
start / finish:	Metro Red Line Vermont/Santa Monica stop		
	1015 N. Vermont Avenue 90029		
Transit:	Metro Red Line		
Best time to walk	Avoid the busy commute hours when doing this walk. Parking would be very difficult daytime college days. A great walk for a Saturday or Sunday afternoon		
Highlights	A midtown feel thoughout- transition from lovely residental zone to gritty to historic-cultural area & back		
Break spots	Numerous bathrooms and food chances along the way		
Please read pg 12-15 for information common to each walk in this book			

The Red Line station at the beginning and end of this walk is actually 1500 feet off the left edge of the map – All else is on **Map page 60**

Walk south on Vermont, then cross at signal to travel left or east on Lockwood to Hoover. Find Manzanita just slightly to your right and take that. Go right on Del Mar then right on Sanborn back to Hoover. Notice street angles and read "D" (page 62). Turn left on Hoover, left on Melrose, left on Lucille and then right on Marathon. Enter Bellevue Park. Walk straight back and slightly right and exit park beyond the ball field-northeast corner at gate to Edgecliff. Turn right on Marcia, left on Maltman, passing the Neutra House at 1317 (E). Turn right on Larissa. Go up **Stairway 3** at 3316. Go straight, then left on Descanso, then right on Robinson to go down **Stairway 7** at 832. Turn right at bottom, then right on Marathon, left on Robinson, right on Ellsworth, left on Micheltorena while passing the Orthodox Church (F). Turn right on Bellevue. At Hoover, the walk is one-third done. Take Hoover south to Temple and down **stairway 12**. You have left Silver Lake and are in Historic Filipinotown. Cross Silver Lake Blvd. carefully and go left up ramp returning to Temple eastbound. Note the Western Exterminator signage (**"G"**). Turn right on Dillon. Before you make a left on Beverly, check out the Medusa Lounge on your right.

From Beverly, take crosswalk at Vendome and go south. Go left on 3rd, right on Occidental. Walk down the grassy median. Arrive 6th Street. Unless it is Sunday, the lovely De Neve Library **(read H and J)** is a good bathroom opportunity. The walk goes to the left of the library and takes a path to enter Lafayette Park. Walk through park staying left of the basketball courts and right of the pool building. Come up to Wilshire and take crosswalk at Hoover coming into a triangle park. Pass courts, find a cool 1930's sculpture, "Power of Water". The Granada Buildings **(U)** are across street.

This is the 5 ½ mile point of the walk. *If leaving early, continue west to the Vermont-Wilshire Metro station.*

If you are not leaving, walk east on Wilshire four blocks to Park View and turn left. MacArthur (once Westlake) Park is on your right and Park Plaza **(K)** on your left. Turn left on 6th Street. Turn right in two blocks on Coronado St. and pass gated **Stairway 14** on your right. Turn right on 3rd cross in the crosswalk beyond Carondelet then hook back right on Carondelet. As it ends in two blocks, descend **Stairway 13**. Turn right on Beverly to check out Brooklyn Bagel; then back west on Beverly to Rampart **("L" & "M")**. Tommy's is the last bathroom opportunity until late in the walk. Turn right on Rampart and walk to Temple enjoying the old street lights.

Turn left on Temple, pass the abandoned precinct station **(R)** and walk a dull one-third mile before turning right on Vendome. Go under freeway and turn right on London.

As London jogs left, go up **Stairway 11** following Reno to Bellevue. Turn right. Take Bellevue a half mile and go up **Stairway 9.** On top is old Queen of Angels. (Q)
The walk is 70% complete.
Turn left on Waterloo then left on Marathon going down **Stairway 8.** Turn right on Benton Way, left on Lafayette Park to curve around this fabulous block. At Marathon turn right. At Silver Lake, cross at signal and make immediate right on Reno. In three short blocks, go left through the park. First find little **Stairway 6** climbing the median, then turn right to locate **The Music Box Stairway 5**. At top turn left to follow divided Descanso. Go down **stairway 4** by 3365. Turn left on Larissa and go down **stairway 2** at 3315. On Sunset turn left and cross to north side of street. **(read "C", "B" then "A" Pg. 62)** At Sunset Junction sign (Sanborn), cross to south side of street. Bear left on Santa Monica and follow to Vermont noticing the Cahuenga Library on the right **("H")** and display of historic street lights at the service yard on the left and the Staples store on the right. Arrive back at Vermont.

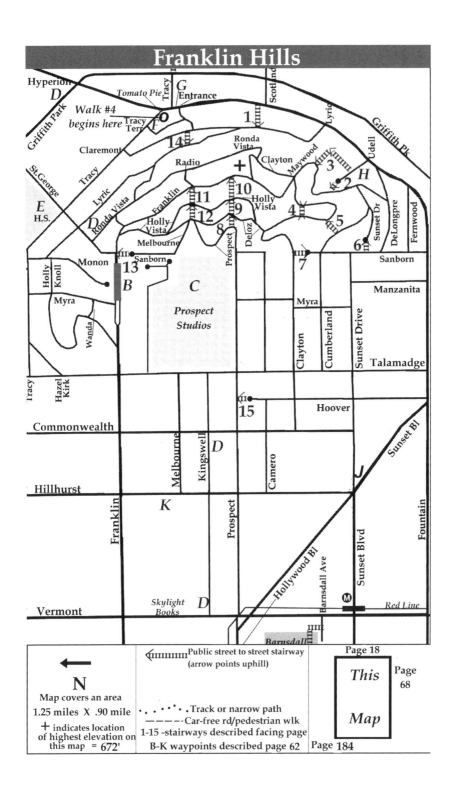

Franklin Hills

Hyperion
D
Tomato Pie
Tracy
G Entrance
Scotl nd

Walk #4 begins here
Tracy
Terr
F
O
1
Lyric
Griffith Pk
Griffith Park
St. George
Claremont
14
Ronda Vista
Radio
Clayton
Maywood
Udell
Tracy
Lyric
+
3
H
Ronda Vista
Franklin
11
10
Holly Vista
2
E
H.S.
D
Ronda Vista
Holly Vista
12
9
4
5
Sunset Dr
DeLongpre
Fernwood
Melbourne
8
DeJoz
Prospect
6
Monon
Sanborn
13
Sanborn
Holly Knoll
B
7
Manzanita
Myra
C
Myra
Prospect Studios
Clayton
Cumberland
Sunset Drive
Talamadge
Wanda
Tracy
Hazel
Kirk
15
Hoover
Commonwealth
Melbourne
Kingswell
D
Camero
Sunset Bl
Hillhurst
J
Franklin
K
Prospect
Sunset Blvd
Fountain
Hollywood Bl
Barnsdall Ave
Skylight Books
D
(M)
Red Line
Vermont
Barnsdall

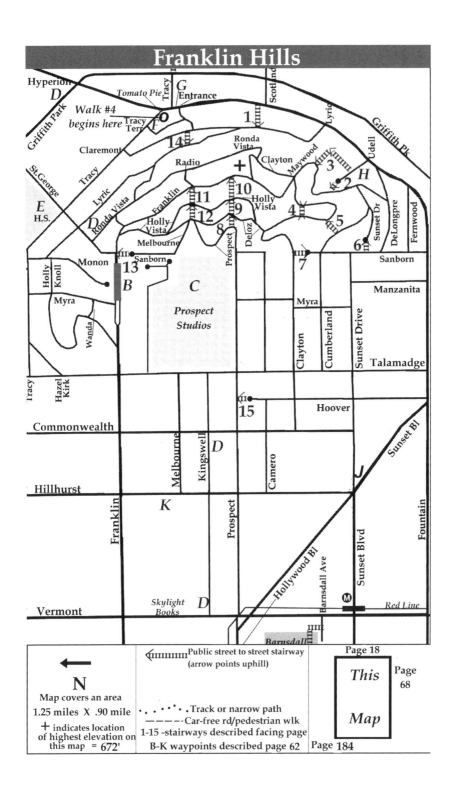

N

Map covers an area
1.25 miles X .90 mile
+ indicates location
of highest elevation on
this map = 672'

〈IIIIIIIIIIII Public street to street stairway
(arrow points uphill)

· · · · · · · Track or narrow path
— — — – Car-free rd/pedestrian wlk
1-15 –stairways described facing page
B-K waypoints described page 62

	stairway	location: top / bottom	steps	
1	Scotland Street	2232 Lyric / 2301 Hyperion	137	B

Compared to the other stairways of this group, Scotland is the only one that connects to a major boulevard. When you climb this steep, straight passage you are likely to find more signs of blight and misuse.

| 2 | Udell Minor | 1982 Mayview / 3870 Udell | 39 | B |

Easy to miss from the top; Udell is a pretty & unique 550 foot long dead-end jewel of a street that walkers would miss entirely without its two stairways.

| 3 | Udell Major | 2040 Mayview / 3838 Udell Court | 206 | B |

Remarkable stairway/pathway that is as long as the street it climbs up from. It twists and turns offering a great view of the west wall of the Silver Lake basin. LA Stairstreet Advocates did a major cleanup here in 2013 *(page 71)*

| 4 | Clayton Avenue | 3819 Clayton Ave / 3915 Clayton Ave | 36 | B |

Quick up & down on just 150 feet of length. If there were no stairway here you would have to walk one-fifth mile on the broad bend of Clayton instead

| 5 | Cumberland Ave | 3884 Clayton Av / 3953 Cumberland | 126 | B |

When you look up or down these stairs their eventual length comes as a surprise because of the concealing dogleg in the middle.

| 6 | Sunset Drive | 3626 Sunset Dr / Ac from 1427 Sanborn | 43 | B |

Provides an entry point to the Franklin Hills stairs from the southwest.

| 7 | Sanborn | 1575 Sanborn / Ac from 4001 Clayton | 41 | B |

A little jewel of a stairway that comes unexpectedly at either end.

8	Prospect walk (L)	1811 Deloz / near 3976 Prospect	57	A
9	Prospect walk (M)	1801 Holly Vista / 1740 Deloz	71	A
10	Prospect walk (U)	3814 Franklin / 1800 Holly Vista	167	A

This set of 3 stairways gives a stair climbing challenge greater than any other location in LA. If you start at the bottom of the hill at Myra and Sanborn and ascend to the top of Prospect Walk, you will have climbed 275 feet. That would be eighty feet more than from Echo Park Ave to the top of Baxter stairs or from West Silver Lake Blvd to the top of the Swan stairs. *(page 72)*

| 11 | Radio Walk (U) | 3860 Franklin / 1848 Holly Vista | 126 | B |
| 12 | Radio Walk (L) | 1849 Holly Vista / 1856 Deloz | 97 | B |

It is a treat to see this great double stairway standing tall in a 1932 Army Signal Corps photo of the area surrounded by no trees and few houses.

| 13 | Shakespeare Bdg | 3970 Franklin / 2056 Sanborn | 85 | B |

Drops down from the southeast corner of this cherished 1926 monumental bridge to a cull de sec bordered on one side by Lycee International

| 14 | Radio Walk East | 2342 Lyric / 2413 Claremont | 110 | B |

Not a particularly memorable stairway other than it is steep and straight!

| 15 | Hoover Walk | 4338 Prospect / 1654 Hoover | 37 | B |

Blessed since 2009 by the Richard Mendoza mural, "Fluid City Rising" *(page 71)*

Franklin Hills

Franklin Hills rises steeply as the last bastion of the central LA hills before the web of streets stretch across the plain towards the sea. In a car, this is an impenetrable thicket; better to go around The stairways invite the walker in. It is the stairs along with the beloved bridge, a beautiful high school building and the associations with Disney that best define what is special about this area. Franklin Hills is a section of the Los Feliz neighborhood; the west part of this mapped chapter would be considered Los Feliz proper, not Franklin Hills.

Interesting places to walk to in Franklin Hills:

B Shakespeare Bridge

An architectural Gothic fantasy, this structure endures as a magic portal into the neighborhood. When the bridge was built in 1926, it crossed a flowing Sacatella Creek that continued south and west to what is now mid-Wilshire where it sometimes flooded the streets. The bridge seems all the more fanciful now that the creek has vanished into a storm drain.

C Vitagraph Studio	Vitagraph was a New York film maker that started a studio here in 1915 on 23 acres. By the mid-20's it was owned by Warner Brothers and parts of "The Jazz Singer" were filmed here. In the 1940's, ABC bought the property and it has been used for much TV production since then. Renamed Prospect Studios, it was acquired by Disney.
D Disney Country	This area is steeped in old Disney lore. Walt & Roy Disney started a studio in their Uncle's garage at 4406 Kingswell and successively moved to bigger accommodation on the same street at 4651 and 4649. From there in 1925, they built a much larger complex where the Gelson's now stands at Hyperion and Griffith Park and occupied that until 1939. "Snow White and the Seven Dwarfs" was made here, the first full length animated film in history. They built around the corner on Griffith Park a courtyard of eight Norman bungalows in 1931 that some of the animators lived in. Walt and Roy had built for themselves matching homes at or next to 2495 Lyric in 1926 – each about 1100 square feet and built from a kit manufactured by Pacific Ready Cut Homes.
E Marshall High Sch	a collegiate gothic main building has become an archetype of what a high school should look like for hundreds of filming crews. Built 1931 and barely rescued from being pulled down after the 1971 quake. Famous alum include Leonardo Dicaprio, will.i.am, Caryl Chessman the Red Light bandit and Frisbee inventor Walter F. Morrison.
F Shepard Fairey	the famous graphic artist has a studio on Sunset and a recent mural, "Make Art, not War" on the wall of Baller's Hardware
G Haven of Rest	Another oddity: a building in the shape of a ship, complete with portholes and gangplanks. Paul Myers, who called himself 1st Mate Bob, broadcast a radio ministry here from 1941 to 1973.

H Udell Ct cottages	While many of the 17 odd properties along this nice street are plain, there are about half a dozen delightful cottages that look as if they belong in the Bohemian woods - early 1920's, some are tiny.
J KCET studios	Filming has been done on this property off and on since 1912 which might make this the oldest surviving studio in LA. The beautiful brick building was built in 1920 and has to be seen from the back on Sunset Drive. The many owners of this site have included Essanay, Charles Ray Productions, Monogram, the Bank of Italy & now, Scientology.
K Los Feliz Village	Between Hillhurst and Los Feliz is a wonderfully walkable zone of lively businesses densely mixed with a pretty assortment of homes and apartments from the early to mid 20th century. This area is corner stoned on the southeast by the beautiful 1923 Vista Theater

Hoover Walk

LA Stairstreet Advocates came to cleanup the Udell stairs March 2013

Shakespeare Bridge

Prospect Walk   *Howard Petersen photos*

WALK 4	FRANKLIN HILLS "TOMATO PIE" CURCUIT	
2.9 miles	elevation gain: ++	14 stairways
start / finish:	Tomato Pie Pizza -2457 Hyperion Avenue 90027	
Transit:	You can take the Red Line to Vermont/Sunset Station and pick up this loop near its middle after walking 7/10 mile (read below)	
Best time to walk	Really anytime day or night (but take a flashlite for after dark) Tuesday night with the group is perfect!	
Break spots	No bathroom or water opportunites on this route	
Please read pgs 8-9 for information common to every walk in this book		

The shortest walk in the book has some serious ups and downs and terrific views, particularly to the north and west. This is the tightest closed loop of stairways in the city. Los Angeles Stairstreet Advocates (Facebook) leads a group on this loop each Tuesday beginning at 6:30pm. Do this walk anytime, including after dark with a flashlight. Be very careful of passing traffic on streets with no sidewalks and when exiting the stairs along this walk.

Entirely on map page 68

Facing Tomato Pie, look at the Shepard Fairey mural to your right **("F", pg. 70)** before you walk left to the near corner and head right or south on Hyperion. You see the ship-shape Haven of Rest studio across Hyperion. As you get near 2301 Hyperion, climb **Stairway 1** on your right. Turn left at the top onto Lyric and follow back down to Hyperion and turn right. Take 2nd right at DeLongpre. Very soon, make another right on Mayview.

Begin to watch on the right for **Stairway #2** in a break in the fence line past address 1458 and go down that. On Udell Court, walk downhill 200 feet and appreciate the colony of old homes **("H").** Find **Stairway 3** on left and follow its wind back up to Mayview and turn right.

Haven of Rest when "1st Mate Bob" was still broadcasting - 1971

Walk steeply up the street to the first intersection and turn left on Clayton. As Clayton dips and curves to the left near 3819, go straight ahead up and over **Stairway #4**, turn left on Clayton again at the bottom.

In just 300 feet, find **Stairway #5** on the right by 3884 and follow it down. Turn left onto Cumberlain. Turn right at an oblique angle onto Sunset Drive, which you follow to the end and down **Stairway #6 to** Sanborn Avenue.

Arriving on Sanborn, this is about 45% of the circuit. If you using transit to reach this walk, you can start and end here. It is 7/10 mile west on Sunset Drive/Sunset Bl. to the Red Line at Vermont and 4/10 mile south from here to Sunset Junction.

Turn right, going north on Sanborn and, where it ends, descend **Stairway #7**. Turn left at the bottom then right on Myra. Again right on Camero where you climb steeply to curve left on Sanborn and make a right on Prospect. As Prospect begins to curve to the left, go up Prospect Walk: **Stairway # 8** on your right, then **Stairways #9 & #10** above.

Reaching the high point, enjoy the view and catch your breath. Turn left and walk just 1/10th mile. Descend Radio Walk **Stairways #11** then **#12**. Coming to the bottom, you arrive at a peculiar 4 way intersection and take the 2nd street from the right which is Melbourne. This curves to the right to become Sanborn. You are on the opposite side of the fence from the Prospect Studios **("C")** and Lycee International. At the end of Sanborn, climb **Stairway #14**. Enjoy, but do not cross the Shakespeare Bridge **("B")**.

Cross busy Franklin walking straight across the crosswalk, and then turn right to take the crosswalk across St. George. Climb up Franklin hugging the left curb to make the first left on Hollyvista then immediately right onto Ronda Vista Drive. Look north in the distance behind you for a good view of the old Earl C. Anthony villa. This has long been a retreat for Catholic priests. Bernard Maybeck, mostly known for his Bay area projects, was the architect. Veer left at a "Y" onto Ronda Vista Place. Then in short time, turn right onto Lyric.

In 500 feet, at 2342, go down **Stairway #14**.
At the bottom, jog to the right then immediately left going down Entrance Drive. Make the next left onto Tracy Terrace. Follow this as it curves down to Tracy Street. Turn right and arrive in front of Tomato Pie.

Shepard Fairey mural at Baller Hardware

West Bank - Glendale Narrows-LA River

The LA River is a walkable resource that recently has seen a lot of added amenities.The river is a hot commodity now with the local government and the media. Described here is a 7.4 mile stretch called the Glendale Narrows This is a river showpiece because much of it has a "soft bottom".The river floor is unpaved, not because the Corps of Engineers was "thinking green", but because there are too many natural springs in this area for a solid concrete river floor to stay intact. This happy event gives us an ecosystem much like the personality of the historic stream.

The west bank is characterized much by the freeway that runs next to 60% of this stretch of river and a bike path that runs along all of this stretch. This means as a plus that there are more places to join and leave the river path, more mini-parks on the way and that one can walk over seven miles without interruption. On the negative side, the freeway is unpleasantly close to the bike path from mile 3 to mile 7.4. Remember it is a BIKE path! There is ample space to walk to the left or right of the bicycle lanes.

You may walk in the channel itself WHEN there is no flood, small stream advisory or thunderstorm watch and when measurable rain has not been predicted for that location. It is the MRCA (Mountain Recreation and Conservation Authority) that governs the public use of the channel itself. As the rules come into place, dogs will not be allowed inside the channel.

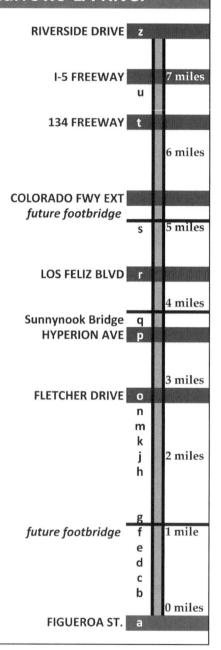

RIVERSIDE DRIVE — z

I-5 FREEWAY — 7 miles
u

134 FREEWAY — t

6 miles

COLORADO FWY EXT
future footbridge
s — 5 miles

LOS FELIZ BLVD — r

4 miles

Sunnynook Bridge — q
HYPERION AVE — p

3 miles

FLETCHER DRIVE — o
n
m
k
j — 2 miles
h

g
future footbridge — f — 1 mile
e
d
c
b
0 miles
FIGUEROA ST. — a

z	7.5	Riverside Drive	bikepath ends; Bette Davis picnic area to north
u	6.76	Zoo Dr gate	river access- close to the soccer ball structure
t	6.47	Zoo Dr gate	river access-south of #134-near on/off ramps
s	4.92	Crystal Springs Equestr'n tunnel	Access point ok for walkers,not bikes; the Mort La Kretz foot, bike & equestrian bridge from the east bank is approved – maybe here 2015?
r	4.28	Los Feliz (north)	The Daum flyover bridge is narrow,best left for
r	4.2	Los Feliz (south)	cyclists, Griffith Park entrance is 1/4 mile away
q	3.83	Sunnynook Bridge	Only footbridge over this part of river; links to 2nd bridge over fwy.Walk 1000' to tennis court office; new Sunnynook Park opened here
p	3.67	Hyperion Bridge	stairway up to bridge 400' from bike path gate
p	3.53	Glendale Blvd	South of the famous 1929 bridge, carefully enter/exit through gap next to freeway ramp
o	2.93	Fletcher Drive	to south: .2 mile to food, .8 mile to Silver Lake
n	2.72	Rattlesnake Park	South side of Fletcher Drive Bridge access with nice park, Great Heron gates & 1927 bridge
n	2.7	Clearwater St	river access with tromp l'oeil murals on bldgs
m	2.33	Marsh St. Park	river access with lovely park, Goldstone gate, water fountain, portable toilets in skate park
k	2.19	Allesandro St	river access
k	2.12	No. Coolidge Av	river access
j	2.05	Derby Ave	river access
j	1.94	Knox Ave	river access- little park with water fountain
h	1.86	Newell Street	river access-direct route to Riverside+Allesandro
g	1.26	Dallas Street	only access point for half mile either direction- One & one-third mile walk to Elysian Heights.
f	1	future bridge	400 foot footbridge to be built here by 2016
e	0.87	Riverdale Ave	river access-2 blocks to neighborhood market
e	0.82	Meadowvale Ave	river access, Goldstone gate, little park
e	0.75	Shoredale Ave	river access - bike path reads 26 km here
d	0.69	Harwood St	river access
d	0.64	Gatewood St	river access
c	0.43	Duvall Street	river access - bike path reads 26.3 km here
c	0.36	Steelhead Park	A pretty park with native vegetation but no water or bathrooms. At the Oros St. access.
b	0.2	Egret Park & Osos Park	The bikepath begins at Egret Park which would have a water fountain if not for the vandals; Larger Osos Park is along Riverside Drive
a	0 mile	Figueroa Street	Historic but flawed 1927 bridge currently being replaced; walkers need to use the shuttle bus. The new bridge is being built next to, not over the old bridge. There is a small movement afoot to keep the old structure for non-motor uses, maybe a park. What a change of thinking for LA!

East Bank - Glendale Narrows-LA River

For the walker, the character of the east bank is very different from the west. You don't need to constantly watch for bicyclists. North of Los Feliz you just need to watch for errant golf balls and perhaps give some space to a horse and rider. The freeway is not the annoyance found on the west bank. Being on the east bank does give the walker some nice neighborhood connections with Atwater Village but nothing as direct as the emersion you get in the Elysian Valley neighborhood on the south end of the west bank. The views of Griffith Park, Silver Lake & Elysian Heights are stellar this side.

The walking environment this side is better but there is less of it. The south end is pretty much a no-go. Taylor Yard that covered 30 acres here is gone but this is still an active rail zone. Access is inconvenient if not patently unlawful. From Fletcher to Colorado, walking is wonderful but that only lasts 2.75 mile plus the back-track to get out. That's much less than you can do on the west bank. North of Colorado is another 1.5 miles of industrial river bank before an unsanctioned exit point. North of I-5 is an attractive but tiny Glendale narrows park.

An exciting benefit when walking the river is the public art. Sculpture, iron gates and benches by Brett Goldstone are the river's artistic signature as are as are sculptures by Michael Amescua. Frank Romero's mural is striking across from Egret Park. Pskaught's murals beneath Hyperion Bridge are a hoot. Rafael Escamilla's Red Car is evocative.

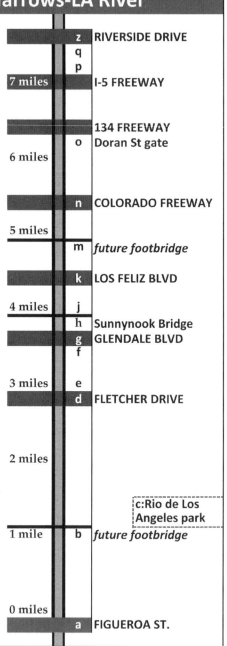

z	RIVERSIDE DRIVE
q	
p	
7 miles	I-5 FREEWAY
	134 FREEWAY
o	Doran St gate
6 miles	
n	COLORADO FREEWAY
5 miles	
m	*future footbridge*
k	LOS FELIZ BLVD
4 miles, j	
h	Sunnynook Bridge
g	GLENDALE BLVD
f	
3 miles, e	
d	FLETCHER DRIVE
2 miles	
	c:Rio de Los Angeles park
1 mile, b	*future footbridge*
0 miles	
a	FIGUEROA ST.

z	7.35	**Riverside Drive**	Bette Davis park is a jewel both sides of street
q	7.25	**(north end) Glendale Narrows Park**	Opened Dec '12, an ambitious "well dressed" park with a bike path that, at six-tenths mile long, is better fit for strolling. Extending this
P	6.66	**(south end)**	riverside park south will be the next phase.
o	6.28	**Doran St. gate**	Used historically, even if it is not official access
n	5.45	**Colorado Bridge**	The 1 ½ miles beyond North Atwater Park is a great stretch of river but it does get increasingly industrial. You can walk 6/10 mile to Colorado to Colorado & another 3/10 if you duck under. and turn back. You can duck under the overpass at Colorado and walk another 9/10 mile before you have to exit near the 134 at Doran Street.
m	4.86	**N.Atwater Park**	Newly enlarged park has great river access and a somewhat isolated feel. Many stables in this vicinity and the new bridge (2014?) will carry bikes, walkers and equestrians to Griffith Park
k	4.18	**Los Feliz (north)**	Enter this less well used part of riverbank by way of a lovely Michael Amescua gate.
k	4.13	**Los Feliz (south)**	Access is from a path through the grassy area
j	4.05	**Dover Street**	river access near a little par course
h	3.81	**Legion Lane**	river access
h	3.69	**Sunnynook Brdg**	Lovely spot; nice view of Griffith Park's Beacon Hill; great access spot from/to Atwater Village
g	3.52	**Hyperion Bridge**	You need to duck under bridge here - murals!
f	3.44	**Red Car park**	On the south side of Hyperion Br, a delightful mural is painted on a former track buttress.
e	3.08	**Acresite Street**	river access through a Goldstone gate
d	2.7	**Fletcher Drive**	Public access begins north of bridge through a Goldstone gate.North & east of here is Glassell Park including Eagle Rock Brewing in 2/3 mile!
c	1.35	**Rio de LA park**	Despite the name, provides no river access
b	1.16	**Metrolink road**	This road (though a RR underpass) is not now meant for public access to river but at some point in future will relate to a new footbridge
a	0	**Figueroa Street**	Northeast of the river is the Home Depot that now serves as one end of the shuttle bus route over the bridge reconstruction. Confluence Park (which celebrates the meeting with the Arroyo Seco) is obliterated by construction. Half a mile from here is the Lincoln/Cypress Gold Line station. A one-third mile walk going up San Fernando takes you to the old Lawry's, now the river center with nice gardens and offices of groups key to river revitalization

This 1953 pre-freeway photo looks up river with Glendale Blvd & Rowena at lower right. Atwater is right of the river. The Red Car crossing, Hyperion Br., Sunnynook Br. and Los Feliz Br. are in view. *Clarence Inman photo*

Top: Marsh Park: middle: riverbed walking; bottom: 1978 high water (C.Inman)

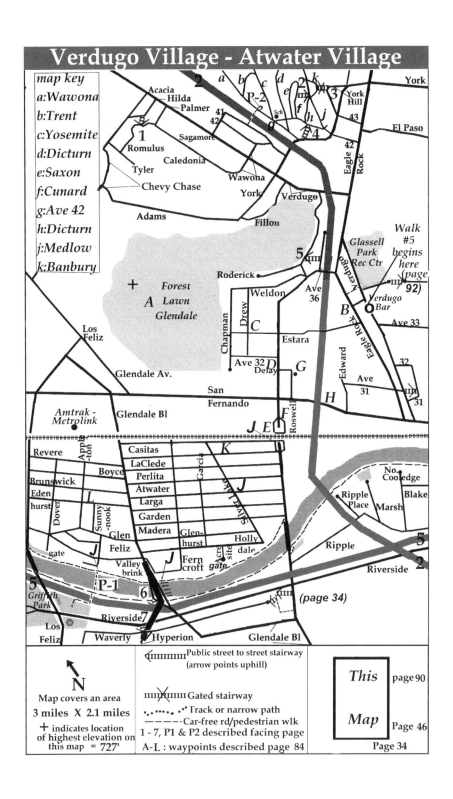

Verdugo Village - Atwater Village

This section of the book covers a zone from Glendale/Eagle Rock on the north to a sliver of Silver Lake just south of the LA river on the south. Much of this section is Glassell Park, a nice neighborhood that seems to get overlooked and confused with bordering neighborhoods with better name recognition . Much of this section is Atwater Village which justly deserves the high name recognition it currently gets. These are flatland communities that benefit visually from their nearness to the hills of Mount Washington, Forest Lawn, Griffith Park and Silver Lake. The river and railroad play heavily in the character of these areas. This is definitely a zone to get out of the car to appreciate.

Walkable assets and distinctive destinations to walk to mapped on pg. 82

	stairway	location: top / bottom	steps	
1	**Hilda Avenue**	1359 Romulus Dr / 1360 Hilda Av	54	B
	In the Adams Hill district of Glendale, a pleasant little set of steps			
2	**Banbury Place**	2669 Medlow Avenue / 2686 Cunard St	132	B
3	**York Hill Place**	2678 Banbury Place / 4051 York Hill Pl	GATED	
	Banbury is a prodigious uninterrupted climb up the west side of a ridge that would be perfectly matched by the descent down the east side if the York Hill stairs were not gated as they have been for decades. York Hill is by a rambling sloping property with a 1924 house that was once home to silent/ sound movie star ZaSu Pitts & later to future 1st Lady Nancy Davis. *(page 86)*			
4	**Delevan Drive**	4035 Avenue 42 / 2872 Delevan Dr	21	C
	Mostly just a tired looking pathway with one end facing a freeway onramp			
5	**Avenue 37**	3700 Roderick Road / 3637 Fletcher Drive	60	B
	On top is a pretty street next to Forest Lawn; below is a busy intersection that includes a corrugated steel skin redesigned commercial building with a 5-kilowatt solar array and live/work space. Tony Unruh is the architect.			
6	**Hyperion /** **Glendale**	top:bridge deck-northbound side bottom: on Glendale next to bike lane gate	39	C
	Not exactly a clean stairway, but much improved from its prior status.			
7	**Hyperion /** **Riverside**	top: 3101 Waverly Drive bottom: behind 3100 Riverside Drive	62	B
	A useful stairway unifies Silver Lake/Franklin Hills with Griffith Park. Built into it is an odd iron channel piece meant to accommodate bicycle tires - an innovation promoted by longtime resident and Councilman Tom Labonge			
	pedestrian bridges			
P1	**Sunnynook Bdg**	An historic and picturesque footbridge that joins Atwater Village on the east bank with the west bank bike path–a 2nd bridge crosses the freeway and lands behind the soccer field in the Rec Center *(page 7)*		
P2	**Wawona crossing**	In Verdugo Village, a nifty pedestrian bridge goes over the Route 2 Freeway near Delavan School -east side has a cool ramp (page 86)		

A Forest Lawn	Included for its looming presence on the land-

scape, although it could be considered a place to walk to. This place was
hugely popular weekend destination to Angelinos in the Depression era.

B Gregory Fount o ink	Lovely 1931 commercial building with art deco flourishes; once housed the west largest supplier

of fountain ink & ink wells. The ink wells were particularly decorative.

C Community garden	A spot raised from the ashes of gang violence.

The Drew St gang terrorized the neighborhood from this location
culminating in a 2008 firefight with LAPD. Eventually Wells Fargo gave the
property to the city which tore down the house and made this garden a
possibility. Ponder this spot not out of sensationalism but appreciation
that "notorious" locations might be tidy homes and proud residents.

D Capitol Records	A non-descript 50's grey manufacturing building is

notable for its participation in mid-20th Century pop culture. That old
vinyl of the Beatle's "I want to hold your hand" may have come from here.

E Valley Dairy	1931- Art Deco with a surprising interior (look

through door) JM Cardin Sprinklers has been a 30 year resident who has
restored and maintained this lovely building.

F Van de Camps	1930 Dutch Renaissance revival style bakery closed

1990. Van de Kamp's was a popular west coast bakery company. The
business included coffee shop style restaurants that had a trademark blue
rotating windmill including one where the Denny's is now. This building
was rescued for adaptive reuse by a coalition and funded by a state bond
issue to be a satellite campus of LA City College. This prompted a huge
political controversy as the community college board backed away from
the neighborhood LACC campus idea to rent site for other uses.

G Eagle Rock Brewing	When son and father Jeremy and Steven Raub started crafting here in 2009, they were the first

LA based brewery operation in 60 years. For the beer enthusiast, their
stature in the local scene is obvious. Even if not, check out their casual
un-barlike taproom and their fascinating production area which offers
tours on Sundays. Open Weds-Saturday evenings – Sunday afternoons.

H Ribet	In the 1920's-40's this building had a more stream-

line moderne angular shape as it housed the Theme Hosiery Factory.

J Rafael Escamilla	Muralist who has contributed much to the Atwater Village scene with work by the tracks near Casitas,

at Vince's Mkt, at the Red Car river crossing and at Sunnynook+Valleybrink

K Atwater Crossing	(ATX) is a five-block creative community bordering

the train tracks with a theater, restaurant, artistic theme space rentals,
artisanal manufacturing and cutting edge live-work townhouses.

L Fantasy Bungalows	Along Brunswick and nearby, a series of mostly 1000 squarefoot, 2-bedroom cottages flamboyantly

designed and built in the mid-1920's. They are heavily influenced by the
exoticism of the films of the day and the then recent discoveries in Egypt

Van De Kamps Bakery Building

Gregory Fount o Ink Building

Banbury stairs

Wawona crossing

WALK 5	GLASSELL PARK, LA RIVER PATHS, ATWATER VILLAGE		
8.7 miles		elevation gain: +	2 stairways
Shorter walk option:		5.7 miles - start/finish at Denny's	
start / finish:	Verdugo Bar - 3408 Verdugo Rd - 90065		
Transit:	Metro 84 bus from Downtown (including Chinatown Gold Line) runs frequently daily (stop ID 1749 is 1 block away)		
Best time to walk	Sunday is perfect because of the Atwater Village Farmers Market and afternoon hours at Eagle Rock Brewing. Weds-Sat afternoons Brewery is also open. Enjoyment of the river is enhanced by recent rain (if not too heavy!)		
Highlights	Charming neighborhoods, LA river paths, nice 1920's era commercial bldgs, Eagle Rock Brewing		
Break spots	At San Fernando+Fletcher and along Glendale Blvd		
Please read pg 12-15 for information common to each walk in this book			

Verdugo Bar is the starting point for both walks 5 & 6. Parking is easy and there are bathrooms at the recreation center two blocks up the street if the bar is closed. When open: a perfect spot to finish! They have great beer and a nice beer garden.

All on map page 82:

Facing Verdugo Road from the bar, turn right and walk to Avenue 35 and turn left. Walk one block to Eagle Rock, cross street in crosswalk and turn right on Eagle Rock. Enjoy the pretty commercial building (**page 84 "B"**). Cross Ave 36 at the signal THEN turn left on the freeway overpass. Pass the building with corrugated steel skin, cross Fletcher and turn right. Find and go up **Stairway 5**. Turn left at top of stairs. On Roderick Road pass an edge of Forest Lawn and follow the curve of the street almost to Fletcher but turn hard right at a "Y" onto Weldon. Turn left on Drew. Look for the community garden before Estara. (**read "C"**) Turn left on Estara and right on Fletcher by the old Capitol Records plant (**"D"**) across from Delay Street

At San Fernando use local businesses if needed as the next bathrooms are 4 miles away.

Shorter option: You could cut 3 miles from this walk by starting and finishing near the Denny's at Fletcher and San Fernando. This would diminish the appreciation of this area.

From in front of McDonald's you walk a few hundred feet towards the tracks to look through the windows of JM Cardin/Valley Dairy and look across at Van de Kamp's **("E"&"F")**. Come back towards McDonald's and walk along the west side of Fletcher under the railroad. In less than half a

mile, before crossing the river, turn right into the river path through the Goldstone gate. As conditions permit **(read page 76)**, drop down to walk on the concrete apron next to the water. As you get close to the next overpass, climb back up to the tarmac road outside the river bowl.

This is Red Car Park with our first Rafael Escamilla mural **(J)**. Duck under the Hyperion Bridge to keep walking in same direction; you have step a bit sideways for a short distance. Stay up on the service road after the bridge as you next walk over Sunnynook Bridge. Turn right on bike path and walk outside the bike lanes. At Los Feliz Blvd, exit the river though a gate and turn right. After crossing over the river, walk on a grassy area and head for a gate that puts you back on the road on the east bank of the river.

Very shortly exit the river path through the gate to Dover Street. Turn right on Valleybrink and left on Sunnynook (Enjoy the Rafael Escamilla detailing on the home at corner). Walk one block on Sunnynook, turn left on Griffith View, right on Glenfeliz and left on Appleton. Turn right on Brunswick and enter the Fantasy bungalow district **("L")** At Glendale Blvd the walk is 60% done. On Sunday, you will want to take in the farmers market across the street. Otherwise, head to the right and perhaps get lunch or coffee.

The walk picks up by "Bill's" at Madera Street. Follow Madera to Garcia and turn left, turn right on Larga and left on Silver Lake. Checkout the mural at Vince's Meat Market, then continue three blocks to Casitas and turn right. Here is Atwater Crossing **("K")**. Beyond here, when you come to Fletcher do a clockwise half-circle to the left to see Escamilla's neighborhood mural near the tracks. Keep going around until you can head north on Fletcher, right side of the street. At San Fernando, a mile and a half remains of the walk. If not going to Eagle Rock Brewing, turn right on San Fernando.

> If Eagle Rock Brewing is open (see "G") keep walking on Fletcher beyond San Fernando, turn right on unlikely looking Delay St, turn right on Roswell and look for the "orange door" on the left. Leaving here you would take Roswell to the left down to San Fernando Rd and turn left.

Shorter option ends here.

Continue east on San Fernando under the freeway and consider the history of the Ribet building **("H")**. Turn left on Edward, turn right on Avenue 31. Take Avenue 31 across Eagle Rock/Verdugo and climb **Stairway 8** (Pg. 90) and enjoy the view. Turn left on top, go to Ave 32 and turn left. Turn right on Verdugo Road and walk a quarter mile back to start.

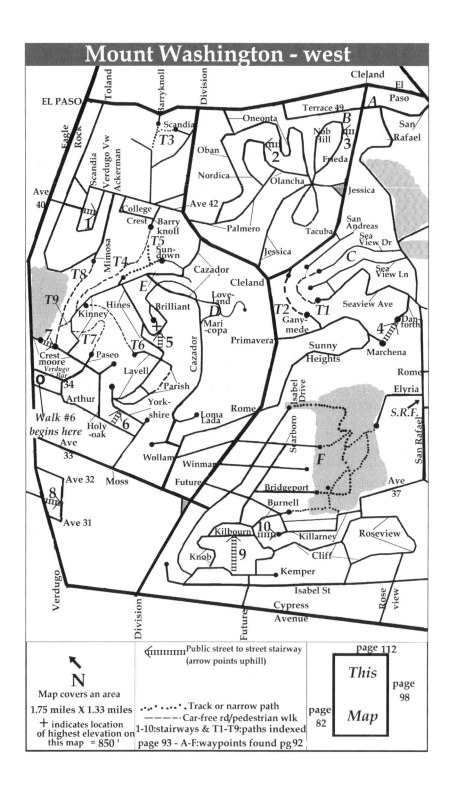

Mount Washington - west

EL PASO

Toland

Barryknoll

Division

Cleland

El Paso

Terrace 49

San Rafael

Eagle Rock

Scandia

Verdugo Vw

Ackerman

Scandia

T3

Oneonta

Nob Hill

XII

B

A

3

Oban

Nordica

Olancha

Frieda

Jessica

2

Ave 40

1

College Crest

Barry knoll

Ave 42

Palmero

Tacuba

San Andreas

Sea View Dr

Mimosa

T4

T5

Sun-down

Jessica

Sea View Ln

C

T8

Cazador

Cleland

Love-land

D

Seaview Ave

T9

E

Hines

Brilliant

T2

T1

Dan forth

Kinney

Mari-copa

Gany-mede

4

7

T7

Paseo

T6

5

Cazador

Primavera

Sunny Heights

Marchena

Crestmoore

Verdugo Bar

34

Lavell

Rome

Arthur

Parish

York-shire

Loma Lada

Rome

Elyria

S.R.F.

Walk #6 begins here

Holy -oak

6

Wollam

Winman

Isabel Drive

San Rafael

Ave 33

Moss

Future

Starboro

F

Ave 37

8

Ave 32

Bridgeport

Burnell

Ave 31

10

Kilbourn

Killarney

Roseview

Knob

9

Cliff

Verdugo

Kemper

Division

Future

Isabel St

Cypress Avenue

Rose view

page 112

This

Map

page 98

page 82

N

Map covers an area
1.75 miles X 1.33 miles

+ indicates location
of highest elevation on
this map = 850 '

⫷ⅠⅠⅠⅠⅠⅠⅠⅠⅠⅠ Public street to street stairway
(arrow points uphill)

••• • •••• • Track or narrow path

– – – – – Car-free rd/pedestrian wlk

1-10:stairways & T1-T9:paths indexed
page 93 - A-F:waypoints found pg 92

	stairway	location: top / bottom	steps	
1	Avenue 40	4001 Verdugo View / 3950 Scandia	35	C
	Two segments of old wood steps joined by a 240-foot asphalt path			
2	Oneonta-Olancha	across fr 1105 Olancha / nr 1085 Oneonta	132	A

A wonderful stairway that possesses interesting design and great views, it is found in a useful spot and is well kept thanks to work parties. The stair-story is portrayed by a sequence of 20 murals by local artist Mike Schelly. *(page 94)*

| 3 | Cleland-Frieda | 4832 Frieda / 4841 Cleland | 66 | B |

Two wood staircases linked by a long, overgrown, almost spooky pathway.

| 4 | Danforth Drive | 776 Danforth / 4018 Marchena | 56 | B |

It would take 2 miles of driving to connect the points joined by this 225' stairway. These stairs are a passage between contrasting neighborhoods.

| 5 | Hines-Brilliant | 3726 Brilliant / 2400 Hines | 106 | B |

Easy to miss on the bottom where the steps are often ankle deep in rubber tree leaves. Across from the top, there is a passage to the summit.

| 6 | Arthur-Yorkshire | 2359 Yorkshire / 2333 Arthur | 106 | B |

Steep stairway with view on top through the Los Feliz gap to Hollywood Hills

| 7 | Crestmoore Place | 2640 Crestmoore Place / 2714 Crestmoore | 93 | B |

Cull de sec stairs that are a good kick off point into the wilds of Mt Washington

| 8 | Avenue 31 | 3147 Verdugo Place / 3140 Verdugo Road | 40 | C |

Wood stairs with surprisingly good view towards Griffith Park and west

| 9 | Tillie Street | 1804 Kilbourn / 1811 Kemper | 135 | A |
| 10 | Kilbourn | 1645 Kilbourn / 3180 Future | 133 | B |

Tillie "Street" is 600 feet long and 400 feet is for walkers only – a great stairway
Turn right at the top and Kilbourn awaits you with great views on top

	pathway	description
	(the Elyria Canyon paths are described on following page)	
T1	Sea View loop	Magical half mile of unfinished walker's road that

links Sea View Drive to Sea View Ave. Described in the Bakalinsky-Gordon seminal stairway walk guide in 1990 and it keeps on giving 23 years later.

T2	Ganymede Dr	650' of nice trail joins two stubs of paved street
T3	Barryknoll	Sketchy when it is wet or weedy, a 1/10 mile path
	to Scandia Dr	helps you to avoid walking on busy Division Street
T4	Kinney St to	Lovely 3/10's mile path with nice views goes from/
	Barryknoll Dr	to 3669 Kinney - has side path to Sundown Drive.
T5	Sundown Drive	Joins 2 stubs & has a 300' weedy path to "T4"
T6	Lavell Drive	Nice 850' woody pathway joins 3663 to 3726 Lavell
T7	The Paseo to	A very special, isolated feeling trail of 1/3 mile that
	El Rosa Drive	Connects 2 deadends. The Paseo side is a deep canyon

with a steep, hairpin turn.El Rosa end has views, maybe even a rope swing!

| T8 | Mimosa Drive | 600' of trail from top Stairway #7 to end of Mimosa |
| T9 | Mimosa-Kinney | from "T8" to near 3628 Kinney; short, rudely steep |

Mount Washington west

This guide has two sections Mount Washington "west" and "east" and I am using those compass identifiers to map the entire physical massive, not just the neighborhood of that name which is found within it. On the "west" map, all to the left of Division St. is part of the neighborhood of Glassell Park; everything to the right is part of the neighborhood of Mount Washington. The massive rises like an island of twisted, complicated ridges and lanes above a sea of streets on a rigid grid. For the walker, this is an urban wilderness that might call for purposeful route finding with concerns about when the next water or comfort stop might be found. The west section with its still unbuilt lots and delightful trails gives the walker a lovely foreground to the great views across canyons and into the city.

Interesting places to walk to in Mount Washington west:

A   Coptic Church   Holy Virgin Mary Coptic Orthodox Church was built in 1988 as the first church in the Coptic style in California.

B   Nob Hill Haus   When completed in 2011, the LA Times coined this "The Greenest House in LA". It has the first permitted grey water system In the city and rain water is harvested in a buried cistern that resembles a small submarine. There's an integrated recycling plus composting system and a stack venting that discharges hot air. This Frank Pasker & Grit Leipert creation is a shining star of sustainable design.-4825 Nob Hill Drive

C   The Sea View's   Lane, Drive & Avenue: 3 narrow streets frame an extraordinary colony of about 75 homes with styles ranging from perfect Craftsman's, a Harwell Harris modern and a Jorge Pardo built for MOCA.

D   "Hidden canyon"   Unique signage and overlook of a dead-end canyon with a little farm. You can walk down road but the overlook satisfies most.

E | BIG & small house | Anonymous Architects specializes in building on challenging lot sizes. This new 950 sq. foot home is on a lot about 44' x 59'. House does not actually touch the ground and is designed as a single room

F   Elyria Canyon   35-acre nature park administered by the Santa Monica Mtn Conservancy with a rare woodland of native California black walnut trees, coastal sage scrub, chaparral and grasslands. Trails here both give enjoyment of park and connect streets and even diverse neighborhds.

Elyria Cyn trails   Start with the notion of a "trunk line" trail three quarter mile long covering a broad crescent from Isabel Dr to Bridgeport Dr From Isabel: 1st jnct goes right 600' to Wollam gate; 2nd jnct goes left 475' to Elyria Dr gate; 3rd jnct is a 600' shortcut right to the barn and water spot; 4th jnct goes left 250' to park bench; At barn & water is a private access rd. then a trail on left that climbs 1/4 mile to Burnell,with 475' path to Kilarney

Holy Virgin Mary Coptic Orthodox Church

The Paseo to El Rosa Drive trail

The Oneonta-Olancha stairs with a detail of one of the 20 murals

WALK 6	MOUNT WASHINGTON WEST	
7.6 miles	elevation gain: +++	8 stairways
start / finish:	Verdugo Bar - 3408 Verdugo Rd - 90065	
Transit:	Metro 84 bus from Downtown (including Chinatown Gold Line) runs frequently daily (stop ID 1749 is 1 block away)	
Best time to walk	Ideal on a clear day but nice anytime it is not too hot. Consider that Self Realization Fellowship is open Tuesday-Saturday 9-5pm and Sunday 1pm to 5pm.	
Highlights	Great hills and stairs, rustic streets, a variety of trails, Self Realization Fellowship, Knob Hill Haus	
Break spots	No water or bathrooms besides Self Realization Felowsh	
Please read pg 12-15 for information common to each walk in this book		

ALL ON MAP PAGE 90

Verdugo Bar is the starting point for both walks 5 & 6. Parking is easy and there are bathrooms at the recreation center two blocks up the street if the bar is closed. When open: a perfect spot to finish! They have great beer and a nice beer garden.

Facing Verdugo Road from the Verdugo Bar, turn right and walk to Crestmoore and turn right. Climb **stairway 7** and continue on Crestmoore until it comes to a "tee". Turn right then shortly left on Arthur. Climb **stairway 6** at 2333 and turn left on top. Coming to a choice of three streets, take the middle. Stay on Lavell until, at a cross street, Lavell goes left and you go straight on Hines. Just as Hines breaks left, find and go up **stairway 5**. Turn right on top. Curve around and, at Cazador, head straight ahead (disregarding the not a through street sign) to stay on Brilliant. As Brilliant hooks back to Cazador again, turn sharp left on Loveland. Meet a smaller street heading down to the left. Enjoy the view over "Hidden Canyon" (page 92 "D"). Loveland is now Maricopa Dr. as you follow it a bit more before you turn right on Cazador.

Follow this north about a quarter mile until you come to a "T". Look at The BIG and small house ("E") to the right of the lovely crossroads Mediterranean Revival home. Turn left at that "T" and walk down hill on Lavell which soon becomes Kinney. At 3669 pickup a trail (T4) on the right that continues 3/10 mile to Barryknoll.

Passing from trail to pavement, curve right on Barryknoll, left on Ave. 42 and right on Barryknoll. At an "End" sign where Verdugo Vista Terrace goes left, go straight on a small trail that curves to the right to meet Scandia. Take Scandia to Verdugo View to Division and turn left. Turn right on busy El Paso. Make the first right on Oneonta and bearing left at the "Y" follow to **stairway 2** on the right. Go up to Olancha Street and turn left. You pass Oneonta on the left then come to a 6-point junction. Take the nearest street on the left. Bear left at a "Y" to stay on Nob Hill Dr. At 4825 is "Nob Hill Haus" **(B)**. Look at that and go down **stairway 3** on left near 4832 Frieda.

The walk is half done and the route turns right at the bottom. Before that, walk 100 yards to the left to see the Coptic Church **(A)**. Turn around and head south on Cleland; watch for traffic and walk carefully. In about half a mile turn left on Ganymede. At its end, continue on a 600' dirt trail (T2). Back on pavement, turn left on Primavera then left on Marchena.

Go up stairway 4 on left past 4018 Marchena.

At top, follow Danforth to San Rafael and turn right. It's a beautiful one-third mile to the Self Realization Fellowship on left **(Read "B", page 100)**. This is the 5 ¼ mile mark.

The route continues on San Rafael until it ends at Ave 37. Turn right; follow the curve to the left which puts you on Killarney. Turn right to stay on Killarney. At a "Y" in the 1600 block of Killarney, bear left on Kilbourn and go down **stairway 10**. Go straight ahead at the bottom of stairs then look on left around 1804 to go down Tillie Street which is **stairway 9**.

Tillie Street stairs

Turn right at bottom and follow the "S" curve of Knob St. until you can turn right on Isabel Drive. Isabel curves to right. Turn left on Ave. 33. Follow this for about two-third mile to Verdugo and turn right. It's a long block then a short block back to the Verdugo Bar.

Mt. Washington - east

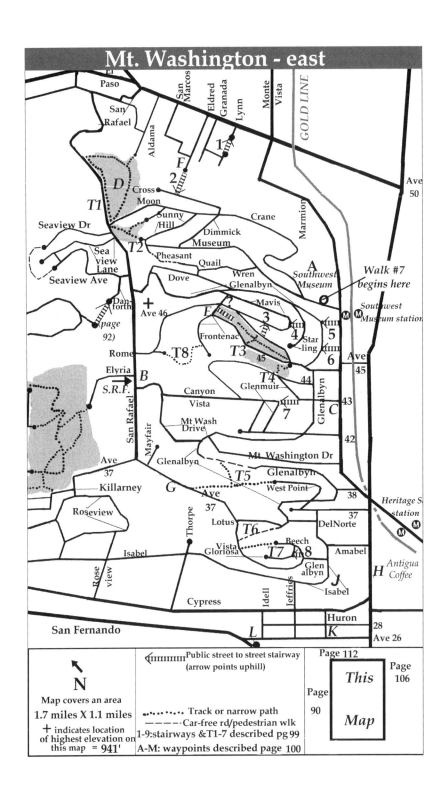

El Paso

San Marcos

Eldred

Granada

Lynn

Monte Vista

GOLD LINE

San Rafael

Aldama

1

F

2

Cross

Moon

D

T1

Crane

Marmion

Ave 50

Seaview Dr

Sunny Hill

Dimmick Museum

Sea view Lane

T2

Pheasant

Quail

Dove

Wren Glenalbyn

A Southwest Museum

Walk #7 begins here

Seaview Ave

Dan- forth

Ave 46

Mavis

Southwest Museum station

(page 92)

Frontenac

F

3

4

5

Star- ling

M

M

Rome

T8

T3

45

6

Ave 45

Elyria

B

S.R.F.

T4

44

Glenmuir

43

C

Canyon Vista

7

42

San Rafael

Mayfair

Mt Wash Drive

Mt. Washington Dr

Glenalbyn

Ave 37

Glenalbyn

T5

Glenalbyn

West Point

38

Heritage S. station

M

Killarney

G

Ave 37

Roseview

Thorpe

Lotus

T6

DelNorte

37

Isabel

Vista Gloriosa

T7

Beech

8

Glen albyn

Amabel

J

H

Antigua Coffee

Rose view

Idell

Jeffries

Isabel

Cypress

Huron

28

L

K

Ave 26

San Fernando

Page 112

Page 106

Page 90

This Map

N

Map covers an area
1.7 miles X 1.1 miles

+ indicates location of highest elevation on this map = **941'**

Public street to street stairway (arrow points uphill)

Track or narrow path
Car-free rd/pedestrian wlk
1-9:stairways &T1-7 described pg 99
A-M: waypoints described page 100

	stairway	location: top / bottom	steps	
1	Lynn	4932 Lynn / 4922 Lynn	60	B
	From Ave 50 the street ends at a cliff and a stairway			
2	Eldred	708 Cross / 4864 Eldred	196	A
	What makes this one of the city's best stairways? It is the longest wood			
	stairway, it is beautifully wooded and rustic, it would take miles of walking			
	to connect the same points and it is found atop LA's steepest street. *(page 103)*			
3	Clermont	438 Avenue 43 / 375 Canon Crest	153	A
	Beautiful; one of the best stairs anywhere. Connects to Carlin Smith Park			
4	Mavis	340 Mavis / 4567 Starling	71	B
	Perhaps the most rustic stairway on the list. Dirt trail & railroad ties.			
?	Carlin Smith	top: 511 West Ave 46	56	
	Not on the "official" list because it is a park stairway - pretty & useful both			
5	Glenalbyn Way	4600 Glenalbyn / 4601 Marmion	58	B
6	Glenalbyn Walk	across fr 4555 Glenalbyn / 4547 Marmion	22	B
	Parallel links from busy Marmion near Gold Line to bucolic Glenalbyn.			
	#7 has a metal sign promoting "garden cottages" that dates back 85 years.			
7	Canyon Vista	331 Canyon Vista / 326 Avenue 43	102	B
	Lovely stairway that once was the right of way of the Mt.Washington Railwy			
8	Vista Gloriosa	434 Vista Gloriosa / near 3440 Glenalbyn	35	C
	You can probably skip this one unless you are intent on getting them all!			
	path	description		
T1	Heidelberg Pk	(read next pg) A fun but faint loop trail of .85 mile		
	length leaves San Rafael at 4430, meets the end of Aldama, passes a deep			
	wood (with swing!) has an exit by the overlook sign on Moon and another			
	exit by way of a few steps at a little garden view area near 4315 S Rafael.			
T2	Moon Canyon	Lovely "Y" shaped trail; from the junction point, it's		
	.08 mile to San Rafael, .06 mile to Crane Blvd & .05 mile to Museum Drive			
T3	Carlin Smith Trl	Combine this one-fifth mile woodsy trail with the		
	stairway it joins (above) and you gain about 250' elevation.			
T4	Ave 44 to Ave 45	A useful narrow zig zag path joins the Sta Monica		
	Mtn Conservancy woods off Ave 45 with Avenue 44 + Glenmuir Ave			
T5	Kite Hill-West Point	This is a wide, well used but steep trail from the dirt pullout on Ave. 37 to the end of West Point. It		
	is about one-fifth mile with a junction in the middle to a narrow trail that			
	joins an unpaved stretch of Glenalbyn Drive in .05 miles (by the Bell cabs)			
T6	Glenalbyn Dr unpaved	Not really path because they can each be driven but the 3600 & 3900 blocks have 800-1000' dirt road bits		
T7	Beech Street	550 foot trail joins Glenalbyn Drive to Vista Gloriosa Drive near stairway #9.		
T8	Rome Court - Frontenac Ave	Nice 1/10mile shortcut top is next to 3932 Rome Ct. Bottom is just beyond 3 mailboxes including "542"		

Mount Washington east

Breaking the physical massive of Mount Washington into two sections, this map covers much of the Mount Washington and Cypress Park neighborhoods; two communities that fuse together geographically even as they split by a "flats verses hills" cultural divide. No other section of Los Angeles is so blessed with such a visual personality of winding streets, great views, rustic open spaces and diverse housing stock.

A	**Southwest Museum**	The 100-year old building that has been a physical landmark for the community stands now as a painful reminder of a local resource that has been eviscerated. The collection was carted off to the Autry. This is now just an archival facility that a visitor may come to Saturdays for the view and a taste of what once was here.
B	**Self Realization Fellowship**	This landmark is important both for its current use and its very different origin.Paramahansa Yoganada purchased the hilltop property in the 1920's to be the Mother Center for the Self Realization Fellowship. It is an immaculate, peaceful setting with lovely gardens and fabulous views of the city. They are closed Monday and before noon Sunday and the author asks that visitors please conduct themselves here in keeping with the tranquil setting. From 1909-1918 this was an 18-room hotel. An incline railroad was built to reach it and the journey from the city was de rigueur for the Angelino of the era.
C	**Mt. Washington Railway**	Stand at the southwest corner of Marmion and Ave. 43 on the step of the original ticket office and imagine a longer version of Angel's Flight heading up/down the slope. Across the Gold Line fence you can see the little power plant building.
D	**Heidelberg Pk**	18 acres of black walnut woodland preserved a decade ago. There is a net work of faint trails, some described page 99
E	**Carlin Smith**	Recreation Ctr with charming building (bathrooms available Mon-Sat afternoons) & a wonderful stairway/trail (read pg. 99)
F	**Eldred Street**	At a 33% grade, steepest in LA, this is one percent more than Fargo/Baxter and 1.5% more than the steepest S.F. streets
G	**Kite Hill**	Along Ave 37 the ridge juts out for fantastic views.
H	**Antigua Coffee**	Great coffee & vibe in a community center setting. Owner Yancey Quinones has been active converting an adjacent disused pedestrian tunnel into an art gallery open 2nd Saturday night monthly
J	**Isabel Street**	The soul of Cypress Park and a great street to walk.
K	**Huron Substation**	1906: built to convert AC to DC to power Yellow Car trolleys. Now a private residence with unforgettable interior rented for weddings, filming, etc.- Compare to the Ivy Substation in Culver City
L	**River Gardens Pk**	From 1961-91 was a flagship tourist destination for Lawry's Seasonings. Now publicly owned with wonderful landscaping.

The 1909 Ticket office and waiting room for the Mt. Washington Railroad

Huron Substation

WALK 7	MOUNT WASHINGTON EAST	
7.8 miles	elevation gain: +++	6 stairways
Shorter walk options: 4 1/2 miles (walk through the Sea View loop then walk to beginning; 6 1/2 miles (cut out last segment at end)		
start / finish:	Southwest Museum - 234 Museum Drive - 90065	
Transit:	Metro Gold Line - Southwest Museum Station	
Best time to walk	Ideal on a clear day but nice anytime it is not too hot. Consider that Self Realization Fellowship is open Tuesday-Saturday 9-5pm and Sunday 1pm to 5pm.	
Highlights	Fantastic neighborhood of homes, stairs & trails; Eldred Street, Sea View loop, Elyria Cyn, Self Realization Fellowship Highland Park Professor's Row and art galleries	
Break spots	No water or bathrooms besides Self Realization Fellowship	
Please read pg 12-15 for information common to each walk in this book		

START ON MAP PAGE 98 BUT SHIFT IMMEDIATELY TO MAP PAGE 106

With your back to the Southwest Museum tunnel, head to the left towards the Gold Line and continue down the steps before and after the tracks. Follow Woodside to Figueroa and climb **stairway #15** (page 108) at the corner to the pedestrian pathway above Figueroa. Go down either side of the double **stairway #12** through the arch. Turn left on Figueroa; you are across the street from Sycamore Grove ("J", page 110). Turn left past the school onto Sycamore Terrace and soon pass "Professor's Row" ("H, Pg. 110). Turn left on Avenue 50 passing across the street from a remnant of the Occidental College Highland Park campus and the art galleries.

NOW BACK ON MAP PAGE 98 FOR THE REST OF WALK

Turn left on Lynn, go down **stairway #1**. Turn right at Ave 49, right on Granada, left on Ave 50 and left on Eldred. Ascend Eldred St (pg. 102, "F") and mighty **stairway #2**. On top turn left on Cross then right on Crane.

Mighty Eldred stairs   *Carl Encke photo*

Make 2nd left on Sunnyhill and follow to Museum Drive at bottom where you turn right and enter the 700′ long Moon Canyon trail up to San Rafael Avenue. Back on pavement, head right 300′ for the Heidelberg Park overlook then come back. Turn right from San Rafael to Sea View Drive. Follow the pavement and continue past the chain onto the trail which makes a loop to your left. Soon, after passing the chain on the other side, turn left on a short alley connecting you to Sea View Lane from Sea View Avenue. Turn right at the end of this lane and follow back to San Rafael Avenue. Turn right.

(half walk option – one mile return start from here): From San Rafael, turn left on Glenalbyn Dr. which curves left. At the first "Y′ bear left on Quail. After passing Dove and Pheasant, at the 2nd "Y", bear left on Wren. At Museum Dr., turn right.)

Moon Canyon - with tower block of Southwest Museum in background

The full route reaches the 4-mile mark a half-mile further at Self Realization Fellowship ("B", pg. 102). From the SRF gate, walk straight across to Elyria Dr. Follow to end and enter Elyria Canyon Park and trail. Walk down straight past (and NOT left at) a park bench. One-third mile from the street, meet a cross trail where you turn left. Then walk a quarter-mile down, passing a side trails to the right then to the left. Coming to the water fountain and the barn, take a trail that climbs to the left by a notice board. About 250' up this slope, take the less well defined trail straight up to Killarney, ignoring the more obvious trail that heads to the right. At Killarney turn left, then left on Ave 37 which curves right and crosses San Rafael. Stay on Ave. 37. You reach Kite Hill along Ave 37 and have done 70% of the walk.

Staying left at a dirt pullout, find a trail that goes steeply 475' down to a junction visible from the top.

Turn left at that junction on another path and soon find yourself on an unpaved part of Glenalbyn Dr, probably seeing some parked taxis. Turn left. Reaching pavement go right at the first junction. Two streets are found at a sharp bend to the right and you need to select the first on your right, Mt. Washington Drive. Walk down to Marmion, turn left, and walk to Ave 43 to the old base of the Mt. Washington RR "C", Pg. 102.

There are 1.3 miles of good stuff remaining to walk including 4 stairways. However, if you need to leave early, the starting point near the Gold Line is just a couple blocks up the street.

Turn left on Ave 43 then left on Glenalbyn and right on Ave 42 and right on Glenmuir. As Glenmuir bends into Canyon Vista left, go down **stairway #7** on the right. At the bottom, turn left (Glenmuir again). Arriving at Glenmuir and Ave 44, look just by the street sign for a zigzag trail down to the bottom (Rainbow Canyon). Follow trail to right to regain pavement and turn left on Ave 45. Soon, at the Carlin Smith park sign, take the trail that goes between Ave 45 and Canon Crest. It flattens out at a cross trail with a small stairway on the right. Take those stairs up to Canon Crest and turn right. Go up **Stairway #3**. At top, turn right on Ave 46 which becomes Mavis. At the middle of a curve to the left, watch for the woodsy stairway on the right and descend on **stairway 4** and trail to Starling. Turn left on Starling, right on Glenalbyn. As Glenalbyn curves to right, go straight down **stairway 5** to Marmion near the Gold Line.

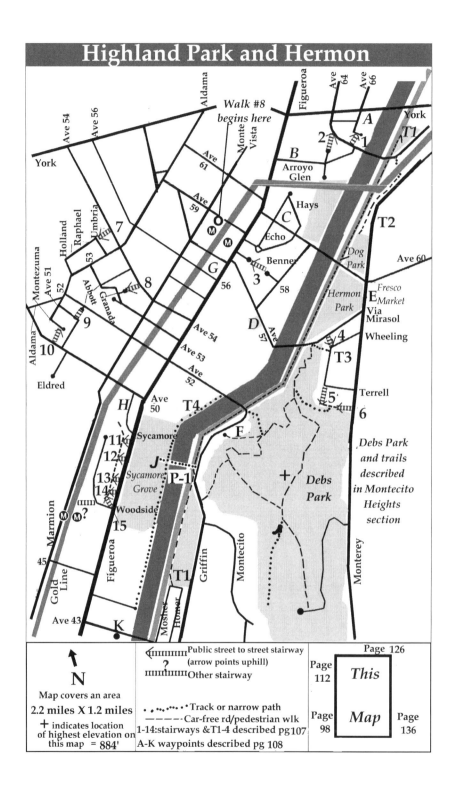

Highland Park and Hermon

Walk #8 begins here

Aldama

Figueroa

Ave 64

Ave 66

York

Ave 54

Ave 56

Monte Vista

A

2

T1

1

York

Ave 61

B

Arroyo Glen

T2

Ave 59

Hays

Raphael

Umbria

C

Holland

7

Echo

53

Benner

Dog Park

Ave 60

Montezuma

Ave 51

52

G

Bennet

3

Fresco Market

Abbott

8

56

58

Granada

D

Hermon Park

E

Via Mirasol

9

Ave 54

Ave 57

Wheeling

Aldama

10

Ave 53

4

T3

Eldred

Ave 52

Terrell

H

Ave 50

T4

5

6

Sycamore

F

Debs Park and trails described in Montecito Heights section

11

J

12

P-1

Sycamore Grove

13

14

Debs Park

Woodside

15

Marmion

?

Monterey

45

Gold Line

Figueroa

Griffin

Montecito

Ave 43

K

T1

Mosher

Homer

Page 126

Page 112

This

Page 98

Map

Page 136

N

Map covers an area
2.2 miles X 1.2 miles
+ indicates location of highest elevation on this map = **884'**

⟨IIIIIIIIII Public street to street stairway
? (arrow points uphill)
IIIIIIIIIII Other stairway

• • •••• • Track or narrow path
— — — — Car-free rd/pedestrian wlk
1-14:stairways &T1-4 described pg107
A-K waypoints described pg 108

	stairway	location: top / bottom	steps	
1	Avenue 66	near 235 Ave. 66 / Marmion & Avenue 66	24	C
	Leaf-covered stairs connect a 5-block pocket with a busy zone near freewy			
2	Avenue 64	139 Avenue 64 / 201 Avenue 64	61	B
	Look beyond the trash and broken glass for a great view down the arroyo			
3	Avenue 58	147 Avenue 58 / 200 Avenue 58	80	B
	Nice design with alternating "pull-outs". Crosses an old rail right of way			
4	Lower Bushnell	403 Wheeling Way / 5571 Via Mirasol	62	B
	Climbs from Hermon Pk. to steeply sloping Wheeling near the elementary			
5	Upper Bushnell	Pullman Pathway / 5417 Bushnell	126	A
	Lovely stairway pointed towards Debs Park- joins the Pullman stairs			
6	Pullman	Pullman pathway / 5401 Monterey Road	140	B
	Runs at a 90 degree angle to stairway 5 - a stairway to "nowhere" that works			
7	Raphael	5363 Raphael / 5374 Raphael	27	D
	Skip this one unless you feel like you just have to "do" every stairway			
8	Granada	5322 Granada / 420 Avenue 54	127	A
	A wonderful wide stairway with stair houses; chaotic at the bottom with a block			
	of beautiful homes and views on top. Has a strong sense of transition. *(page 111)*			
9	Abbott Place	429 Avenue 51 / 432 Avenue 52	56	C
10	Salient	5027 Montezuma / 701 Avenue 50	132	C
	Abbott & Salient might be forgettable stairways except that they are links			
	on a successive chain of north to south stairways. #10 is in pretty bad shape			
11	Figueroa Walk N.	Top: 4733 Figueroa	45	C
12	Glen Mary Arch	Top: 4733 Figueroa	55	B
13	Figueroa brick	Top: 4645 Figueroa	21	D
14	Casa de Adobe	Top: 4605 Figueroa	19	C
15	Ziegler Estate	Top: 4601 Figueroa	16	B
	These 5 stairways join a quarter mile pedestrian pathway with street level			
	Figueroa across from Sycamore Grove. Glen-Mary is the jewel of the set.			
	A century old archway was an early trolley waiting station. It has double			
	stairs, a shrine & a 2010 mural "Haramoknga – Place Where People Gather".			
?	Goldline platform stairs			
	I don't count these on the list but they get you from Woodside to Marmion.			
	Bridge			
P1	Sycamore Grove	Fwy/Arroyo overpass: Sycamore Grove to Griffin Av		
	pathway			
T1	Arroyo bike path	Runs inside the basin mostly next to water. Starting		
	by a stable next to Marmion, it's 2/3 mile to Hermon Dog Pk exit, then 1.5			
	mile to exit the basin by Sycamore Grv footbridge, then .3 mile to end at			
	Mosher. A pretty space to walk in but loud. Path is closed when stormy. *(page 111)*			
T2	Marmion to Hermon Dog Pk	6/10 mile service rd ends at a tunnel by dog park. Be safe on the Marmion side –is next to freeway ramp!		
T3	Wheeling trail	from V.Mirasol, a 600' path thru trees to Wheeling		
T4	Ave 44 to Ave 52	9/10 mile path that was once Union Pacific roadbed		

Highland Park

What is commonly called the Highland Park neighborhood is large, about 4 square miles. This book section includes Hermon, central Highland Park and the Sycamore Grove area. York Valley, Mt. Angelus and Garvanza are included elsewhere in the book. One of the city's oldest suburbs and the first one to be annexed, Highland Park has an enormous amount of historic character and has been a nourishing home for the regional arts for over a century. 2013 sees it ranked as the nation's hottest market for real estate activity. Highland Park arrives belatedly and perhaps a bit reluctantly to the roster of "cool" neighborhoods of LA. As a one time resident of twelve years, I like to use the phrase "soulful streets" to describe what you will find here.

A	**Judson Studios**	105 years ago, the Arroyo Guild of fellow Craftsmen was founded here to build "useful things of superlative excellence and beauty". This was one the USC School of Fine Arts and remains a producer of stained, leaded and architectural glass. *(page 143)*
B	**Abbey San Encino**	A 90 year old home hand built by master craftsman printer Clyde Browne with inspiration that ranged from California missions to an Edinburgh palace. It has a pipe organ and a dungeon. Still family held by grandson Severin Browne who spent some youth here as did his brother Jackson. The album cover of "For Everyman" by the famed singer-song writer features a photograph made in the patio of the Abbey. *(110)*
C	**Echo - Hayes**	Six blocks in this trapezoid shaped mini-district contains a particularly fine collection of old houses and interest. Walk by the Pisgah Home Historic District north of Ave. 60. It was founded in the early 1900's by a faith healer and social reformer Finus Yoakum and carries a colorful background. Today you still find a very unusual village here with a senior center and even a Tuesday afternoon farmers market.
D	**La Tierra de la Cuelbra park**	A privately owned and developed community art park. ACLA= art, community, land , activism!
E	**Hermon**	One of those secret LA neighborhoods, Hermon grew a century ago from a Methodist camp. It has fought to keep its own identity; a fight not helped when Hermon Ave. was renamed after a daughter of a local politician. It has a few odd listed historic assets like a trailer park and a wall made from car parts. A dog park keeps the Hermon name active and Hermon Park also includes a WPA built little theater.
F	**Dragonfly**	Local artist L.T. Mustardseed has a thick Burning Man resume and her home/studio here is graced with installations.
G	**HP downtown**	A zone from Figueroa to Monte Vista between Avenues 54 and 58 is a visual collage for the wanderer moving at walking speed. Iconic signage, old bank and church buildings and business fronts

H **Professors Row**	Occidental College was in Highland Park for 16 yrs. near Ave. 50+Figueroa (including Robinson Jeffers' student days) and a cluster of 1912-era craftsman's were perhaps commissioned for faculty. Notice a surviving college building that now is apartments north of Ave 50. *(page 110)*

(page 110)

J **Sycamore Grove**	A nice park with a sleepy atmosphere that conceals how this spot has had an active role in Los Angeles history for 130 years. In the late 1800's Sycamore Grove was back country between LA and Pasadena where highwaymen harassed travelers. The area also became known for the brothels that thrived where the rule of law was casual at best. Highland Park elected to give up its civic independence in 1895 partly because the unruly conditions including a beer garden where the park is now. By 1910, the Sycamore Grove area was home to seven film companies; the spot preceded Edendale as a movie making mecca. From the 1910's through the forties, the area was famous for state reunion picnics, particularly for Midwestern transplants. Concerts were popular in the park's band shell; even John Phillip Souza played here.

K **Lummis House**	Named "El Alisal" by its builder, Charles Fletcher Lummis who was a journalist, Indian activist; historian and raconteur. He was a promoter and "tastemaker" for all the regional Southwestern & California arts as he held court here from the late 1800's when he began building this home. It is a tour-de-force in Arroyo rusticity inside and out. The surrounding gardens of native plants are lovingly tended to. The home is open Thursday to Sunday noon to 4pm and is a must see.

El Alisal - the Lummis Home

Professor's Row (1974 photo)   (page 109)

Abbey San Encino   (page 108)

Granada stairs

Arroyo Seco bike path

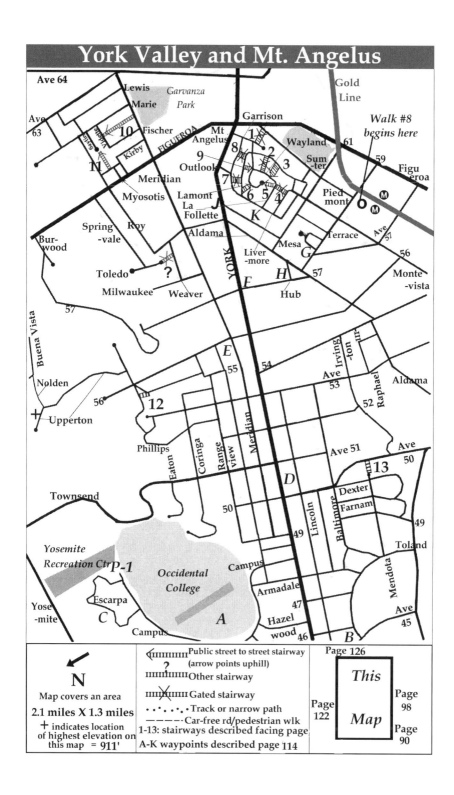

York Valley and Mt. Angelus

Ave 64

Lewis
*Garvanza
Park*

Marie

Ave 63

10   Fischer
FIGUEROA
Kirby
11

Mt Angelus
9
Outlook
8
7
6   5   4
Meridian
Myosotis   Lamont
La Follette
K

Garrison

Gold Line

Walk #8 begins here

Wayland   61
Sum -ter   59   Figueroa
3
Pied mont   M
M

Spring -vale   Roy
Aldama

Bur- wood
Toledo
Milwaukee   Weaver

?

Liver -more
Mesa   G
F   H   Hub

Terrace   Ave 57
56
Monte -vista
57

Buena Vista
57

Nolden
56
Upperton

12

E
55   54

Ave 53
52   Raphael   Aldama

Phillips
Eaton   Coringa   Range view   Meridian

Irving   -ton

Ave 51   Ave 50
13

Townsend

50
D
49   Lincoln   Baltimore   Dexter   Farnam   49
Toland

Yosemite Recreation Ctr   P-1
Occidental College
Campus

Yose -mite
Escarpa
C
Campus
A   Armadale
47
Hazel wood   46
B
Mendota
Ave 45

N	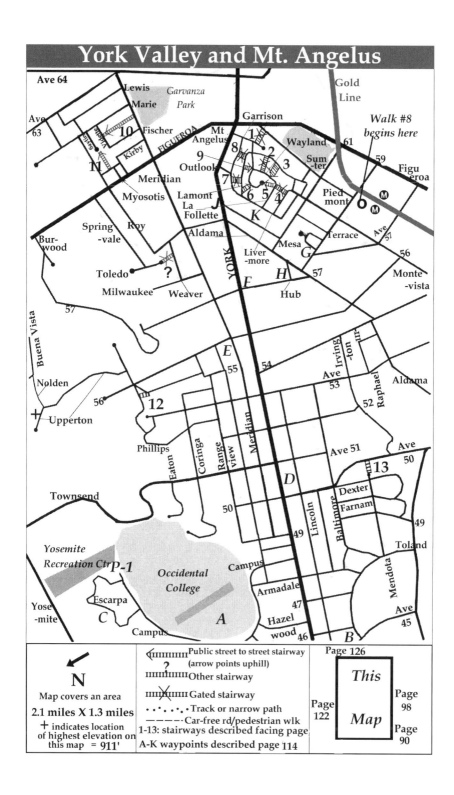	Public street to street stairway (arrow points uphill)	Page 126

Legend box:

N

Map covers an area

2.1 miles X 1.3 miles

+ indicates location
of highest elevation on
this map = **911'**

|‖‖‖‖‖‖‖ Public street to street stairway
? (arrow points uphill)
‖‖‖‖‖‖‖‖ Other stairway
‖‖‖X‖‖‖‖ Gated stairway
• • • • • • Track or narrow path
– – – – Car-free rd/pedestrian wlk
1-13: stairways described facing page
A-K waypoints described page 114

Page 126

Page 122   This Map   Page 98

Page 90

	stairway	location: top / bottom	steps	
		The Mount Angelus stairways, #1-9, are a special case; read pg. 114 & 116		
1	Mt. Angelus	6218 Mt.Angelus Pl / 6171 Piedmont	48	gated
		Sometimes unlocked Saturday; It WOULD be a primary entry passage.		
2	Hosmer walk	243 Lafollette/across fr 6200 MtAng.Dr		gated
		Gates always locked; named perhaps for 19th C. sculptor, Harriet Hosmer		
3	Sterling Walk	271 Lafollette/6155 Mt Angelus Drive	66	B
		The longest of the Mt. Angelus stairways; peeks southeast down the Arroyo		
4	Lwr Monte Vista	281 Lafollette / 246 Livermore	27	gated
		steel gates always closed		
5	Upr Monte Vista	281 Wayland / across from 281 Lafollette	22	B
		Tiny and pretty - reaches the "peak" of Mt Angelus at a cull de sac		
6	Grimke Walk	242 Wayland / corner Outlook+Lamont	45	B
		Easy to miss from the top - looks down on the Police Museum on York		
7	Emerson Walk	Across fr 263 Lamont / 6176 Outlook	26	gated
		Concealed behind wooden gates; not even open for the Stairstreet Ghosts		
8	Andes Walk	244 Lamont / 6134 Garrison	46	gated
		Gates here are just about never locked and I have led groups through many		
		times. Lying along the steps is a wonderful Andes Walk street-sign.		
9	Lafollette Walk	222 Wayland / 263 Lamont	30	B
		Short & direct - "Fighting" Bob Lafollette was a famous Progressive Senator		
10	Vista Place	Across fr 6215 Vidette / 6247 Meridian	23	C
		Only a few steps at the top of long, steep path - great seasonal tangerines!		
11	Myosotis	6203 Saylin / 6179 Kirby	114	B
		"Forget me not" -neighborhood on top is surprisingly peaceful and remote		
?	Toledo-Weaver	1100 Toledo / 5903 Weaver	gone	
		The treads have been stolen and the path is now gated - this one is delisted		
12	Avenue 55	5331 Raber / 1847 Avenue 55	21	C
		Far from any other stairway; high on the north slope of York Valley		
13	Mendota Street	4976 Mendota / across from 950 Ave. 50	14	C
		Easy to pass on this one; I do like the improvements on the adjoining home		
	passage			
P1	Campus Road to Yosemite gate	When is a gate in a chain link fence like a public stairway? This spot is similar to a mountain pass		
		with limited access. The gate is locked/unlocked by park employees		
		on the same schedule as the rec center hours. It is closed at night, closed		
		Sunday mornings and closed when they neglect to unlock it. Since it takes		
		1.2 miles to walk around it when locked, it can be frustrating. When I ran		
		this gap nighttime during college years, the gates were never locked.		
		This is similar to the history we have had with gated stairways.		

York Valley and Mount Angelus

"York Valley" is used in this guidebook to define that part of Highland Park (and a bit of Eagle Rock) that orients towards York instead of Figueroa. Mercifully the promise that York was the "next Melrose" still seems a ways off. There are a number of vibrant forces at work here (not necessarily in harmony) that add vitality unimaginable a decade ago. On one end of this zone is tiny Mt. Angelus with a unique history and stairway theme. Occidental College on the other end is said to be in Eagle Rock; a walker will likely associate it with the York side of the hill.

A	Occidental	The college has been here for nearly a century now

on a beautiful campus. The quad is perfectly proportioned for a delightful stroll. Newly dedicated is a one mega-watt solar array built as a ground hugging, flowing sculpture on the flank of 867 foot tall Fiji Hill.

B	Sparkletts	An icon of LA's 1920's school of the exotic, this

was one of several water companies here on the Cienega del Garvanza. In "Moorish" style to symbolize an oasis. Wonderful mosaic over door.

C	Escarpa Drive	Any walk in the area should include this .4 mile

loop of views and architecture ranging from modernists to pueblos.

D	York Boulevard	Besides the cool businesses between Ave 50 and

Ave 54, York has been a laboratory for alternative traffic uses. 4 car lanes evolved to 2 car lanes + 2 bike lanes; 1st use of a bike coral & a street porch A recent Conde Nast article said of York, "it's the new coolest street in L.A". Coming to the quarter-acre vacant lot at Ave 50 will be a public space that one committee member has promised will be "the most pimped-out city pocket park in Los Angeles". Hmm, can't wait.

E	Avenue 56 mural	Activist artist Judy Baca created this Highland Park

history mural in 1976 and it was wonderfully restored in 2011. Enchanting!

F	Galco's	Local hero John Nese had the genius idea to make-

over a family market into a soda pop emporium - a great place to walk to

G	Smith Estate	Beautiful 1887 Queen Anne mansion on a hilltop
H	One block home	A 560 square foot home that occupies its own block
J	Police Museum	inside a 1926 precinct station that once was target

of a Symbionese Liberation Army bomb - open Mon-Friday & 3rd Saturday

K	Mt Angelus	Mt. Angelus is a knob poking above the Highland

Park plateau that measures only 1500' by 900'. Ten narrow streets wind around each other amidst a colony of small, mostly 1920's homes. In the early 1900's, this plot was developed by Cora Scott Pond-Pope, a New Englander of suffragist-abolitionist lineage. She named streets and stairs after her heroes. This is the only place in LA where the stairs have names unrelated to the area streets. Each one had a "street" sign on a post. Today access to five of the nine surviving stairs is inhibited by gates. The posts have been stripped of their signs. The locals appealed to the city in 1985 as they were concerned that the stairways were linked to crime. The city council voted to leave the choice about closing the stairs to the neighbors and made no provision for a review of that policy in the next generation.

The Stair Street Ghosts

The most ingenious and inclusive event to honor the public stairways of Los Angeles took place in 2011 on October 30.

Louisa Van Leer is an artist and a resident of Mount Angelus. She won a grant from the "Artist Bailout" for this project and got assistance from the city and the Highland Park Heritage Trust. This was an afternoon that combined the celebration of her neighborhood stairways with a Halloween carnival and a commemoration of the 100 years of Women's Suffrage in California. A block was closed to traffic; eight stairways were freshly cleaned and signed including four that typically have locked gates. Independent walking was encouraged and group tours were led by such stair-celebrities as Charles Fleming. Replica suffrage ribbons were worn and period songs sung. The kids had a parade and a costume contest. Alas, the closed stairways were closed again after the event but the day earned city appreciation for our stairs.

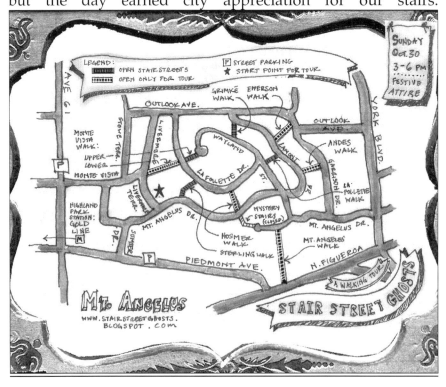

WALK 8	HIGHLAND PARK - HERMON		
8.4 miles		elevation gain: ++	15 stairways
Shorter walk option:	6 miles - cut off last segment		
start / finish:	Highland Pk. Gold Line station: 151 N. Avenue 57, 90042		
Transit:	Metro Gold Line - Highland Park Station		
Best time to walk	Just about anytime when not too hot. Not a "big view" walk so cloudy/hazy days are not an issue.		
Highlights	15 stairways, unique Mt. Angelus, Galco's Soda Pop shop cool commercial districts along York and Figueroa,		
Break spots	Soda pop shop, York+Ave 50, downtown Highland Park		
Please read pg 12-15 for information common to each walk in this book			

START ON MAP PAGE 112 AND REFER TO MAP PAGE 116
Walking off the Gold Line platform on the Avenue 59 (north) side, turn left on Ave. 59 then immediately right on Piedmont. Reaching the Recreation Center in a couple blocks, there is a last chance for a bathroom. Across from the Rec Center, go up Sumter St on the left to enter Mt Angelus **(read pg. 114 "K" and refer to the map pg. 116).** Turn right on Mt. Angelus Dr., then left up the **stairway #3** near 6155 and turn right on top. Examine the top of gated **stairway #2** at 243 Lafollette then, when you come to a "T", go straight down **stairway #9**. You will proceed left on Lamont but know that you are near the tops of two gated stairways **(#8 and #7).** Near 282, go up **stairway #6** and turn right on top which leads you to a cul-de-sac. Descend **stairway #5** and notice the gates on its continuation **stairway#4**. Turn right in front of those gates on Lafollette, left on Outlook, left on Livermore. Admire a mural where you turn right on Monte Vista. You leave Mt. Angelus at Ave 61.

Turn right on Ave. 61 and left on Terrace and right on Ave 59. You should turn right on El Mio and do the 360 degree around the dramatic hilltop Smith Estate **("G")**

Back at Ave. 59 turn right. This soon intersects Ave. 57.

Bear right and at Aldama go either right or left around the **"one block house" ("H")** and pickup Ave. 57 again other side. At York, find **Galco's** Soda Pop Store on right. ("F")

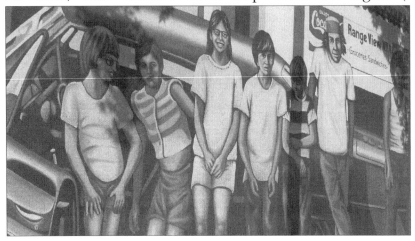

You can shave a mile off the route (but cheat yourself) by turning left on York and head to Ave. 50. Otherwise, cross York and take Ave 57 three blocks to Meridian and turn left. At Ave. 56 before you turn right, look at the **mural (pg. 114 "E").** Go uphill on Ave. 56 one block to Stratford and turn left, then right on Ave 55. Follow Ave. 55 as it shifts to the right and walk uphill to **stairway #12**. Turn left at top of stairs and take the first left from Raber to Barker. At Ave. 53 turn right and follow to York. Enjoy colorful York to Avenue 50 where you should plan a break. This completes 40% of the full route; over half of the shorter route.

From Café de Leche, walk to Ave 50 and turn left. Past the school, where Ave. 50 curves to left, take Dexter which is smaller and straight ahead. Climb to Mendota and turn left, soon picking up a little sidewalk on the right and then down **stairway #13**. Turn right on Ave. 50. At El Paso, cross over to be on the east side of Avenue 50 (geology above you!).

REST OF WALK ON MAP PAGE 106

Past 701 Ave. 50, climb **stairway #10**. Turn left on top at Montezuma which curves right, Turn right on Ave. 51. Go down **stairway #9** on the left at 429. Bottom of stairs, turn left and climb up Ave. 52. Turn right on top at Aldama ST. then left on Aldama TERRACE then right on Raphael to end at **stairway #7**. At Ave. 54, turn right and follow to wonderful **stairway #8** at the Granada St. sign. Climb to reach Granada St. Follow to Ave. 53 and turn left to go steep down to Monte Vista where you turn left. Go right on Ave. 56 reaching Gold Line. Short version of walk ends. The station is a block to left.

The full walk is another 2 ¼ mile. Taking Ave. 56 further to Figueroa turn left, cross street and turn right at Ave 57. Check out **La Tierra de la Culebra ("D")** downhill on right. Keep following Ave. 57 making a left on Via Mirasol before the freeway. Cross over freeway and enter **Hermon (read "E" pg. 108).** On right, in front of closed gate for Debs Park, pick-up the narrow path that parallels Via Mirasol through trees as it climbs and reaches where Wheeling meets Bushnell. Turn right walking up Bushnell and soon see your next objective, **stairway #5** straight ahead. Climb this to a walkway that turns into **stairway #6** going down to Monterey Rd. Turn left, following Monterey to one-way Wheeling Street and turn left. At 403, go down **stairway #4**, cross street and enter Hermon Park. Follow pathway to the right of the first group of tennis courts and to the left of the 2nd group (bathrooms here). The path curves to left and meets a walkway that climbs on right up to Ave. 60. Take that, turn left on Ave. 60 and cross over the Arroyo and freeway. Turn left on Benner and right on Ave. 58. Climb **stairway #3** meeting Ave. 58 on top. Meet and cross Figueroa. Jog a bit right and continue to Gold Line.

Eagle Rock

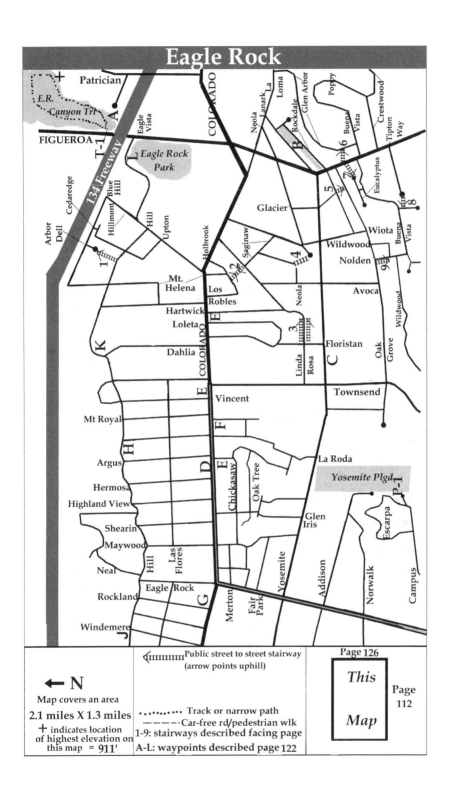

Patrician

E.R. Canyon Trl

FIGUEROA

Eagle Rock Park

Eagle Vista

Blue Hill

Cedaredge

Arbor Dell

Hillmont

Hill

Upton

Holbrook

Saginaw

Glacier

Mt. Helena

Los Robles

Hartwick

Loleta

Dahlia

Neola

Janark La

Loma

Glen Arbor

Rockdale

Poppy

Buena Vista

Crestwood

Tipton Way

Eucalyptus

Wiota

Wildwood

Nolden

Buena Vista

Neola

Linda Rosa

Floristan

Avoca

Wildwood Grove

Oak Grove

Vincent

Townsend

Mt Royal

Argus

Hermosa

Highland View

Shearin

Maywood

Neal

Rockland

Windemere

Hill

Las Flores

Eagle Rock

Chickasaw

Oak Tree

La Roda

Yosemite Plgd

Glen Iris

Escarpa

Merton

Fair Park

Yosemite

Addison

Norwalk

Campus

COLORADO

134 Freeway

COLORADO

COLORADO

Page 126

This Map

Page 112

← N

Map covers an area
2.1 miles X 1.3 miles
+ indicates location of highest elevation on this map = **911'**

⊲ꟷꟷꟷꟷ Public street to street stairway (arrow points uphill)

•••••••••• Track or narrow path
– – – – – Car-free rd/pedestrian wlk
1-9: stairways described facing page
A-L: waypoints described page 122

	stairway	location: top / bottom	steps	
1	Arbor Dell	1100 Arbor Dell/ 1371 Hill Drive	78	B
		Very pretty stairway; at the bottom is lovely Hill Drive; standing on top you see skyscrapers and get a hint of what the pre-freeway hills were like.		
2	Saginaw	1301 Linda Rosa / 1450 Holbrook	60	B
		A special stairway that climbs from each end and has a paved pathway across the ridge top. I like to credit the merits of this stairway mentioning that the LA Times architecture critic lived alongside it until recently		
3	Linda Rosa	1507 Linda Rosa / 1531 Linda Rosa	39	B
		Stairs built into the sidewalk on either side of this pretty street		
4	Neola	near 4827 Neola Pl / 1321 Neola St	47	B
		I am always intrigued by the 90 year old river rock/brick home at the base of these stairs behind Rockdale School. Stairs have an unusual design.		
5	Oak Grove	near 1040 Oak Grove in the meridian	20	B
		Oak Grove is a pretty, well-named double street with a median stairway		
6	Tai chi	1007 Glen Arbor / across fr 7149 Figueroa	64	B
		These stairs plus Glen Arbor Ave. take you from Figueroa into the La Loma district and those stairs. Named after a mural by artist Roger Dolin that was funded by a neighborhood group. First painted 2004, refurbished 2011 *pg 124*		
7	Eucalyptus	6035 Eucalyptus Lane / 7149 Figueroa	39	C
		Faces the Tai Chi stairs and lifts you into a rustic little Topanga-like lane		
8	Tipton	800 block Tipton Terr. / 5811 Tipton Way	15	C
		Easy to pass on this one but the old, isolated wood steps are alluring		
9	Nolden	1961 Nolden / 1983 Nolden	79	C
		Very steep street with sidewalk stairs running up halfway on the west side.		
	pathway			
T1	Eagle Rock Canyon Trail	As a rule, the pathways described in this book are selected because they function like the stairways; they are good street to street options to give the walker an avenue that the motorist cannot use. This trail is an exception; the only place it takes you is right back to where you started. A walker should visit this this trail, if for no other reason, than is was so artfully designed and built. Master trail builder Peter Schaller and a band of volunteers in 2007 crafted a one mile loop trail with a great view that is fun to walk. The high point looks down to the top of the Eagle Rock and the views expand far to the west and south. Notice the striking 100-year old sandstone colored power station. A rail line was extended just to get the materials up the canyon. I recommend doing the loop counter-clockwise staying right at the start. Come up these and sit for the sunset. *(page 124)*		
	passage			
P1	Yosemite Plgd Campus Rd gate	An important pass through point available when Yosemite playground is open - read page 113		

Eagle Rock

Eagle Rock has realized benefits from being on one hand one of the central LA neighborhoods and on the other staying tucked away from the fray that comes from being central. Independent until 1923, Eagle Rock was annexed to LA relatively late in the game. It has a central business district that has purposefully avoided the cliché and national retailers. There is a back drop of high, empty (but for the arrival of the 134 Freeway in 1970) hills that create both barrier and back drop. Ridges define east, south and west boundaries. These enhance the pleasant walkability in this neighborhood of a diverse population of 35,000 (including the author for 25 years).

A	The Rock	A 50' tall rock formation where the shadow beneath an outcropping will resemble the outstretched wings of an eagle. The top and rear of the rock are on private property but a 1989 threat to develop the property in front of the rock galvanized the community to "save the rock". Bandito Tiburcio Vasquez may have hid in the cave here in 1874 before his capture & there are photos of Chinese soldiers training here in 1904 under a Capt. O'Bannion in anticipation of the 1911 Rebellion.
B	Rockdale Garden	Beautiful community garden and art park that is more than just garden plots. Stretches along an abandoned rail line.
C	Rock Row	A newer trend in LA housing development is to use the small-lot subdivision code and the Wronske brothers are architects that have excelled in making it work. Each of these 15 homes is about 1300-1600 sq.foot with high marks for minimal energy use. Appearances aside, each is free-standing with about a five inch gap from its neighbor.
D	Colorado Blvd	Like so many boulevards in LA (San Vicente, Venice, Glendale, Huntington, et all) the presence of a center median is a dead give-away that a trolley once ran here. Colorado and Townsend was the end of the line for an LA Railroad Yellow car that ran clear to Inglewood. Colorado is where the restaurant/retail renaissance of Eagle Rock has been active in the past 15 years. Colorado's six lanes of ever flowing cars has been a traffic engineer's dream but a nightmare for many locals looking for a less auto-centered environment. A movement called "Take back the Boulevard" grew out of the thirst for some traffic calming. The issue has been extremely contentious but in October 2013, the bike lanes and sensitivity to the needs of the pedestrian have arrived.
E	Adaptive reuse	Colorado Blvd has some good examples including a a 1911 bungalow now Little Beast & the 1939 Pillars Department Store that is now Renaissance Arts Academy. Also the 1931 car showroom that was Fatty's and will soon be Eagle Rock Brewing.
F	Casa Bianca	Almost 60 years in this storefront with famous pizza and timeless pink and blue neon advertising "Pizza Pie"

G Carnegie Library	Built 1915 & remodeled 1927 - now is a community center. This Mission/Spanish Colonial building is a beauty - inside and out.
H Hill Drive	undulates softly for 2 miles at the top of the Eagle Rock valley and perhaps is one of the great walking streets in the city. Together with the 20 straight streets that connect Hill to Colorado, this leafy and palm studded district is full of interesting homes.
J Brauch House	2327 Hill: another home with fairytale detailing in the sleepy hollow arches. Popular culture demands that this home be best known for its one time renters: Ben Affleck (once an OXY student) and Matt Damon when they were writing "Good Will Hunting".
K Bekins Mansion	This 1927 sprawling chateau dominates this part of Hill Dr. and has been on and off the market in the $3-$5 million range for a few years. It includes a bistro. Those faux-wood handrails were made by shooting cement into fire hoses and letting it dry before hose is cut away.
L Eagle Rock Park	A Richard Neutra designed gym building built in 1953 has roll back doors that can transform it into an open air pavilion.

Tai Chi stairs

Eagle Rock Canyon Trail

Casa Bianca   *pg 122*

Rock Row   *pg 122*

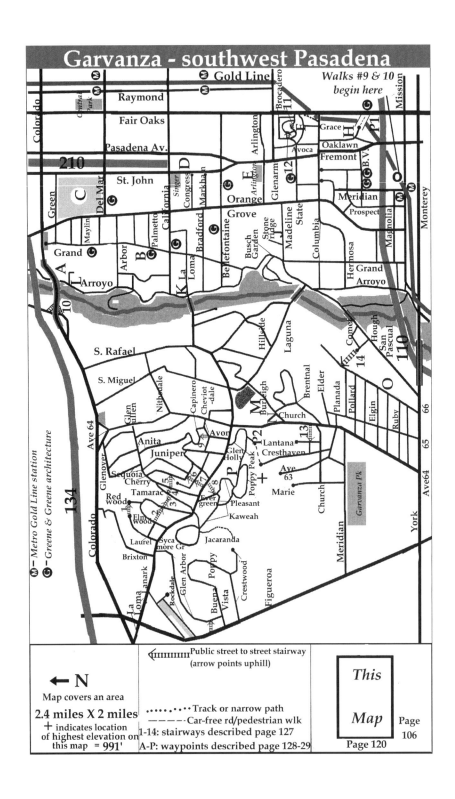

Garvanza - southwest Pasadena

Gold Line

Walks #9 & 10 begin here

Colorado

Central Park Ⓜ

Ⓜ Raymond

Fair Oaks

Pasadena Av.

210

Green

Del Mar Ⓖ

St. John

Maylin

Grand Ⓖ

Arbor

B Ⓖ

Palmetto

California

Singer

Congress

Markham

Bradford

La Loma

K

Arroyo

A

10

Brocadero

Arlington

Mission

Grace

Avoca

Oaklawn

Fremont

Ⓖ B.V.

P1

Arlington

Glenarm

Ⓖ 12

ⒼⒼ

O

Ⓜ

Orange

Grove

Stone Ridge

Busch Garden

Madeline

State

Columbia

Meridian

Prospect

Magnolia

Monterey

Belfontaine

Hermosa

Grand

Arroyo

Hillside

Laguna

Comet

Hough

San Pascual

14

110

66

S. Rafael

S. Miguel

Nithdale

Glen Suffen

Capinero

Cheviot-dale

Burleigh

Church

Brentnal

Elder

Planada

Pollard

Elgin

Ruby

O

Ave 64

Glenover

Anita

Juniper

Avon

Lantana

Cresthaven

13

P2

M

Glen Holly

Poppy Peak

Ave 63

Marie

Church

Garvanza Pk

Ave64

York

Colorado

134

Sequoia

Cherry

Tamarac

Red wood

Elm wood

Laurel

Brixton

Evergreen

Pleasant

Kaweah

Syca more Gr

Jacaranda

Meridian

La Loma

anark

Rockdale

Glen Arbor

Buena Vista

Poppy

Crestwood

Figueroa

Metro Gold Line station

Ⓜ –

Ⓖ – *Greene & Greene architecture*

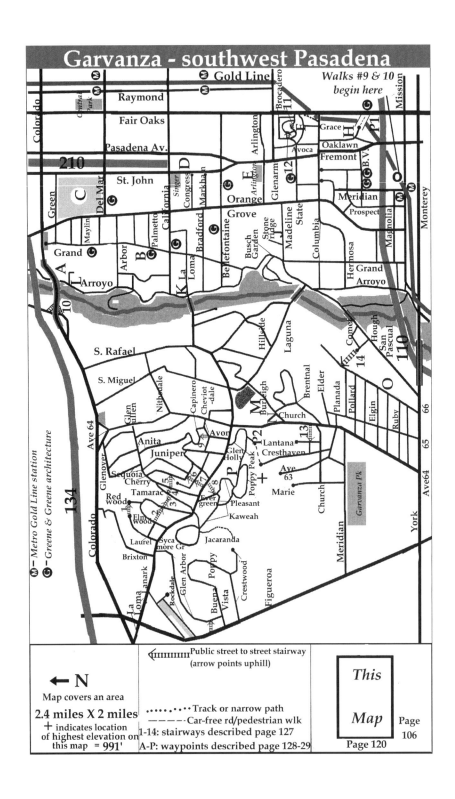

⤚🚶‏‏Public street to street stairway
(arrow points uphill)

← N

Map covers an area

2.4 miles X 2 miles

+ indicates location
of highest elevation on
this map = **991'**

┈┈┈┈Track or narrow path

─ ─ ─ ─ Car-free rd/pedestrian wlk

1-14: stairways described page 127

A-P: waypoints described page 128-29

This

Map

Page 120

Page
106

	stairway	location: top / bottom	steps	
1	Sycamore Glen	240 Redwood Dr / 252 Sycamore Glen	60	B
		Nice stairway that joins 2 cul-de-sacs. "Secret Stairs" missed this one.		
2	Elmwood-Redwood	395 Redwood Dr / 420 Elmwood Dr	98	A
3	Redwood-Tamarac	365 Tamarac Dr / 390 Redwood Dr	99	A
4	Tamarac-Glenullen	362 Tamarac Dr / 363 Glenullen Dr	90	A
5	Glenullen-Cherry	351 Cherry Dr / 360 Glenullen Dr	99	A

Four stairways line up for an exceptional "chain" of stair walking. Counting the 3 narrow streets it crosses, this is just over 1000 feet long. That is not quite the linear stair passage that Loma Vista Place is but close. Finding such stair dedication in such an upscale neighborhood is unusual.

6	Upper Cherry Dr	437 Cherry Drive / Cherry Alley	53	B
7	Lower Cherry Dr	Cherry Alley / 1587 La Loma Road	43	B

Debatable whether this should count as one stairway or two.

8	Evergreen Dr	610 Evergreen Dr / 1560 La Loma Rd	45	C

Of this group of 9 stairways, the only one south of La Loma Road. Very hard to see from the La Loma end. Combine this with a walk up Poppy Peak.

9	Avon Avenue	1428 Capinero Dr / 1437 Cheviotdale	44	B

Another pretty one off on its own.

10	Colorado Bridge	Colorado Bridge / Linda Vista Av	34	C

Towards the west side of the bridge on the east bound traffic side. A twin stairway is on the west bound side but there is no pedestrian way there.

11	Grace Walk	88 Grace Terrace / 54 Grace Walk	63	B

Pretty - stretches out in step clusters melting into a Moreton Fig tree

12	Grace - Brocadero	95 Grace Terrace / ac fr Brocodero	37	B

A west facing stairway on fabulous Grace Hill

13	Rosewood Terrace	1102 Lantana / 1113 Avenue 64	50	B

Nice to go down these as you gaze at the Church of the Angels

14	Hough	760 Avenue 66 / 6635 Hough	126	A

One of the best: the only way up or down this hill, nice view and charming tile work on the risers.We can thank nearby San Pascual Elementary. *(Illus. back cover)*

P-1	Oaklawn Bridge	400 block Fair Oaks - 400 block Oaklawn Ave		

A graceful, perhaps whimsical, bridge built for cars by Greene and Greene in 1906 is now open for foot use only. It now bridges the Gold Line, but the Santa Fe passenger trains and freights ran here. Look north at a trail to the left of the tracks and see what is the right of way of the famous but short-lived Pasadena Cycleway from around 1897 to 1910.

P-2	Cresthaven Drive	About 300 feet of pavement removed from auto

use in one of those odd boundary zones between Los Angeles and Pasadena. Nice shortcut from the Church of the Angels area to the lovely Poppy Peak residential zone. A "no trespassing or loitering" sign on the LA side seems pretty silly - you can be the judge.

Arroyo Seco trail and access paths: covered on page 130

Garvanza and southwest Pasadena

This 4 square mile area is consolidated in this book as one section. That part of Pasadena near the lower Arroyo Seco relates to the Los Angeles neighborhood of Garvanza in a way that is apparent to someone on foot even as someone in a car might think that there is no connection. This area has a district of historic homes as significant as anywhere in the country. It has a wonderful tight cluster of stairways very uncommon for the wealthy post WWII neighborhood they are found in. It has 120-year old remnants of rustic Annandale and Garvanza.

It is the deep canyon and trails of the Arroyo Seco that command and a walker's focus as he or she explores what is beyond.

A Colorado Bridge	You can walk across it, under it on a path, under it on the adorable Parker Mayberry Bridge or take the twin stairways to reach it. This 100-year old iconic landmark has a particular walking component because the adjacent freeway attracts most of the traffic. Ghoulishly nick-named for fifty suicides that occurred here 1933-1937.
B Pasadena Heritage	There are scores of connected blocks (not all named on map) with an extraordinary trove of early 20th century homes. This is a walker's paradise; eye candy at every turn. West of Orange Grove try the zone bordered by Colorado, Arroyo and about Madeline. East of Orange Grove, I recommend the area bordered by California, Fair Oaks and Mission. There are wide streets, some made all the more walkable with barriers against auto passage on one end.
C Ambassador	32 acre campus of nice pathways and landscaping. Property assembled from estates for Evangelical college 60 years ago. Now, some of this is high school campus so visitation is limited in spots.
D 710 Extension	Like an obnoxious guest that just won't leave, the specter of freeway construction and the fervent fight against it has influenced different parts of this section for more than forty years. Consider as you walk anywhere between Orange Grove and Fair Oaks.
E Arlington Garden	A jewel - and one that would not exist but for the uncertainty cast on this property during the freeway threat. This 3-acre botanical garden of paths and drought tolerant plants is a relatively unknown treasure for the walker to wander. Walk the labyrinth!
F Grace Hill	Just a pimple on the Pasadena plain rising one hundred feet above what surrounds it. A lovely, eclectic zone to walk through on narrow lane and stairway to enjoy the view. This was once a 19[th]century estate. A 45 foot tall wood-shingled water tower that is now a 4-story home is the feature neighborhood attraction.
G Greene & Greene	Brother architects who dominated the California Arts and Crafts movement with a long list of masterpieces mostly built in less than a decade. Although their best work is just north or east of this mapped section, they were very active in this zone 1900-1915 and their works that can be seen while walking are marked with a letter "G".

H Oaklawn	A posh residential tract begun in 1904 is lined with
sensational homes and anchored on east end by a distinctive bridge (now
closed to autos) and trolley waiting station designed by Greene & Greene.
The walker can promenade up the 75 foot wide, often car-free, avenue.
J Busch Gardens	Brewery patriarch Adolphus Busch wintered in his mansion on Orange Grove north of Madeline and
built 32 acres of public gardens. A popular destination in the years
around WWI, the entire area was subdivided for homes in the 1930's
and it would take a true local archeologist to turn up much evidence of
this historic attraction. At 1025 Arroyo Dr., the unusual half circle framing
now built into a home was once part of the Greek pergola. From Stone
Ridge 100 feet north of Madeline, you can see the "Old Mill", now a home.
K Batchelder	Look for the handmade craftsman tiles on the path
and chimney of a lovely "chalet". Here was the home and studio of Ernst
Batchelder, who was a leader of the local arts and crafts movement.
L La Casita	Perched on the Arroyo edge, this is a pretty garden
and lodge designed by Myron Hunt and built during the Depression years.
M Johnson Lake & Beaudry Tunnel	Although the lake looks to be just a suburban amenity in a gated community, this is an historical
feature of the landscape and there are photos of San Rafael Winery lake-
side from the 1870's. The Campbell-Johnson family from Britain centered
their 23 thousand acre ranch here on land purchased 1883. In 1876 Victor
Beaudry, an early LA mayor and land baron, built a 480' foot long tunnel
In the narrows of Burleigh Street to open up the inaccessible "vale" of
Annandale. The tailings from the tunnel dig contributed to enlarge
the lake. The tunnel is long since blasted away to become an open slot.
N Church of the Angels	Built from San Fernando valley sandstone in 1890 as memorial to the pater of the Campbell-Johnson
clan who died on a return visit from Britain to the cattle ranch. The design
is based on a church in Surrey and the builder was Alexander Coxshead.
O Avenue 66	An historic spine of Garvanza; I love these grand
80-foot wide avenues that get little traffic. A few too many unfortunate
apartments keeps this from being ranked as really fine assembly of homes.
P Poppy Peak	At a thousand foot elevation, this hill has much
influenced how the area has developed. The legend is that early explorers
anchored offshore could see a blaze of California poppies on the summit
and so named the feature. Of interest to the walker is the historic district
of exemplary modern period architecture north of the peak and south of
La Loma along Kaweah, Poppy Peak Dr. and Pleasant. One favorite is the
1300 sqft. home that Richard Neutra built for Occidental College Art
Professor Constance Perkins in 1947. Located at 1540 Poppy Peak, Mr.
Neutra produced a work that was custom suited to a diminutive lady who
wanted a space she could create in, not a traditional family floor plan.

Lower Arroyo Seco

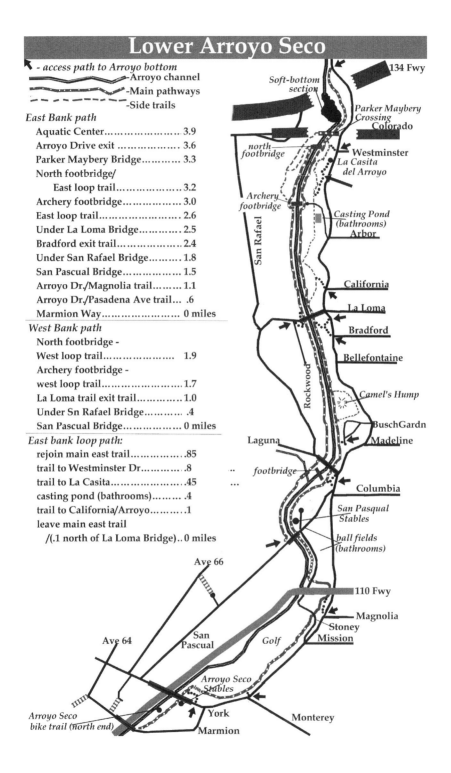

↖ - access path to Arroyo bottom

⟿ -Arroyo channel

≈≈≈ -Main pathways

- - - - - - - -Side trails

East Bank path

Aquatic Center.........................3.9
Arroyo Drive exit 3.6
Parker Maybery Bridge............3.3
North footbridge/
    East loop trail....................3.2
Archery footbridge..................3.0
East loop trail..........................2.6
Under La Loma Bridge.............2.5
Bradford exit trail....................2.4
Under San Rafael Bridge..........1.8
San Pascual Bridge..................1.5
Arroyo Dr./Magnolia trail........1.1
Arroyo Dr./Pasadena Ave trail... .6
Marmion Way........................ 0 miles

West Bank path

North footbridge -
West loop trail...................... 1.9
Archery footbridge -
west loop trail........................1.7
La Loma trail exit trail.............1.0
Under Sn Rafael Bridge............ .4
San Pascual Bridge................. 0 miles

East bank loop path:

rejoin main east trail.................85
trail to Westminster Dr.............8
trail to La Casita.....................45
casting pond (bathrooms).........4
trail to California/Arroyo...........1
leave main east trail
   /(.1 north of La Loma Bridge)..0 miles

WALK 9	SOUTH PASADENA TO ARROYO TERRACE		
6.2 miles		elevation gain: +	5 stairways
Shorter walk option:	4 miles: loop back early		
start	Metro Gold Line - South Pasadena station		
finish	Metro Gold Line - Memorial Park station		
Transit:	Metro Gold Line		
Best time to walk	Thursday afternoon has the farmer's market; one key passage towards end of walk gets locked at 7pm; perfect in spring but delightful any season or hour		
Highlights	Fabulous districts of historic homes; Arlington garden; Arroyo Seco pathways		
Break spots	bathroom by the casting pond-Lower Arroyo Seco park		
Please read pg 12-15 for information common to each walk in this book			

The Gold Line stop and surrounding Mission and Meridian is the start point for both walks 9 and 10. Both of these walks are NOT loops but end at a different Gold Line station for an easy ride back to the start. Walk 9 goes north, Walk 10 goes south. With cool businesses like Buster's Cafe, this is a great spot to start or finish a walk. The Farmers Market is Thursday open 4pm to 8pm.

If my only goal was to maximize attendance on a walk I led or suggested in a book, Walk 9 is the low-hanging fruit. The beauty and walkability of this area is attractive to the max.

ALL ON MAP PAGE 126 (more detail lies on the Arroyo Seco *map page 130* and the north "annex" map for the end of walk) Looking at Mission from Buster's, turn left and walk east 4/10's mile to Fair Oaks enjoying the storefronts then turn left and walk north 3/10's on heavily used Fair Oaks. Turn left on the obvious car-less Oaklawn Bridge admiring the waiting station as you pass. Off the bridge walk ahead through Oaklawn ("H") and stay right in a block. Coming to the formal gates as you exit onto Columbia, cross the street carefully and jog slightly left to keep going north on Avoca.

At State Street, take the diagonal right ahead to Grace Terrace and begin to climb. Take a hairpin turn to the right. Curving left, pass "88" on right and "80" on left to find **stairway #11**. Go down stairs then take the hairpin turn back left that keeps you on Grace Terrace. Pass the Water Tower House on left (read "F", Pg. 128) before turning right down **stairway 12** at "75". Turn left then right doing 250 feet of backtracking. Turn right on Avoca and left on Glenarm. It is important that you take the cross walk straight ahead crossing Pasadena Ave

a preemptive victim of the 710

before turning right on Pasadena. Ponder that this might have become freeway ("D"). As you reach Arlington, cross it and walk another 90 feet north and enter the garden on a path. Take as long on whatever path attracts you but eventually exit far to the left back out on Arlington where you turn right walking west. Turn left on Orange Grove and cross diagonally to the southwest corner Madeline+Orange Grove.
This is about the one third point of the walk.
Walk down hill on the left side of Madeline enjoying the Cravens Mansion (Red Cross) best viewed from their west driveway. Eventually shuffle over to the right side of the street before "485". The gate leads your gaze to a Busch Garden relic, "The Old Mill" **("J")**. At Stoneridge turn right

and walk only 200 feet and back for a better view of the Old Mill.

Back on Madeline, walk down to the junction with Arroyo Bl. and cross street going straight ahead to stay on Arroyo on the right hand side of the street. As it curves left, the San Rafael Bridge appears beautifully on the

stairs into the Arroyo Seco

right. Cross San Rafael and just beyond the plaque find a trail that takes you up, then down 73 steps into the Arroyo Seco.

You could bail out early here: walk down the arroyo past the stables to meet and follow the start of Walk 10 in reverse.

The complete route, however, asks you to turn right on the trail and walk upstream on the right side of the culvert.

Walk 6/10's mile on path. As the next bridge gets close, watch carefully for a trail that cuts right at an oblique angle and climb path and 54 steps to Arroyo Dr. (bear left at junction).

Turn left on Arroyo Drive, cross La Loma and appreciate the homes, particularly the Batchelder Home on right at 626 ("K"). At California, find a path back down into the Arroyo and turn right as you reach the first trail.

a Batchelder tile (4" square)

Colorado Street Bridge

In about 1/3 mile are the casting pond and a park building with bathrooms and water.

Leaving here, continue up the Arroyo on the same trail, crossing pavement to pick it up on the other side. In about 150 feet find an obvious side trail to right that will climb out of the Arroyo again to reach La Casita at the rim ("L").

From the front door, walk further north through the parking lot to reach Arroyo Drive again.

At Westminster, get a good view up at the old Arroyo View Hotel building (now the US Court of Appeals) before finding a trail on left that takes you back down.

Reaching the trail on the bottom, turn right and soon find the junction with the main trail along the culvert. Continue upstream first under the Colorado Bridge ("A") and then the 134 Freeway Bridge. Enjoy the area beyond Scoville Dam where the creek flows freely in a more natural soft bottom channel. Follow the trail as it eventually climbs up to meet Arroyo Drive. Walk on the gravel left side of the road until you see a flat grassy area across the street. Cross carefully here. The Aquatics center looms nearby. Walk across the grass then to the right of the Aquatics center via a narrow passage.

Soon, as you are just about even with the diving platform, make a 180 degree right turn around a tree to pick up a path with 21 steps that curves to the left.

Reach a 4-way junction with other paths, turn right.

Still walking uphill, ignore a path that splits off to the left in 100 feet. Eventually (about 1500 feet from Arroyo Dr.) you reach a gate. This gets locked nightly at 7pm by private security. Find a different route if you are late.

You've arrived in Arroyo Terrace district with its treasure of Greene & Greene and Myron Hunt homes. Turn right at the gate. Turn left on Grand which returns to Arroyo Terrace where you turn right following its curve right to pass Scott. Just after Scott, turn left into a walkway behind the neighborhood church. Turn right at the grand stone chimney and left on the walkway beside the parking lot. Walk to the Gamble House. This is one of the most marvelous and important attractions in this entire book. I did not describe it in the area notes since it is just off the chapter map. It can be seen any day or hour from the outside – tours available to view the interior Thursday-Sunday.

When satisfied, go out to Orange Grove. From here it's a mile on auto-pilot: right on Orange Grove left on Walnut. At Raymond enter Memorial Park walk diagonally to the right of the band shell to reach Gold Line where it is 3 stops back to the start.

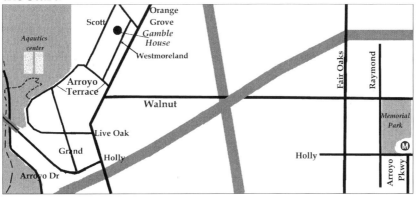

Montecito Heights - Lincoln Heights

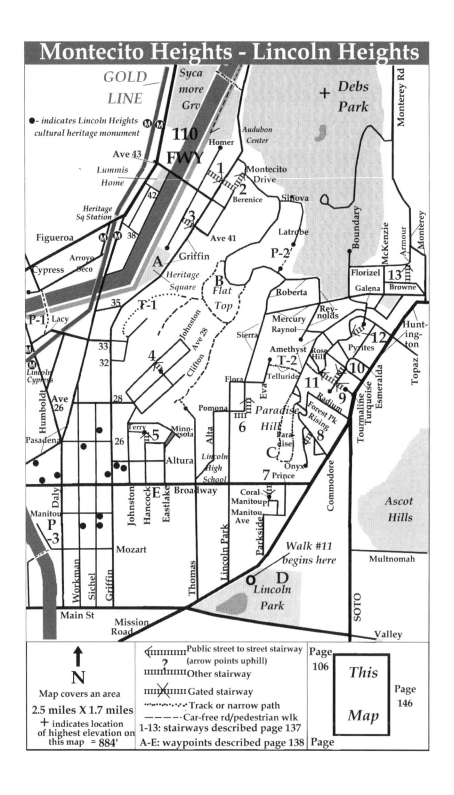

GOLD
LINE

● - indicates Lincoln Heights
cultural heritage monument

Syca
more
Grv

110
FWY

Debs
Park

Monterey Rd

Homer

Audubon
Center

Ave 43

Lummis
Home

42

Montecito
Drive

1

2

Berenice

Sinova

Heritage
Sq Station

Figueroa

38

Ave 41

Latrobe

3

Boundary

McKenzie
Armour
Monterey

Arroyo
Seco

Cypress

A

Griffin

Heritage
Square

P-2

Florizel

Galena

13

Browne

B
Flat
Top

Roberta

35

T-1

Johnston

Rey-
nolds

Mercury
Raynol

Hunt-
ing-
ton

P-1 Lacy

Ave 28

Sierra

12

33

Clifton

Amethyst

Rose
Hill

Pyrites

32

4

T-2

10

Flora

Telluride

11

9

Humboldt

Ave
26

28

Pomona

Eva

Paradise

Radium

Forest Pk
Rising

Tourmaline
Turquoise
Esmeralda

Topaz

Pasadena

26

Terry

5

Minn-
esota

Alta

6

Hill

Para-
dise

8

C

Onyx

Altura

Lincoln
High
School

7 Prince

Commodore

Ascot
Hills

Daly

Manitou

P
-3

Johnston
Hancock
Eastlake

E Broadway

Coral
Manitoup

Manitou
Ave

Parkside

Multnomah

Mozart

Lincoln Park

Walk #11
begins here

Workman
Sichel
Griffin

Thomas

D
Lincoln
Park

SOTO

Main St

Mission
Road

Valley

N

Map covers an area

2.5 miles X 1.7 miles

+ indicates location
of highest elevation on
this map = 884'

⊄ıııııııı Public street to street stairway
      (arrow points uphill)
ıııııııııı Other stairway

ııııⅪıııı Gated stairway

······· Track or narrow path
————·Car-free rd/pedestrian wlk
1-13: stairways described page 137
A-E: waypoints described page 138

Page
106

Page

This

Map

Page
146

	stairway	location: top / bottom	steps	
1	Homer-Griffin	4433 Griffin Ave / 4426 Homer	63	B

Picks up across street from stairway #2. From the steps, notice kind of a greenbelt right and left. Dan Koeppel's research turned up that this might have been the Pasadena Cycleway route had it not been abandoned a century ago. A corridor here was held as right of way for some time after the first segment went bust four miles north. *(page 145)*

	stairway	location: top / bottom	steps	
2	Griffin-Berenice	4507 Montecito Dr / 4430 Griffin Av	60	B

An L shaped stairway: Montecito (hard to spot) down to Berenice, turn right - then stairs and pathway past a 100-year old home to Griffin.

	stairway	location: top / bottom	steps	
3	Avenue 41	4103 Griffin / 4102 Homer	63	B

Close to Heritage Square - straight up. This one really looks like a ladder.

	stairway	location: top / bottom	steps	
4	Montecito Street	near 3029 Johnston / 2817 Montecito	78	B

Draped by conifers; remote in a Lincoln Heights box canyon.

	stairway	location: top / bottom	steps	
5	Hancock-Terry	3033 Terry Place / 2537 Hancock St	24	C

Odd little shortcut that kind of looks gated at Hancock but is not

	stairway	location: top / bottom	steps	
6	Sierra Sidewalk	2826 Sierra / 3628 Pomona	14	C

An elevated walkway reached by steps that runs along the east side of Sierra & south side of Pomona. Numerous little stairs access this.

	stairway	location: top / bottom	steps	
7	Coral Street	2351 Coral St / near 3830 Broadway	96	B

Different: free standing steel structure joined to bluff top by bridge.

Stairways 8 through 12 are in the "Gem Streets" district

	stairway	location: top / bottom	steps	
8	Mallard - Onyx	2602 Onyx / 2539 Mallard	123	B

Kind of off on its own - long and narrow

	stairway	location: top / bottom	steps	
9	Lower Tourmaline	Across from 2929 Pyrites	31	C
10	Pyrites	2929 Pyrites St / 3033 Pyrites St	34	C

A sidewalk stair high above Pyrites street - joins stairway #11

	stairway	location: top / bottom	steps	
11	Upper Tourmaline	near 4404 W.Rose Hill/2929 Pyrites	191	B

Start from Huntington, walk up steep Tourmaline to the lower stairway, climb that, cross Pyrites and take the upper stairway, then climb rudely steep Tourmaline: you will have ascended 380 feet. That is almost double the ascent from Echo Park Avenue to Park Avenue above the Baxter Stairs.

	stairway	location: top / bottom	steps	
12	Galena Street	4521 East Rose Hill / 3420 Galena	106	B

Pretty rustic around here - the barking dogs are a permanent feature.

	stairway	location: top / bottom	steps	
13	Browne-Florizel	4534 Florizel St / 4537 Browne Ave	103	B

Nice view towards County-USC Hospital and beyond-open lot west side.

	other pedestrian assets:		
P-1	Graffiti Bridge	From Ave 34 near Lacy to Ave 26 & Arroyo Seco -

800 foot pedway crosses freeway and Arroyo. Looks sketchy but is well used

P-2	Latrobe shortcut	Walker friendly barrier against car passage
P-3	Mozart overpass	nifty spiral then ramp over the 5 Freeway
T-1	Ave 33 to Flat-top	4/10 mile from VonKeithian to across fr school
T-2	Telluride Street	Almost a comically steep track climbs 240 feet

elevation in 740' of distance. There are a couple of wood stair sections on one side that look as if they belong in a Rocky Mountain mining town.

Lincoln Heights and Montecito Heights

These two neighborhoods fuse together on a map and in this book section but are different from each other. Lincoln Heights can be characterized by a flat grid of streets flowing away from downtown that tuck up against the surrounding hills. It is a product of the late 19th century and retains a nice inventory of homes, churches and commercial structures more than a century old. Montecito Heights is largely mid-20th century, and almost entirely residential. To the explorer on foot, it is best characterized by empty spaces and sensational views found in Debs Park, Flat Top and Paradise Hill.

A Heritage Square	This is a repository of 19th century LA and Pasadena

structures with restored interiors that were destined for a wrecking ball. There are about 10 buildings including a rail depot from Palms, a church from northwest Pasadena and homes that once stood in a number of LA neighborhoods. The museum is a product of the 1960's-70's when the city was at last becoming aware how quickly it's built history was vanishing. Open Friday to Sunday afternoons, the $10 entrance makes this more of a destination than a casual walker's pass-by

B Flat top	Also known as Radio Hill and Mt. Olympus, this is

300 mostly undeveloped parcels on 100 acres. Encompassing two ridge-lines, this is the premier unprotected open space in the city combining great views, proximity to several densely populated neighborhoods and the resemblance to the bald grassy hilltops the 18th century settlers would have found. Accessible mainly from Thomas St. on the southeast and at the end of a bend of Montecito Dr. on the north. The Four Square Church of Echo Park holds title to much of this land. At the end of 2011, some new fencing and signage was added to discourage the walking patterns that the locals had enjoyed. While walking this wonderful hilltop persists, the visitor who comes at the suggestion of this book should understand that access is a bit in flux and should do as the locals do. From Montecito Dr., enter walking to the right of the remote gate arrangement. Regaining dirt road, you can walk out on the mesa about 700 feet before reaching a "Y". To the right would be the junction with Fenn which extends a lovely 1/5 mile to a dead end from which you would need to return. Past Fenn is the start of trail "T-1" described on the previous page. A left turn at the "Y" then right at the next "Y" takes you eventually to pavement at Thomas St, beyond an auto barrier. It's half a mile walk from Montecito to Thomas.

C Paradise Hill	Another mostly bare hilltop with spectacular views

Like Flat Top, this sixty acre mountain top consists mostly of privately owned, undeveloped lots. This area was evaluated by the Santa Monica Mountain Conservancy a decade ago for possible park conversion. For now, a walker may enjoy the emptiness. On top, Amethyst ends at a gate chained against autos. From here, a rugged 3000' private dirt road makes a long loop to connect with Rising Dr. where there is no gate.

Flat Top (Radio Hill)

D	Lincoln Park	The park and surrounding area is now a forgotten

corner relative to the importance it held for LA recreation in the early 1900's. Dedicated as Eastlake Park in 1901. A 5 cent Yellow Car ride would get 1900-era Angelinos out of Downtown and into the public park and adjoining independent attractions like the Selig Zoo and the Ostrich Farm. A walk through the park today yields some reminders of the early 20th century. There is a distinctive 1920's boathouse, a WPA sculpture of Florence Nightingale and wonderfully restored deco entry gates facing Mission. Alas, the 1930 era carrousel, installed here with great fanfare in 2005 to replace a historic predecessor that had burned down, is unused. It sits shuttered, listed for sale on ebay for $110,000 a few years back.

E	HM 157	which stands for Historic Cultural Monument #157

is a Victorian in the heart of Lincoln Hts. In its fifth year striving to be a music venue, gallery, live/work space, farm, and location for public and private events, film/photo shoots, cinema screenings, & eco-workshops.

•	Lincoln Heights Historical monumts	Back in the 1880's when Lincoln Heights was a "suburb", not a neighborhood, the fashionable

moved here as a refuge from the city center. A solid dot indicates the location of some of the many "HCM"'s located here. From Victorian homes and churches, to a recycled Federal Bank Bldg., to a fire house and a water department office in 1920's moderne style to a Carnegie library. Design a casual, flat walk of only about 2 miles length to capture these landmarks.

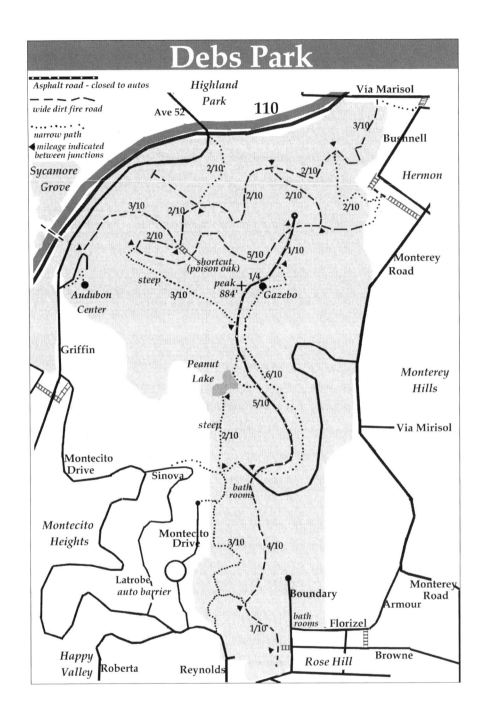

Debs Park

Asphalt road - closed to autos

- - - **wide dirt fire road**

.... **narrow path**

◄ **mileage indicated between junctions**

Highland Park

Ave 52

110

Via Marisol

3/10

Bushnell

Hermon

Sycamore Grove

2/10

2/10

2/10

2/10

3/10

2/10

2/10

2/10

2/10

5/10

1/10

Monterey Road

2/10

shortcut (poison oak)

steep

peak 884'

1/4

Gazebo

Audubon Center

3/10

Griffin

Peanut Lake

6/10

Monterey Hills

5/10

steep

Via Mirisol

2/10

Montecito Drive

Sinova

bath rooms

Montecito Heights

Montecito Drive

3/10

4/10

Latrobe auto barrier

Boundary

Monterey Road

bath rooms

Florizel

Armour

1/10

Browne

Happy Valley

Roberta

Reynolds

Rose Hill

WALK 10	SOUTH PASADENA TO MONTECITO HEIGHTS		
9.5 miles		elevation gain: +	8 stairways
Shorter walk option:	5.6 miles (including walk back)		
start	Metro Gold Line - South Pasadena station		
finish	Metro Gold Line - Heritage Square station		
Transit:	Metro Gold Line		
Best time to walk	The Lummis Home is open noon-4pm Thurs-Sunday and that should be a priority if you've never been. Otherwise Audubon center open Tues-Sunday 9am 5pm		
Highlights	Johnson Lake and Church of Angels, Arroyo Seco bottom on bike path, Debs Park, Audubon center, Lummis Home		
Break spots	Hermon Park & Fresco Market; Audubon center		
Please read pg 12-15 for information common to each walk in this book			

The Gold Line stop and surrounding Mission and Meridian is the start point for both walks 9 and 10. Both of these walks are NOT loops but end at a different Gold Line station for an easy ride back to the start. Walk 9 goes north, Walk 10 goes south. With cool businesses like Buster's Cafe, this is a great spot to start or finish a walk. The Farmers Market is Thursday open 4pm to 8pm.

This is a good companion for walk 9. It stretches along the Arroyo Seco visiting parts of three chapters of this book. So you need to flip well back in the book at times for descriptions.

START ON MAP Pg. 126 (soon on the Arroyo map Pg. 130)

Looking at Mission from Buster's, turn right and walk west. Turn right on Meridian and then left on Magnolia. Follow Magnolia to the Arroyo rim – about a half mile off. At Arroyo Dr., cross the street and look slightly right for a park access path that will lead to the bridal trail. Turn right on Bridal Path and walk the vaguely spooky passage under the 110 Freeway. The horse trail curves left and down, passing to the left of a ball field then intersects Stoney Drive Follow the trail as it crosses Stoney and turns right. The bathroom here might be useful.

Church of the Angels *page 129*

STILL MAP PG 126 When the trail meets the car bridge on left for San Pascual, take that, crossing bridge and entering Los Angeles. Next turn right on little Comet St. and follow around to the left. Intersect Hough and climb up **Stairway 14.**

On top walk straight ahead on Meridian and turn right where it ends at Ave. 65. Coming to a "T", turn left on Elder and right on Avenue 64. Arrive and explore, when open, the Church of the Angels (read "N", page 129). Leaving here, walk up Church St. that runs behind the church and bear left on Brentnal at the split. Come down to Burleigh and turn right. Almost immediately you are aware of the narrows that was once the Beaudry tunnel. Beyond that, pass Johnson Lake on your left (page 129,"M") as you walk along Burleigh and turn left on Laguna. Take Laguna to La Loma and turn left. At the signal, cross to west side of street and turn left to walk downhill on Avenue 64. After about a third of a mile you've reentered Garvanza and pass a colony of old homes on the right. Across from the church, climb **stairway 13** at the Rosewood Terrace sign. At the top, go straight ahead on Lantana and turn left where it ends on Cresthaven. Head downhill and follow this until you hit Planada and turn left. At Avenue 64 turn right. Walk down to Meridian, cross to the east side of street at signal and turn right again then left on Pollard. Walk until it ends at Ave. 66. Turn right and reach York after six interesting blocks.

You have come 4 1/2 miles. Recommended lunch location is still 2 miles away. There are food/bathroom chances on right.

Thinking about a shorter walk? Turn left on York; walk on the right side over the freeway and arroyo. Turn left on Pasadena Avenue and then right on Mission. That would be 1.4 miles back to the South Pasadena Gold Line. It is a 9/10's mile walk the other direction on York, Figueroa and Piedmont to get to the Highland Park Gold Line.

NOW ON MAP PAGE 106

Staying on route, jog left on York to cross at the signal then right and left again to regain Ave 66. Pass the Judson Studios (Pg. 108,"A") on left and follow Ave 66 as it ends on a curve left. Go down **stairway 1** (pg. 106).

The next two-third mile is a circle that winds back at this spot. Cross carefully at the island and walk towards the freeway onramp then turn right on La Riba, left on Ave. 64 and right on Arroyo Glen. Walk two blocks to find the Abbey San Encino on the right. ("B"). Turn around, go back to turn left on Ave. 64 and **climb stairway #2**. On top turn right on Ave 64 and come back to where you were, crossing at the island again, and back to the bottom of stairway #1. Continue walking over the freeway and arroyo and enter Hermon. On the left hand side, you start to pass a grassy section of Arroyo Seco Park; look for a gap in the wall to get into park.

Walk diagonally left and find the gate to enter the Arroyo Seco bike path. Turn into that, walking the bike path along the stream. In 2/3 mile, take the first exit on left up a ramp to the gate by the Hermon Dog Park. Turn right walking under Avenue 60.

Judson stain glass at Abbey San Encino

The walk is two-thirds complete; this is a good lunch spot. If you are not carrying food, try walking back up to Ave 60 over head and east 1000 feet to Fresco Market which has good fresh prepared items and sandwiches.

After your break, follow the paved path that angles left then right past the theater building to the right of some tennis courts. Continue through the park to the left of the next group of courts until you are at Via Mirasol. Take the crosswalk and go up **Stairway #4 (still page 106)** to the left of the crosswalk. Walk ahead, up Bushnell St. and **stairway #5** comes in view at the end of the block. Go up this and find the beginning of **stairway 6** on your left. Just go up 22 steps of this and find on the right side an obvious path into Debs Park.

NOW ON DEBS TRAIL MAP PAGE 140

One hundred feet up, stay right at the fork and follow a narrow path (past some old planters that look like wells) to join a wide Debs Park main trail about a fifth mile from the stairway. Climb this; there is a major junction in about one thousand feet where you stay right and start going downhill. Enjoy the view of Highland Park. At the next trail junction (another one of those planters) ignore the two trails on the right (one small, one paved) and continue on the main trail ahead left. The next junction by some green stairs is a "Y"; take the trail going down to the right. Finally, after about a mile of dirt since stairway #6, you reach pavement and bear left past the parking to walk directly to Audubon Center. Open Tuesday to Saturday 9am to 5pm, it's free entry and has a refreshing patio and good bathrooms. Leaving here, walk left from Audubon exit and there is a path option to the road to get you down to the Debs Park gate.

NOW ON MAP PAGE 136 Facing Griffin Ave. from the Debs Park gate take the crosswalk and turn left on other side of street walking by Montecito Heights Park.

At Montecito Drive, turn left crossing Griffin again in a crosswalk. **Stairway#2 (Pg. 136)** is the next objective and a bit hard to locate. From Griffin, walk on right side up Montecito 600 feet, and look for a stairway across the front of "4507". Take a few steps down, turn right and walk the other steps plus pathway to come back to Griffin. Cross street and take **stairway #1** further down the slope. Notice the gap and greenway that would have been the Pasadena Cycleway route had it been built this far. Turn left on Homer St. Turn right on Avenue 43 and cross arroyo and freeway. Just beyond the freeway, turn left on Carlotta and enter the Lummis House grounds (described page 109,"K"). Leaving here through the same gate, turn right on Carlotta, right on Ave. 42 and left on Midland. At a "T" with Ave. 38 turn right and meet Pasadena Avenue. Turn left. Past Ave. 36 there is a crosswalk that takes to the Gold Line Heritage Square station.

Homer-Griffin stairs   *Steve Matsuda photo*

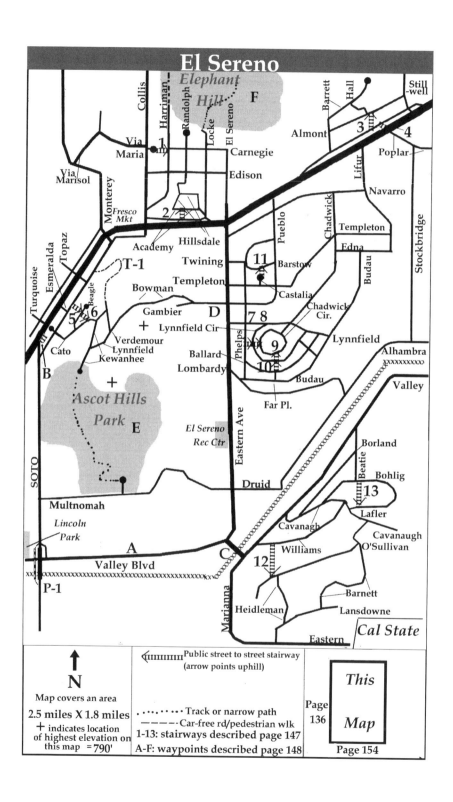

El Sereno

Elephant Hill

Collis
Harriman
Randolph
Locke
El Sereno
F

Via Maria
1
Carnegie
Edison

Via Marisol

Barrett
Hall
Still-well
Almont
3
4
Poplar
Lifur
Navarro

Monterey

Fresco Mkt
2
Academy
Hillsdale
Twining
Templeton
Bowman
Gambier
Lynnfield Cir
D

Esmeralda
Topaz
Turquoise
Beagle
T-1

Pueblo
Chadwick
Templeton
Edna
11
Barstow
Castalia
Budau
Chadwick Cir.
7 8
Lynnfield
Alhambra
xxxxxxxxxx

Stockbridge

5 6
Cato
Verdemour
Lynnfield
Kewanhee
Ballard
Lombardy
Phelps
9
10
Budau
Valley

B

Ascot Hills Park
E

El Sereno Rec Ctr

Far Pl.

Eastern Ave

Borland
Beatie
Bohlig
13
Lafler

SOTO

Multnomah

Lincoln Park
A
Valley Blvd
C
Druid
12
Williams
Cavanagh
Cavanaugh
O'Sullivan

P-1
xxxxxxxxxxxxxxxxxxxxxxxxxxxxxxxxxxxxxxxxxxx

Marianna
Heidleman
Barnett
Lansdowne
Eastern
Cal State

↑
N

Map covers an area
2.5 miles X 1.8 miles
+ indicates location of highest elevation on this map = 790'

⊲ımımım Public street to street stairway (arrow points uphill)

· · · · · · · · · Track or narrow path
— — — - Car-free rd/pedestrian wlk
1-13: stairways described page 147
A-F: waypoints described page 148

Page 136

This
Map

Page 154

	stairway	location: top / bottom	steps	
1	**Carnegie Street**	3757 Harriman/Collis+Carnegie	20	C
	Railroad tie steps in valley defined by Elephant Hill and Monterey Hills			
2	**Academy Street**	4762 Academy/4765 Huntington Dr N.	129	B
	Nice long isolated stairway to a interesting hilltop residential area			
	From the top, It's about a third mile to the edge of Elephant Hill. *(page 152)*			
3	**Edison Walk**	5246 Almont / 5253 Huntington Dr N.	75	B
	This is really out of the way and it is surprising to find a long stairway with			
	stair houses and a unique name unrelated to the street names in the			
	the area. Create a stair walk that includes this one and you have achieved			
	some sort of stair-fanatic status.			
4	**Huntington median**	5303 Hunt.Dr N/Huntington+Poplar Links well with stairway #3	21	C
5	**Lower Beagle**	4418 Beagle/4388 Huntington Dr. So.	77	B
6	**Upper Beagle**	4419 Cato St / 4418 Beagle St	95	B
	These ascend near the high entrance to Ascot Park and are very slender for			
	their long length. I always recall a friend's observation as we squeezed our			
	way up, " I'd like to see Laurel and Hardy get that piano up these stairs!"			
7	**Lower Phelps**	2736 Lynnfield / 2852 Phelps	99	B
8	**Upper Phelps**	2746 Chadwick Cir/2735 Lynnfield Cir	83	B
9	**Upper Far Place**	2779 Chadwick Cr/2815 Lynfield Cir	95	B
10	**Lower Far Place**	2815 Lynnfield Cr/2763 Ballard St	73	B
	Chadwick Circle tops an only partially built hillock that rises 200 feet above			
	Eastern Ave. and these 4 stairs that climb it on the northwest and south			
	side are a matched set. Great views of the area of the surrounding hills			
	and the old Farmdale School Building below. Larry Gordan and Adah			
	Bakalinsky's 1990 stairway guide led me up here my first time. Thanks!			
11	**Castalia Ave**	across fr 4953 Barstow/3240 Castalia	19	C
	I think you can throw this one back.			
12	**Heidleman Road**	near 4948 O'Sullivan/5010 Williams PL	234	A
	More steps than Baxter, which is generally considered the "tallest" LA			
	stairway. By my admittedly primitive tools, I believe the climb is a few feet			
	greater as well. This area is called University Hills. Walk up or down			
	O'Sullivan Street on top and the view of the downtown is unusual. The city			
	hall is typically seen as to the right of the financial district from East LA and			
	to the left of the financial district from Silver Lake. From here, it looks to			
	be foreground-middle (see photo page 150).			
13	**Beatie Place**	2221 Lafler Rd / 5140 Bohlig Rd	54	B
	An old wood one with steps on each end and walkway between			
	other pedestrian assets:			
T-1	**Topaz St - Pvt**	4464 Huntington Dr. South to the junction of Cato &		
	Dudley, a 900' walkers route of rutted dirt road and pavement that's worse.			
P-1	**Valley overpass**	Not exactly "Rails to trails" but if you keep to		
	the west of the Soto motorway overcrossing of Valley, you can walk on an			
	an abandoned trolley bridge, once part of Pacific Electric's Northern Division			

El Sereno

The eastern most section of Los Angeles City, El Sereno is about four square miles with about 45,000 residents. There is much early LA history here, but compared to the other northeast neighborhoods, most of that historic character is not to be seen in the contemporary homes and avenues except for the central business area near Huntington & Eastern. Something El Sereno does possess is a neighborhood passion for their own identity. This has played out in ongoing battles as sub-sections try to rename themselves. This passion has benefited walkers in the area as two battles have been won in the past decade against the city and developers to preserve to large areas of open space. Los Angeles is a better city for their perseverance to win parkland status for Ascot Hill and Elephant Hill.

A	Ming Ya Buddhist Assoc.	A real surprise along Valley in an industrial building that they had to fight the city over the right to use for their purposes. This is one of those resources that you really enjoy coming upon when on foot. The outdoor plaza holds most of the interest
B	Soto Viaduct	Something else interesting you tend to overlook unless you are on foot. Cars are now routed clumsily over this structure that was built with Federal Funds in 1937 for Pacific Electric's Northern District trolleys between Pasadena and Downtown. You can see stairways leading to the raised surface for trolley commuters to access the train.
C	Valley Blvd. Overpass	Not exactly a walking destination but this recent public works project addressed an historic issue of freight trains cutting off passage. The fire department would roust two engine companies on one fire to make sure one could get through. The sidewalk mosaics are gathered from neighborhood historical photos.
D	Farmdale School	A beautiful 1889 wood school house with a bell tower has been preserved inside the middle school campus. It can be viewed from Gambier Street a few hundred feet west of Eastern.
E	Ascot Park	93 acres of unstructured open space. This is mostly grasslands on two ridgelines with a shady canyon in the center. It's nearly a mile walk with great views from the corner of Lynnfield+Kewanhee just north of the park to the Multnomah entry area on the south. An open space park instead of an "activity" park, this departure from the parks and recreation culture may help explain why this sat behind locked gates for five years after the ribbon cutting. It does have bathrooms and water.
F	Elephant Hill	The Elephant hill complex of open space is about 100 acres, most of which is still privately owned but can be walked on steep, dusty trail. LA purchased 20 of these acres recently and assigned five of those over to the Mountain Resource Conservation Authority to develop a dedicated west-east trail from Pullman to Lathrop. The hill actually extends (and climbs) into South Pasadena but that is inaccessible. The views and semi-wild grasslands up here are special.

Elephant Hill

There are other tracks on Elephant Hill not shown on map that have been carved by ATV use that are too Steep to walk comfortably.

◄ - indicates junction point for mileage segments

Elephant Hill on the whole is not a public park. Some acreage has been purchased by the city for future adaptation to trail use by the Mountain Resource Conservation Agency

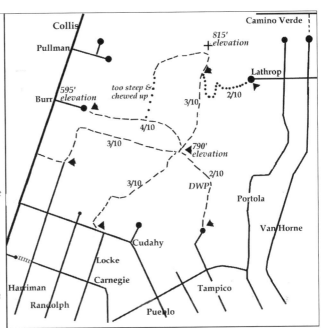

Ascot Hills Park

Additional route: some walkers make a loop within the park by following the fence line - does not look like too much fun

◄ - indicates junction point for mileage segments

✱ location of Ascot Park Speedway - 5/8 mile banked oval oiled dirt track with grandstand active 1924-1936

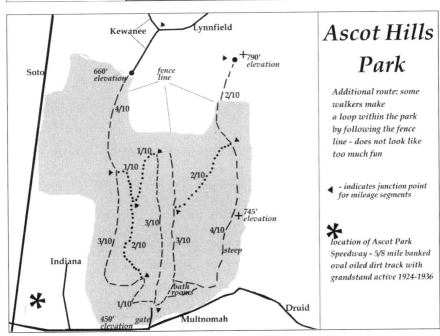

Walk 11	Lincoln Park - El Sereno		
10.4 miles		Elevation gain: +++	12 stairways
Shorter walk option:	6.4 miles (bus back to start)		
start / finish:	Lincoln Park - Mission & Selig 90031 (park by skate park)		
Transit:	Metro 78,79 bus from Downtown including near Union Statn		
Best time to walk	Day time when it is not too hot. A clear day would help enjoyment of hills on top of University, Paradise & Ascot		
Highlights	remote stairways, Ascot Park, Paradise Hill, Lincoln Park		
Break spots	Donut shop Valley +Eastern, Fresco Market at Monterey Rd+Huntington, Rose Hill Park		
Please read pg 12-15 for information common to each walk in this book			

WALK BEGINS ON MAP PAGE 136

From the parking lot facing the skate park, walk on the paths to your right through the trees and back out to Mission Road to see the Art Deco Lincoln Park portal. Then turn around and follow paths taking you to left side of the lake and towards the far left corner (south east) passing the Nightingale sculpture and what was the carousel. Leave the park and turn left on Valley. Pass under Soto.

WALK CONTINES ON MAP PAGE 146

Walk on left side of Valley and break up this mile of dull walking from the Soto viaduct to Eastern Avenue with a visit to the Ming Ya Temple (page 148 "A") Reaching the complicated intersection with Eastern, cross Valley on your right, then turn left, then stay right to go over the RR overpass. ("C"). Across the viaduct is a memorial to actress Lupe Velez. Cross left to a landscaped island with a memorial to pianist Eddie Cano. Across this, you are walking northeast on Marianna and soon turn right on Williams Place. 100' on the right climb **stairway #12**. On top turn left on O'Sullivan and follow that to a "T". Turn left staying on O'Sullivan and walk to another "T" turning left on Cavanagh. Soon turn right on Lafler and find **stairway #13**.

At bottom of stairs, turn left on Bohlig, right on Cavanaugh and left on Marianna. Back at the island with the Eddie Cano plaque, this time take the crosswalk to the right. Turn left on the other side going over the railroad and cross again towards the doughnut sign. You have walked 3.3 miles.

Leaving the little mall, head right or north on Eastern about ¾ mile before turning right on Lombardy.

Cross the street at the small island, and turn right on Bideu. At Far Place, turn left and climb stairways **#10 and #9**. Turn right and walk around much of Chadwick Circle before descending stairways **#8 and #7**. This great view includes the 1889 Farmdale School were you are headed next. At bottom of two stairways, turn right on Phelps, left on Lynnfield and right on Eastern. Cross Eastern at Gambier and continue along the north side of school just far enough for a good look through the fence at Farmdale School. Turn around and take Gambier back to Eastern and turn left. Arriving at Huntington, cross this wide street at the crosswalk. Here, like so often in LA, the green median is a tip-off that a streetcar once ran here. Across Huntington, go straight on El Sereno Ave. for a block and turn left on Edison. At crest of hill, turn left on Randolph and follow its "S" curve until you turn right on Hillsdale. As Hillsdale begins its curve left, bear right and take **stairway#2** down to turn right and follow Huntington Drive (N) to Monterey Road. You have come 6 miles. You could get a snack and use the bathrooms here (at bus plaza or gas station).

Farmdale School - 1889

You could also push on another 1/3 mile to a park and another bathroom.

From here you can leave early taking bus 78, 79 back to the start or walking 1.4 miles on Huntington/Mission.

Academy stairs

RETURN TO MAP PG 136

At Huntington and Monterey, cross Monterey and take Browne St. to the right of the church parking lot. Climb **stairway #13**. Turn left on Florizel and walk into Rose Hill Park. Here is your next chance for a bathroom and picnic stop. Turn left down Boundary and go up the small stairs across from Victorine. Turn left on the trail. Around May there is sometimes a nice growth of Matillija poppies around here.

Bear to the right and go down the steps to Mercury Street. Cross Mercury turning right then quickly left onto Sardonyx as you enter the "Gem Streets".

At the next intersection, take the middle option, jogging slightly right which puts you on Galena. Down the hill, you arrive at a 5 point intersection - turn very slightly left then right to stay on Galena. Climb **stairway 12**.

Bear left at the top going up then steeply down on East Rose Hill. This curves to the left becoming Esmeralda. Coming to a church with an old cupola, go right. At the 2nd right turn is Pyrites. At this corner you go up **stairway #10** following an elevated sidewalk.

Find on your right **stairway #11**.

Climbing this monster, you bear to the left on top and soon stay left at a "Y" going up the dirt part of Tourmaline which is a tougher climb than even the stairway was. Finally, summit at Amethyst. Turn left and walk along the ridge top of Paradise Hill. Gaze down Telluride on your right (read Pg. 137, T-2). Amethyst curves left at a chain when it meets dirt Paradise Drive. Walk out here past the chain a few hundred feet to get the benefit of one of the best views in the city. Flat Top is to your right, Ascot Hill to your left. The route as suggested turns around and starts downhill on pavement. If you want to add half a mile of wonderful view, keep following the dirt road in a counter-clockwise circle for 6/10 mile until you meet pavement at Rising Dr.

Taking the more direct route, return to Amethyst and make the first right. Turn right on the paved part of Paradise Dr. Where the dirt Paradise loop comes out meeting Rising, turn left. Coming to a "Y", bear left on Forest Park and follow this until it ends at Radium. Take Radium downhill until you are facing the Soto viaduct (148 "B"). Cross the one way streets carefully as you walk beneath the viaduct.

On Map Page 146 again: Pickup Huntington Dr. South by the market and take it to 4388 where you find and climb **stairways 5 & 6.** Turn left on top at Cato and take to a radical right turn onto Kewanee. Come to its junction with Lynnfield, bear right.

Now, refer to the Ascot Hills Park Map page 149.

Stick to the main trail which gets you to the front gate in 8/10 mile.

Turn right on Multnomah. Meeting Soto, turn left (do not cross Soto).

In 1000 feet, bear left on the ramp going down off of the Soto over pass and to Valley Blvd. Turn right. Very shortly, you are back at Lincoln Park. Head back to where you started, perhaps taking the path through the trees that appears at the nearest boundary of the park.

East Los Angeles - Arts District

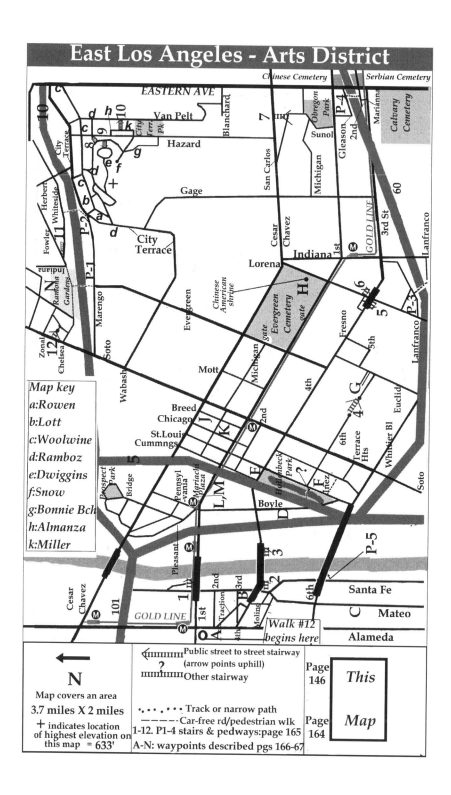

Chinese Cemetery   Serbian Cemetery

EASTERN AVE

Van Pelt

Blanchard

Chinese Cemetery

Obregon Park

Calvary Cemetery

Marianna

10

10

City Terrace Pk

Hazard

San Carlos

7

Sunol

Gleason

2nd

P-4

d   h

c   k

9

c   g

8

e   f

d

c

b   P-2

a

d

Herbert

Whiteside

City Terrace

Fowler

11

Gage

City Terrace

Cesar Chavez

Michigan

3rd St

60

Lanfranco

GOLD LINE

Indiana   1st   M

Lorena

Indiana

P-1

Ramona Gardens

Chinese American shrine

Evergreen Cemetery

gate   H.

gate

6

5

P-3

Marengo

Zonal

12

Chelsea

Soto

Wabash

Evergreen

Fresno

5th

Lanfranco

Mott

Michigan

4th

5th

Euclid

Map key
a:Rowen
b:Lott
c:Woolwine
d:Ramboz
e:Dwiggins
f:Snow
g:Bonnie Bch
h:Almanza
k:Miller

Breed

Chicago

St.Louis

Cummngs

J

K

M

2nd

G

4

6th

Terrace Hts

Whittier Bl

Soto

Prospect Park

Bridge

Pennsyl-vania

Mariachi Plaza

M

L,M

Holbeck Park

?

E

F

Inez

D

Boyle

Cesar Chavez

101

M

Pleasant

1

2nd

3rd

Traction

Moline

3

2

B

4th

1st

6th

P-5

Santa Fe

Mateo

III

GOLD LINE

M

Q   A

Walk #12 begins here

C

Alameda

N

Map covers an area
3.7 miles X 2 miles
+ indicates location
of highest elevation on
this map = 633'

Public street to street stairway
(arrow points uphill)
Other stairway

•••••••• Track or narrow path
———– Car-free rd/pedestrian wlk
1-12. P1-4 stairs & pedways:page 165
A-N: waypoints described pgs 166-67

Page 146

Page 164

This

Map

	stairway	location: top / bottom	steps	
1	1st Street Bridge	NW bridge deck / 132 Center	44	B

These steps have been rebuilt during the bridge modifications for the Gold Line. There are also stairs on the southwest side but now cordoned off.

2	4th St Bridge Wst	SW bridge deck / near 500 S. Mateo	53	C
3	4th St Bridge East	SE Bridge deck / near 401 S. Anderson	51	D

Both of these stairs can get extremely filthy, the east one in particular

4	East 6th Street	2755 E. 6th / 2728 E. 6th	67	B

Pretty nice stairway climbs out of the low area where Roosevelt H.S. is. Very close to the massive mural on 6th

5	4thLorena west	SW bridge deck / near 404 S. Bernal	42	C
6	4th Lorena east	NE bridge deck / across fr 321 Lorena	46	B

This spectacular bridge needs to be seen from underneath, take the stairs!

7	Sunol Street	north:4030 CesarChavez/south:332 Sunol	103	B

Comes as a complete surprise: how can a 100 step stairway be found in such a flat neighborhood? It climbs 41 steps one side, 62 on the other.

8	Ramboz	across fr 1265 BonnieBch/3999 Ramboz	23	C

The "street" this climbs up from looks like an alley, typical of the area.

9	"The 100 steps"	3958 Dwiggins / 1243 Bonnie Beach	133	B

Actually it is well over one hundred, but when walking "The 300" in 2012 we spoke to two different people in City Terrace that named this as such.

10	Miller-Van Pelt	1179 Van Pelt / 1174 Miller	87	B

Pleasant, unexpected stairs in happy proximity to City Terrace Park

11	Fowler sidewalk	in front of 3233 Whiteside	10	C

Just outside of Ramona Gardens, these barely count as they line the sidewalk around a curve. The signage is the story; see the cover page.

12	Verde	2400 Verde / 1200 block N. Soto	29	C

Kind of a remote, throwaway unit but it does have the flourish of double "take your pick" steps on top.

?	Hollenbeck Park		75	

A nice length of steps above the southeast side of the lake and it is great to see the frequent use it gets by locals out for exercise. A "park" stairway

	pedways			

The abundance of useful overpasses reminds one of how victimized this area has been by freeway construction through the years.

P1	Ramona Gardens to Evergreen Avenue

Crosses the 10 Fwy; starts from a Ramona Gardens path

P2	Whiteside to City Terrace Drive

Crosses the 10 Fwy and comes to the foot of the City Terrace hills

P3	Lanfranco Street / Estudillo Avenue

Crosses the 60 Fwy, a fifth mile from the 4th & Lorena Bridge

P4	Mariana Avenue

Crosses the 60 Fwy; very close to both the Chinese and Serbian cemeteries

P5	Santa Fe Ave river access	Beneath the 6th St viaduct is the driveway that you can follow to the river basin- only access this area

Arts District and East Los Angeles

Most of what is covered in this book section is Boyle Heights, which is really neither Arts District or East Los Angeles. East LA is actually a large unincorporated area that includes the east third of this map. Boyle Heights is an historic Los Angeles city neighborhood that, for about five decades ending with WWII, was a lively transitional zone. Immigrant ethnic groups, particularly Jewish, Italian, Japanese, Armenian, Mexican, and African-American settled here as their first Los Angeles stop before gradually filtering into other neighborhoods. Boyle Heights is now 94% Latino and that already dynamic neighborhood culture is invigorated by the proximity to downtown and some influence from the other ethnicities that one shared this area. From a walker's perspective the Arts District can be associated with Boyle Heights because of the enticing river bridges and handy Gold Line service that links the two.

The viaducts	Five of Los Angeles' iconic concrete arch bridges are included in this mapped section indicated by a heavy black line. Space limitations prevent the author from detailing how wonderful and unique each of these monuments is. There are resources (like bridgehunter.com) that support the notion that, surprising to many, Los Angeles is a city of beautiful bridges. A product of the "city beautiful" movement, these five bridges were all built in the space of a decade. 6th Street is the signature masterpiece of the group and we will lose it in the new future because a fatal flaw in the 1932 concrete. The winning design for its replacement has in it some good pedestrian elements that will only slightly deflect the pain we all share for the loss of its predecessor
A J.A.Roebling	This 1913 warehouse (home to Angel City Brewery) was once a distribution center for the builders of the Brooklyn Bridge and manufacturers of wire rope. Peeking through the windows of the unused lobby, you can observe a beautiful tile interior that incorporates work from Ernst Batchelder. Also in view is a wire rope banister.
B SCI-Arc	Pure genius use of a building that is a quarter mile long and only 37 feet wide. In its past life, Santa Fe Railroad cars were were transloaded into trucks on the other side. Now an architecture school
C National Biscuit	A 7-floor factory from 1925 is a good example of loft conversion in the area. Resplendent at night as seen from the bridges.
D Boyle Avenue	This street from 3rd Street south to the freeway has a nice collection of early 20th century homes and institutional bldgs.
E Hollenbeck Park	Like its period brethren Westlake and Eastlake parks, this lovely spot conjures up a notion of late 19th century gentility. Today the area around the lake is full of life and it is a fun place to sit and watch. The floating bridge was reconditioned in 2009 and since named Best Spot for a First Kiss in a *LA Weekly* survey. It always seems to be locked away by Rec & Parks to prevent its being enjoyed.

F Santa Fe Hospital	Originally a railroad hospital, this 1928 bluff-top
building always had a "nourish" look. Since it closed in the 1990's it has	
had an active life as a filming location and a hot spot for chasers of	
paranormal activity. It is now being converted to senior apartments.	

G Casa de Mexicano	This odd shaped building started as a Methodist
Church in 1904. The Mexican consulate in 1931 established this location to	
support the Mexican diaspora. If open, a mural can be seen in the hall.	

H Evergreen	Established in the 1870's, this is the oldest
continuingly operated cemetery in Los Angeles. Buried here are very few	
of the celebrities that visitors often want to locate in graveyards but	
instead an enormous variety (like the population who lived around here)	
of Angelinos including some of the area's pioneers. Here you will find a	
memorial to the Japanese American solidiers of the "442nd" and a	
memorial to the Pacific Coast Showmen's Association (the circus people).	
There is a restored 19th century shrine where Chinese American pioneers	
burned gold and silver paper–symbolizing money–and the deceased's	
personal effects and favorite clothing in the Shrine's burners. Visit these	
grounds with respect; the cemetery is still actively used.	

J Breed Street Shul	Largest Orthodox Synagogue west of Chicago from
from 1915 to 1950. The stone and brick building facing the street is actually	
the successor Shul, built 1924. The original wood congregation house built	
1915 was lifted and moved back intact to accommodate. The older building	
has made for more attainable restoration and is used from time to time for	
community events and religious services. The "newer" shul presents a	
dramatic, evocative interior the very few times that it is open. Stabilization	
and restoration is a noble cause that will take many years. The Breed St.	
congregation may have moved west but these buildings still maintain a	
vital connection with the neighborhood and the evolving community.	

K Hollenbeck	1884-Craftsman with Gothic and Romanesque details
Presbyterian	Another drop-dead gorgeous religious building
remains where the historic congregation is long departed.	

L Mariachi	This plaza as dedicated open space has existed only
Plaza	about 15 years but before that a corner donut shop
here historically was the spot were Mariachi were recruited to play at gigs.A	
bandstand has been contributed by the state of Jalisco, where the Mariachi	
style was born. Across the street is the 7 story Cummings Block, once the	
hotel of choice by the Mariachi, now refurbished by a redevelopment grant	
with the intention if maybe not the reality of attracting the Mariachi back.	

L Libros	open Wednesday through Saturday afternoons:
Schmibros	This is a unique neighborhood treasure founded and
run by David Kipen. It's a bookshop, lending library and local literary center.	

N Ramona	A public housing project with history of a drug trade
Gardens	and a testy relationship wth the LAPD is not your
typical recommended zone to walk through. A visit here will prove both	
surprising and rewarding while you use the pedway, admire the murals and	
see what was, when opened in 1940, recognized as important architecture.	

Walk 12	Arts District / Boyle Heights		
9.7 miles		Elevation gain: +	6 stairways
Shorter walk option:	4, 6 or 8 miles taking Gold Line back		
start / finish:	Metro Gold Line: Little Tokyo/Arts District Station		
Transit:	Metro Gold Line		
Best time to walk	Not at commute hour; Saturday and Sunday are best for lively atmosphere; a nice walk, hot or cold.		
Highlights	cool Arts District, dramatic view from bridges, Hispanic culture, artifacts from past cultures here, Evergreen Cem		
Break spots	Hollenbeck Park, Evergreen Cemetery, Mariachi Plaza		

One of my favorite areas in Los Angeles to explore.

ENTIRE WALK ON MAP PAGE 154

Start at the southwest corner of 1st and Alameda. If it has not been removed (for transit line improvements) by the time you read this, this building has a colorful history as the Atomic Café as a hangout for LA's punk rock scene in the 1980's. Walk down Alameda and at 2nd St. cross diagonally so that you are at the corner of Alameda and Traction. Look in the lobby windows of the old Roebling Building ("A" Pg. 156). Walk southeast on Traction until you come to the back side of SCIArc ("B") and need to turn right. Make a diagonal left, cross 4th St. and proceed pretty much straight ahead on Molina. Make the first left on 4th Place and a 2nd left on Mateo. Coming on a 3-way intersection, cross Mateo carefully and aim for **stairway 2** up to the bridge deck.

Heading over the river, you have a good chance to appreciate the 6th and 7th street viaducts to your right and 1st St. on your left. After crossing the river and the tracks, you are across from the beer distributor. You can decide if you want to take **stairway 3** down. If too dirty just stay on bridge and walk to east end.

Continuing east on 4th St., now it's a dull third mile that crosses over freeway climbs up to what was "Paredon Blanca" or white bluffs to enter Boyle Heights at Boyle Avenue.

Cross Boyle, walking towards the gas station and turn right. Walk about a quarter mile on Boyle.

This historic area includes the Max Factor House at 432 and the International Institute across the street at 435 which was established 1914 by YWCA to "serve women and girls coming from Europe and the Orient and to assist the foreign communities in their adjustments to life in US." At 504 was the 1906 home of the Elmer Simons, a brick manufacturing tycoon. Across the street is a newer version of Hollenbeck Palms, California's first licensed senior home when opened in 1890 at the bluff edge location.

Passing under freeway, watch for a path on left to Hollenbeck Park. If lucky to find it open, walk across the floating bridge. Otherwise walk around the end of lake to your right. Climb the 75 steps. Since these are "park stairs", not a street to street stairs, they don't make "the list". You have come two miles and the bathrooms on the left are the last for another 3 miles. From the top of the stairs consider the history of Hollenbeck Park and the hospital across St. Louis Street. ("E" and "F").

Exit park and turn right on St. Louis. Cross street carefully mid-block and walk in front of hospital. Turn left on Inez and walk this pedestrian alley to Chicago turning right then left on Terrace Heights. Walk this to Soto and turn left. Walk to 6th St. and cross Soto to be in front of an ancient power substation.

Proceed east on 6th passing between the middle school on the right and Roosevelt H.S. on the left. Appreciate the moderne flourishes on the Middle School and then the Anahuanc mural painted by artist Nelyollotl Toltecatl in the 1990's. 6th St. ends eventually at **stairway 4** which you go up. On top, keep going straight on 6th. Turn left on Euclid.
Passing the somewhat audacious double Calle Pedro Infante, you have a worthy view of Casa de Mexicano ("G") which is open from time to time to view the mural and the unusual space.

Continue up Euclid to 4th Street and turn right. Cross to the north side of 4th. Approaching the 4th and Lorena Bridge, stay to the left of the bridge at Concord. Turn right to pass underneath it and appreciate the arches. From Bernal under the bridge you can climb **stairway 5** landing on the bridge deck. Now cross bridge on south side of 4th St. Cross at 2 signals to be on the northeast side of the bridge. Take **stairway 6** down to Lorena. Turn right. Walk up to 1st St.

You have come 4 miles and could walk a long, curving block to your right to reach the Indiana Street Gold Line platform. Otherwise cross to the northwest corner and read the info signs about the impact of subway digging on the potter's field. Turn left. Walking west on 1st you appreciate the soft surface of the running track. If you are fortunate, find the pedestrian gate open into Evergreen Cemetery opposite Fresno Street. There is no single correct way to visit an historic cemetery ("H") but I generally lead groups to the right of the chapel then diagonally left passing an interesting group of Armenian headstones with photos. Further in that direction, find the 1880's Chinese shrine. Turn and walk west towards the exit via the auto gate after checking out the Japanese-American soldier memorial to the right of the exit. By the exit is a bathroom open except on Sunday; other bathrooms are available on Cesar Chavez in half a mile if this is closed.

Evergreen Cemetery

Inside the new Shul *page 157*

Leave Evergreen through the gates and cross Evergreen Street carefully, continuing ahead on Michigan. Turn right on Mott and left on Cesar Chavez, once named Brooklyn Avenue when Boyle Heights had a large Jewish population. After passing Soto, turn left on Breed Street and just walk 250 feet to look at the Shul on the right. ("J") You will only be able to enter the property if there is an event.

Turn back on Breed and return to Cesar Chavez and turn left. The next block is likely to busy with foot traffic before you turn left on Chicago. Walk to 1st St., passing the wonderful 19th century church on your left ("K"). At 1st Street, you have a little pocket park on your left and the newer LAPD precinct station on your right designed by architect AC Martin.
This is 7 miles into the walk and there is a metro station 2 blocks to your left at Soto and 1st.
Turn right on 1st and begin to appreciate this fairly vibrant commercial street on either side of the 5 Freeway. Mariachi Plaza is less than a half mile west on 1st from the pocket park on Chicago and you will find some good refreshment choices approaching there.

At 1st and Boyle, take time to enjoy the plaza area ("L") and be sure to drop in on Libros Schmibros ("M").

Banner at Libros Schmibros - a fitting motto for this book too page 157

From here, the shorter options are to take the metro back or to walk a mile and a half straight back. The full walk includes a three quarter mile loop to the right to the historic Mount Pleasant district. That loop will return right back to this spot.

Leave the plaza facing Boyle and turn right. Make a left on Pennsylvania, then a right on Echandia. Follow this four blocks to the bottom of tear drop shaped Prospect Park (another Brooklyn throw back). Walk up and left through the park leaving at "9 o'clock" taking Mitchell Place. Turn left on Gillette, right on Bridge and right on Cesar Chavez. You are headed for that triangle space on your left but you may need to walk to the signal at Pleasant to cross Cesar Chavez. Aliso Triangle suggests a pocket park that has been taken over by motorist realities. Walking on Pleasant, notice the sign for historic Mt. Pleasant Bakery on your right at 1418.

Back to 1st St., turn right. Walk to and over the First Street Bridge, staying on the right side. Over the river, take **stairway 1** off the bridge on your right and come down to Center St. Walk away from the river to come out to Santa Fe Ave here. Turn left, going south. Approaching the front side of SCIArc, turn right on 3rd St. just short of there. Walk 3 blocks to Hewitt where you turn right unless you are tempted by Wurstkuche on your left. Hewitt ends at 1st, where you turn left and come back to 1st and Alameda where you started.

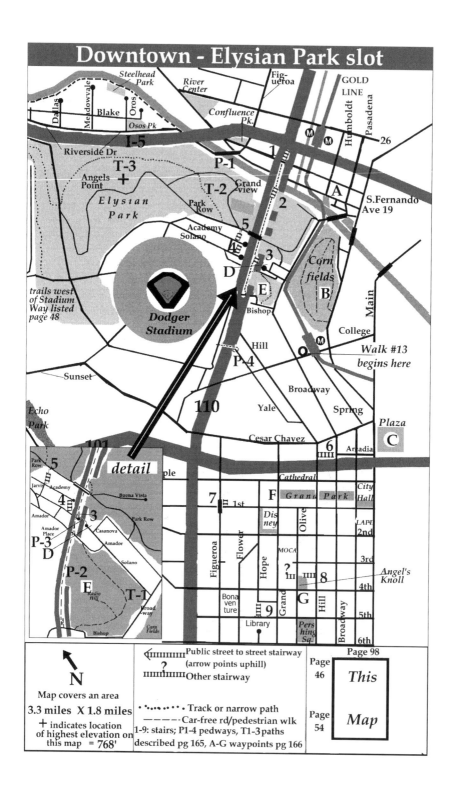

Downtown - Elysian Park slot

Steelhead Park
River Center
Fig-ueroa
GOLD LINE
Pasadena
Humboldt
26

Dallas
Meldowvale
Blake
Oros
Osos Pk
Confluence Pk.

Riverside Dr
I-5

T-3
+
Angels Point

Elysian Park

Grand view
T-2
P-1
1
2
A
S.Fernando Ave 19

Park Row
Academy Solano
5
4
3
D
E
Corn fields
B

trails west of Stadium Way listed page 48

Dodger Stadium

Bishop
Hill
College
Walk #13 begins here

M
P-4

Sunset

Echo Park

Broadway
Yale
Spring

110
Cesar Chavez
6
Arcadia
Plaza
C

detail

Park Row
5
Jarvi
Academy
Buena Vista
4
Amador
Park Row
3
Amador Place
Casanova
P-3
D
Amador
Solano
P-2
E
Radio Hill
T-1
Broad-way
Corn Fields
Bishop

ple
Cathedral
7
1st
F
Grand Park
City Hall

Dis ney
Olive
LAPI
2nd

Figueroa
Flower
Hope
MOCA
?
8
3rd
Angel's Knoll
4th

Bona ven ture
Grand
G
Hill
Broadway
5th

9
Library
Pers hing Sq.
6th

Legend

N

Map covers an area
3.3 miles X 1.8 miles
+ indicates location of highest elevation on this map = 768'

⊏IIIIIIIIII Public street to street stairway
? (arrow points uphill)
IIIIIIIIIIII Other stairway

•`•••• •••`• Track or narrow path
– – – – Car-free rd/pedestrian wlk
1-9: stairs; P1-4 pedways, T1-3 paths
described pg 165, A-G waypoints pg 166

Page 46

Page 54

Page 98

This Map

	stairway	location: top / bottom	steps	
1	San Fernando/110	110 pedestrian route / 4575 Sn Fernando	45	C
2	110 Spiral Stairs	Southbound side/Northbound side	49	B
3	110 Solano Strs	110 pedestrian route / near 545 Solano	46	C

3 stairs that are part of the 110 pedestrian route: #1 is where you would not expect, between the freeway lanes and can be filthy. #2 the spiral stairs is in a dramatic, gritty setting that I am surprised is not used often for film shoots. Stairs #3 is sporadically locked at the bottom – you can use the ramp. Read P-2.

4	Solano School	Across fr 617 Academy / 615 Solano	21	B

Nice little stairs east of the campus, be careful on top for the offramp traffic.

5	Jarvis Street	near 628 Park Row / 702 Academy	42	C

Look as if they have been excavated; from top of steps to street, take a path.

6	Acadia Street	near 400 N. Hill / near 401 N. Broadway	55	B

Across from the Fort Moore monument waterfall-that has not worked in yrs.

7	1st St/Figueroa	near 900 W. 1st / near 100 N. Figueroa	47	C

Simple switch back stairs, easy to miss

8	Angels Flight	351 S. Hill St. / 350 S. Olive Street	121	B

The Big Parade always starts here. They are locked after hours. *(page 167)*

?	Water Crt stairs	Water Court / 300 block Olive Street	32	

Continues across from #8 but I call these plaza stairs, not street to street strs

9	Bunker Hill	400 S. Hope / across from 630 W. 5th	101	A

Before Lawrence Halprin designed these lovely stairs for the Library Square redevelopment, there was an old zigzag stairway here that split two Art Deco beauties: Edison (still there) and the Sunkist Building (demolished)

	pedways			
P-1	Figueroa shuttle	Not a pedway, but until 2015 when bridge is rebuilt,		

you need to take the free shuttle running between Home Depot & Oros St.

P-2	110 Pedestrian Route	Many are excited by this passage but the noise & nearness to speeding cars is not for everyone. From

Bishop St., there is an immediate ramp up, then 3/10 mile to another ramp leading down to Amador, then 1/10 mile to an open gate to stairway #3, then 4/10 mile to Spiral stairway #2, then 2/10 mile to the north end Stairway #1.

P-3	Solano tunnel	Goes under the northbound lanes, next to the garden
p-4	Yale Street	From across from 970 Yale to around 1570 Stadium Wy

900 degrees of spiral gives this one a high score on the "Guggenheim index"

	pathways			
T-1	Radio Hill Gardens			

Broad trail with great views: 4/10 mile Amador to Stadium Way plus 1/3 mile each way on the spur trail that leads to the "Gardens" - such as they are.

T-2	Park Row to Grandview

Wide dirt trail nicely wooded but heavily tagged.

T-3	Portrero Trail	A scenic Elysian Park skinny path that is not for

everyone's taste. It is 1.1 miles running between Grandview Rd and the jnct of Stadium Way and Angels Point. Most of it is narrow with a steep drop off on the north side. There is one spot where you need to climb steeply down and back up to get around a landslide. Avoid this route if it is muddy. *(172)*

Downtown - Elysian Park slot

The area covered by this section is pure invention for the purposes of this book. Lovely Solano Canyon village tucks in the recesses near Elysian Park, but much of this section concerns the non-residential expanse of Elysian Park and the Cornfields Park. Description of the walkable historic and architectural features within the boundaries of this area could fill a large book. Our comments will be limited to the viaducts and parklands.

The viaducts	Three more examples of Los Angeles's string of beautiful concrete arch bridges over the LA River are found on this map and indicated by thick black lines (read pg. 156). The "Buena Vista" or Broadway Bridge built 1913 is especially fine and best viewed while standing on the 1928 Spring St. viaduct. Spring St. has been the subject of a preservation battle when a proposal planned to add 40 feet of width to the bridge surface. That's been reduced to the satisfaction of the LA Conservancy. Main St. Bridge, built 1910 is still open to pedestrians and traffic as it is now being rehabilitated. Unlike the other 9 bridges in this group, Main St. is not a viaduct; it does not pass over rail or motor traffic.
A Humboldt Street	A decade ago, this was a "no-go" zone; now we are seeing amenities. Still under construction, a one acre greenway is adding a path, a bridge and a means to filter storm water runoff enroute to the river.
B The Cornfields	Here are 32 acres of unstructured green space that have been recovered from a century of use as a rail yard. This is an important historical site. The pre-colonial village of Yaanagna was here and the Zanga Madre carried water from the river to the pueblo through here. Great views of the LA skyline. It is a 3/4 mile walk from Chinatown Gold Line platform to the north end by the Buena Vista and Spring Street viaducts.
C The Plaza	This circular open space has been used for 190 years in its current configuration but its history dates further back to 1780 as the center of the original Spanish settlement. It is surrounded by the oldest surviving buildings of LA, the revered Placita Church and Olivera Street.
D Solano Canyon Community Gardens	It is normally locked but the mosaics, the orchard and the garden plots can be appreciated through the fence from Solano or from Casanova Street. Beautiful village resource.
E Radio Hill	This lovely spot gets abused by taggers but has great views and a real sense of distance from its urban surroundings (see pg. 165)
F Grand Park	Here is an heroic transformation of dead space and a predecessor park that was a slave to a parking lot. Opened last year, it is deservedly getting international attention for the genius work by the landscape architects. This is a county park and the team that recreated this space carefully studied the cultural heritage of the county's citizenry in making choices. This is a book about walking but come here just to linger!
G Angel's Knoll	A little green space off 4th and Olive was beloved to locals (yes, including the homeless) for a decade before the agency that owns this property closed it in August 2013, reportedly to make it more presentable to a buyer. Made famous by "500 Days of Summer".

Angels Flight stairs - Angels Knoll on left - funicular on right

110 pedestrian route under the Park Row viaduct   *Howard Petersen photo*

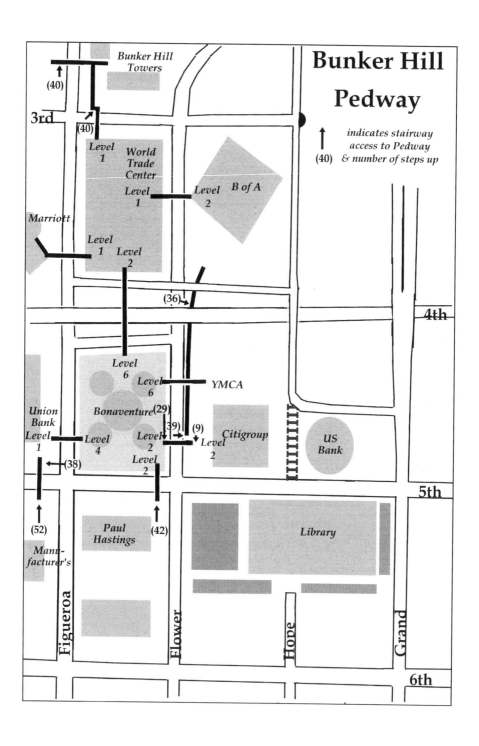

The Pedway This book uses the expression "pedway" to describe a number of pedestrian assets all around the city. To some locals, the true claimant to this descriptive name is the elevated walkway network built in the 1970's as part of the west Bunker Hill redevelopment project. Comprised of 11 elevated overpasses, this was an innovation of Calvin Hamilton, who served as the city's planning director for two decades ending 1985.

When the community of Bunker Hill was razed in favor of redevelopment in the 1970's (a pedestrian nightmare in itself – different story) the planning department's thought was to give pedestrians their own passageways between the new buildings to prevent their interfering with motor traffic flow. This foot corridor is problematic because walking it means passing in and out of office and hotel buildings where the "path" is likely to be lost or where passage can be interrupted by a locked security door. The Bunker Hill pedway runs at several different levels. The total length of the pedway is about 2200' but the longest segment not interrupted by a building is only about a tenth of a mile.

The walking community has been of two minds about the pedway. It represents accommodation to pedestrians in their own space. That's the good view and these bridges are getting some of the affection that the stairways get. On the other hand, if you consider the desirability of an urban street being a lively, organic component of the city, removing the pedestrians from that zone is far from ideal. It is very LA that the "street" was associated with the motorway while the pedestrians were considered the conflicting element to be removed. Consider central Madrid, for example: the "street" was maintained above ground with its foot traffic; it was the motorway that got removed and placed underground.

Walk 13	CHINATOWN, ELYSIAN, FROGTOWN, CYPRESS		
10.5 miles		Elevation gain: ++	2 stairways
Shorter walk option:		cut 2 miles via Lincoln/Cypress Gold L	
start / finish:	Metro Gold Line: Chinatown Station		
Transit:	Metro Gold Line		
Best time to walk	Better on weekends when there are fewer cars and more companions on foot; not when it muddy. River Gardens Park at the 3/4 point of walk closes at sunset.		
Highlights	Solano Canyon, Elysian Pk trails, Elysian Hts, river path, River Gardens Park, viaducts, the Cornfields		
Break spots	Elysian picnic area, River Gardens Park		
Please read pg 12-15 for information common to each walk in this book			

WALK BEGINS ON MAP PAGE 164

This walk is a clockwise loop combining many styles of pedestrian corridors: a Chinatown alley, a spiral, two ramps, two stairways, a classic foot trail, a street chained against cars, a hidden pedestrian pass-through, the river bike trail and a wide park path through a reclaimed rail yard. This walk has several sections that will seem particularly isolated without an "escape" route for someone who is skittish. Bring friends and stick to weekends if that makes you more comfortable.

With your back turned to the escalator down from the Gold Line platform, turn right on College St., walk a block and cross Broadway at the signal then turn right. Turn left under the pagoda gate and enter the Central Plaza. Walk through the plaza, shifting slightly right to come out on Hill St. Take the crosswalk across and enter another plaza. You need to come out on the other side at Yale St. There is no direct passage; the easy way is to turn left in a pedestrian alley, walk to a parking lot and turn right. There is perhaps a more exciting path through the warren impossible for me to describe. Arriving Yale St, locate and take the spiral pedway that climbs up and over 110 Freeway. Turn right on Stadium Way. At Lookout St., cross to the far side of Stadium Way. Continue to right.

A half mile after that pedway, turn left onto a paved path immediately after passing under the freeway southbound and before passing over the freeway northbound. Ascend ramp to be on the 110 pedestrian-way. Walk this for about 2000' and take the first departure opportunity on a ramp on right. That will bring you to Amador STREET. Turn right and walk under the freeway entering Solano Canyon. At Amador PLACE turn right then turn left in front of the pretty school. At the next corner, turn right on Jarvis. As you come up to Academy, you are looking at intriguing Stairway #5 which we will not use on this walk. Instead turn right on Academy, carefully watching cars exiting the freeway. Turn right down **Stairway #4** on the far side of the school. Turn left on Solano, walking under the southbound lanes again and straight for a dead-end at the northbound lanes. Turn left and look for the steps down the pedestrian subway.

On the other side, enjoy what you can of the lovely 5-acre Solano Canyon Community Garden. The gate is typically locked, perhaps you get lucky. Proceed beyond the garden and turn left onto Casanova which climbs and curves to the right. In one-tenth mile, you should be able to enter a park area with some stairs that climbs above to Park Row Dr. (If for some reason, the park gate is locked, you can walk a few feet further to turn left on Park Row street). As you reach the graceful 1941 Park Row arch bridge, you have one of the really unique views of downtown down the slot. Continue up Park Row passing a path leading to Stairway #5 on left.

Portrero Trail

1000 feet from the bridge, you come to a trail entrance on your right. Leave pavement and walk the nicely wooded trail for about half a mile until it meets a paved road. This is the three mile point. Cross the road to find the Portrero Trail. This is a narrow track through grass and woodland high above Elysian Valley and lasts 1.1 miles until you meet the road again. The trail ends at Stadium Way. You carefully cross then turn left. Walk the grassy area between Stadium Way and Elysian Park Drive. There is a bathroom building in about 900 feet, just downslope from the Grace Simons Lodge.

This is the 40% point of the full walk and the next bathroom is 3 ½ miles away. Carry a snack as there is no food here.

WALK CONTINUES ON MAP PAGE 46

Walk towards Grace Simons Lodge and just right of the gate; follow a path that goes around the right side of the enclosure. The path becomes more obvious in a couple hundred yards curving left and soon connecting with the wide Elysian Park path where you turn right. Take this dirt road as it climbs nearer to Park Drive and, just before Marion Harlow Grove, take the 5 step path that puts you on pavement. With Park Drive to your left, and a driveway marked private to your right, head across and down Avon Park Terrace.

You are passing the Atwater Property on your right (page 48 "B") with the two pueblo bungalows. Turn right on Avon.

Go left on Cerro Gordo and right on Valentine. Go up the **Curran Stairs** (#1, page 46) on the left. On top follow Curran down to Echo Park Avenue and turn right. This ends at a "T" with Landa. Turn right. In 750 feet, you reach a chain across the road that lets you proceed without the company of autos. Soon pass another chain. Go left and left onto Stadium Way.

Reaching Riverside Dr. you want to be headed to the right on Riverside but on the other side of the street. Immediately after passing under the 5-Freeway, find a short walker's alley on the left that takes you out to Blimp Street. Turn right on Blimp and right on Blake. Walk 12 blocks on Blake which I always find to be a pleasant and interesting mainstream of Frogtown. When you get to lovely St. Ann Parish Church, you will be turning left on Riverdale. But first maybe walk a few more feet on Blake to tiny "Heavenly Service" market for a cold drink.

WALK RETURNS TO MAP PAGE 164 (Top edge)
Take Riverdale and enter the LA River Bike Path and turn right. Walk down river just over half a mile until you leave it for Oros Street at the far edge of Steelhead Park. Reaching Riverside and Oros, look for a van that looks like a rental car shuttle. That will take you through the construction zone for the bridge which is likely to endure through 2015. The bus might be sitting on other side so don't be surprised if you have to wait 20 minutes. When new bride is complete, turn left on Riverside and walk over it. If the city comes to its senses, you might walk across a pedestrianized old bridge.

De Anza mural by Frank Romero

The shuttle drops you in front of Home Depot. Walk to the left of the store towards the river and turn right on San Fernando Road. In one tenth of a mile, turn right into the Los Angeles River Center Gardens. You will be exiting out the main driveway to Avenue 26 but take your time enjoying this, the old Lawry's California Center (Pg. 100 "M") Before sunset, you should be able to find open bathrooms here near the gate. The complete walk is three-quarters done.

Leaving out the main gate, turn left to find a crosswalk to the north side of Avenue 26. Head east on Ave 26, turn left on Huron (notice how wide these residential streets are – wider than busy Melrose!). At Avenue 28 you turn right appreciating two sides of the Huron substation (Pg. 100 "K").

At Figueroa, it gets hectic. Turn right on Figueroa, left on Avenue 26 and, after walking over the last of the Arroyo Seco creek and under the Arroyo Seco Parkway, you are at the Lincoln/Cypress Gold Line station.

You've walked 8 ½ miles. From here it's one Metro stop to the start of the walk or 2 more miles of walking.

The full route turns right on Humboldt Street. At San Fernando, the Fuller Lofts loom impressively on your left. Keep walking on Humboldt to Ave 19 where you find the unexpected Ed Reyes River Greenway. Walk through the greenway and turn left to exit on Ave. 18. (If not open, turn left on Ave 19 and right on Barranca) Turn right at Pasadena Avenue. Where Pasadena Ave. ends at Broadway, cross over to and walk through the Downey Recreation Center (down then up steps) to Spring Street on the far side. Turn right and cross over the Spring St. Viaduct. After the bridge, make the first right on Aurora St. and enter the Cornfields Park at its north end. Turn left. Take the near, the middle or the far trail to the left and walk three-quarters of a mile back to Chinatown Gold Line.

Little Tokyo to Watts Towers

The other chapters of this book are organized with a map of the area and one to three index pages that describe the stairways, pathways, pedways and some the great places to walk to. For this chapter, the map is drawn specific to a wonderful walk: no stairs or paths but many landmarks of Los Angeles history, culture and art. The long linear 10 mile corridor of this walk would create a surrounding area too massive to map in this book as the other sections are mapped.

WALK 14	LITTLE TOKYO TO THE WATTS TOWERS
12.2 miles	elevation gain: none
Shorter walk option: 5.5 miles (take transit to Watts after 1st 4 miles	
start	LAPD Building - 100 West 1st Street 90012
finish	Metro Blue Line - 103rd St./Watts Towers station
Transit:	Metro Red Line - Civic Center Station
Best time to walk	Fall, winter, spring when not hot; Towers are only open Friday to Sunday; Friday has perhaps too much work day traffic on streets, Sunday the Produce Market would be inactive - Saturday is best. Need to start early 8:30-9am to make the final 3pm tours of the Towers.
Highlights	Little Tokyo, Produce Market area, Central Avenue land-marks, Watts Towers
Break spots	Gilbert Lindsay Park at 5 mile mark, fast food locations at 4 mile, 8 mile and 12 mile marks
Please read pg 12-15 for information common to each walk in this book	

This excursion is the invention of Dean Okrand who is one of our core group. We had a wonderful day doing it on an April Saturday with a group of 25. The first half of the walk is a series of interesting sights. Individually none of which would be a particularly exciting stand-alone attraction; collectively they compose a sumptuous concert of local history. The next half has its spots but is admittedly dull. Doing this stretch on foot will certainly help you come to grips with the vastness of the LA basin and see some busy communities that escape recognition. Expect some blight; walkers who are able to look beyond the veneer to see and hear the ghosts of the 1930's and 40's will get the most out of the day.

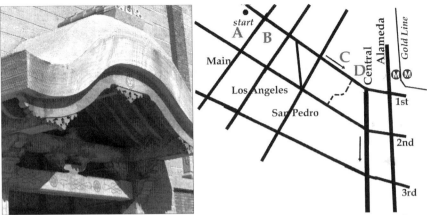

Stand in front of the sensational LAPD building "A" from AECOM architects and face across to the City Hall, turn right walking east on 1st. Across Main is another dynamic addition to Civic Center architecture, the CalTrans building from Thom Mayne "B". Walk on the north side of 1st after San Pedro St. to get close to the 13 brick buildings that comprise a National Historic District "C". In this area is found of one of the largest concentrations of Nikkei (Japanese Heritage) in America. At its peak before the internment during World War II, more than 30,000 Little Tokyo residents lived in this one square mile and were forced to leave their homes and businesses. Pass on your left the 1924 Hompa Hongwanji Buddhist Temple "D", now incorporated in the Japanese American National Museum.

Turn right on Central and find at 3rd the Higashi Honganji Buddhist Temple "E", built here 1976 after moving from Boyle Heights. Before 1939, you would have found the Los Angeles Central Train Station across Alameda around 3rd & 4th streets. Union Station was built then to unify the rail lines, LA had three train stations and the one used by Southern Pacific and (a shorter period) Union Pacific was here.

Coming to 7th you find the Union Terminal Market and Wholesale warehouses "E" built 1915 to 1923 by John and Donald Parkinson who were same architects as for the city hall, Bullocks Wilshire and Union Station.

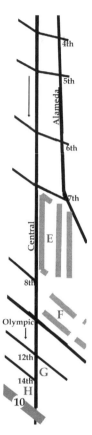

Walk east on 7th and look down the aisle of the "7th Street" Market which has been here almost 100 years. The warehouse buildings to your left are now the headquarters and factory of American Apparel, an astounding example of adaptive reuse.

It is possible that the guard will let you walk down the produce market aisle to exit on the south end at 8th Street. If not, return to Central, turn left and walk around the outside, peering through the portal gates.

At 8th Street, the old market ends and the LA Wholesale Produce Terminal begins "F". Industry changes towards palletization, larger trucks, sanitation and refrigeration doomed the older market to a marginal role.

Further south on Central is the foremost icon of LA industrial architecture, the Coca Cola Bottling Plant "G". It was designed 1939 by Streamline Moderne devotee architect Robert Derrah.

At 14th is Fire Station No. 30 "H". It was designed in the Prairie School style and was built in 1913. In 1924 it became the first of two all-black segregated city fire stations and remained segregated until 1956.

Enduring legacy of African American history along Central Avenue
Engine Co 30, 2nd Baptist Church, 27th St Historical District, 28th St YMCA

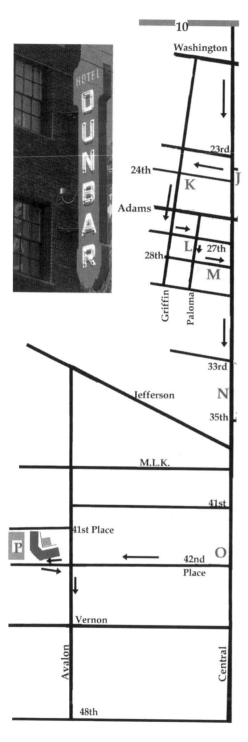

South of Washington starts a mile of the Central Ave. Corridor where a legacy of vibrant African-American arts and music thrived from about 1920-1955.

Past 23rd, find the Moorish Lincoln Theatre Building ("J") the "West Coast Apollo". For more than 30 years, the Lincoln featured theater, music, vaudeville, and movies. Lionel Hampton, Duke Ellington, Billie Holiday and Nat King Cole all played here.

Leave Central turning right on 24th; turn left on Griffith, left on 27th, right on Paloma, left on 28th and return to Central.

Paul Williams built 2nd Baptist Church ("K") a pivotal location in the civil rights movement. Martin Luther King spoke here often 1956-68. Malcolm X spoke here in 1962.

Centred on 27th and Paloma is the 27th St. Historical district ("L") of 1890's-1900's Queen Anne Victorians.

28th Street YMCA ("M") was built 1926 by Paul Williams in an era when most public facilities were segregated. The Y gave access to African Americans to a gymnasium, swimming pool, and 52 dormitory rooms. It is now refurbished into lofts.

Back on Central, look right at Jefferson towards the Angelus Funeral Home (Williams again), the first Black owned business to be incorporated in California. At Jefferson, the diagonal street grid ends (read page 62 "D"). Alameda St., just yards away at First St. is now a mile east running due south.

Fire Station #14 ("N") at 34th is the 2nd of the once segregated all Black Fire houses. At 40th is a fast food place and bathroom chance. At 42nd is the Dunbar Hotel, built entirely by Black craftsmen and laborers in 1928. It featured a lavish Spanish arcade with open balconies and grillwork. This was the LA home away from home at times for Ellington, Basie, Armstrong, Horne, Fitzgerald, Calloway and more.

You have walked four miles. I recommend doing the entire walk but a way to cut it down is to now take the Dash bus across from the Dunbar to the Metro Blue Line Vernon station (about a 6 minute ride-runs every 20 minutes). Then take the Blue Line south to 103rd St station and the Watts Towers.

After the Dunbar, turn right on 42nd Place and walk ¾ mile to Gilbert Lindsay Park, past Avalon, and take a lunch break. LA's Wrigley Field stood here, oriented as shown on the map. The Pacific Coast League LA Angeles played here for 40 years after 1925 and the Major League Angels played here one year. Brooklyn Dodger owner Walter O'Malley got his first toehold in the LA market by trading his Fort Worth Cats franchise for the minor league LA Angels, including their stadium. The city of LA accepted Wrigley Field in exchange for Chavez Ravine where Dodger Stadium would eventually be built.

Leaving the park, turn left on 42nd Place and right on Avalon.

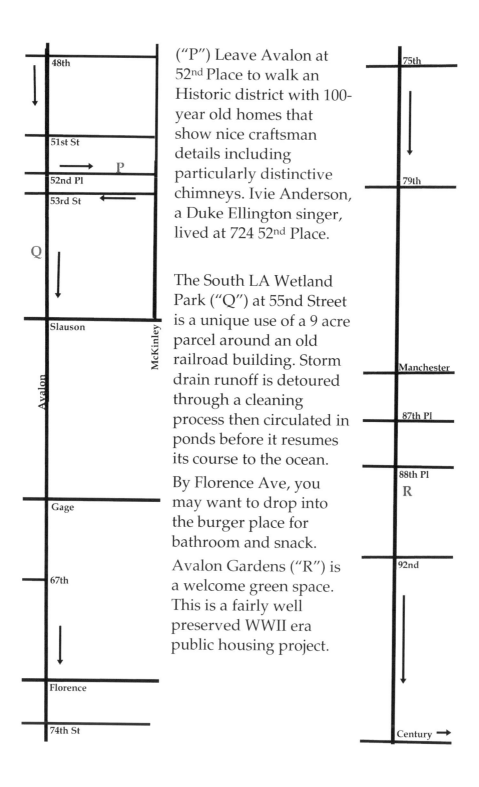

48th

51st St

P

52nd Pl

53rd St

Q

Slauson

McKinley

Avalon

Gage

67th

Florence

74th St

("P") Leave Avalon at 52nd Place to walk an Historic district with 100-year old homes that show nice craftsman details including particularly distinctive chimneys. Ivie Anderson, a Duke Ellington singer, lived at 724 52nd Place.

The South LA Wetland Park ("Q") at 55nd Street is a unique use of a 9 acre parcel around an old railroad building. Storm drain runoff is detoured through a cleaning process then circulated in ponds before it resumes its course to the ocean.

By Florence Ave, you may want to drop into the burger place for bathroom and snack.

Avalon Gardens ("R") is a welcome green space. This is a fairly well preserved WWII era public housing project.

75th

79th

Manchester

87th Pl

88th Pl

R

92nd

Century

52nd Place Historical District

Finally leave Avalon at Century headed southeast to the Towers as shown. Simon Rodia's towers are often thought of as the pinnacle of Los Angeles Fantasy art. Part whimsy, part rock solid construction, it is a mix of concrete, iron, soda pop bottles and broken ceramics done with amazing flair.

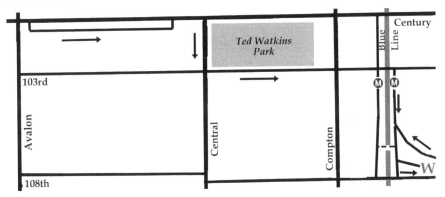

The Blue Line takes you back to the Red Line at

7th.

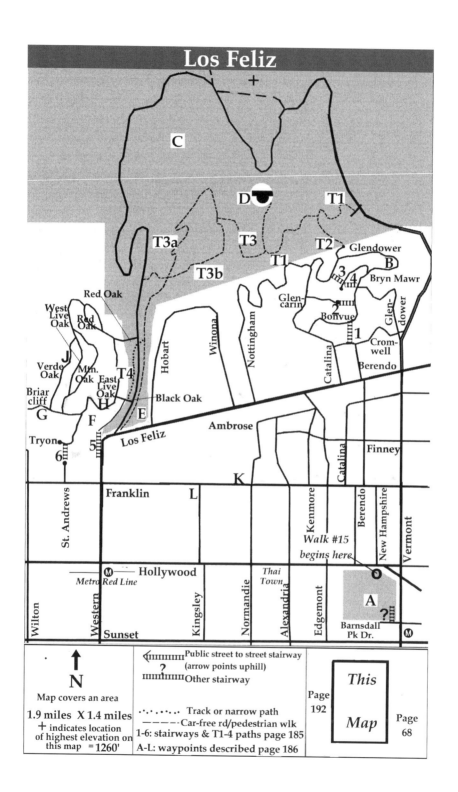

Los Feliz

C

D

T1

T3a

T3

T1

T2

Glendower

B

T3b

Red Oak

Glen-carin

Bryn Mawr

West Live Oak

Red Oak

Winona

Nottingham

Bonvue

3

4

Glen-dower

Verde Oak

Mtn. Oak

J

Hobart

Catalina

1

Crom-well

Briar cliff

East Live Oak

T4

Black Oak

Berendo

G

H

F

E

Ambrose

Tryon

Catalina

Finney

6

5

Los Feliz

St. Andrews

Franklin

L

K

Kenmore

Berendo

New Hampshire

Vermont

Walk #15 begins here

Ⓜ

Hollywood

Metro Red Line

Wilton

Western

Kingsley

Normandie

Alexandria

Edgemont

Thai Town

A

?

Barnsdall Pk Dr.

Ⓜ

Sunset

N

Map covers an area

1.9 miles X 1.4 miles

+ indicates location of highest elevation on this map = 1260'

Public street to street stairway
(arrow points uphill)
Other stairway

········· Track or narrow path
————- Car-free rd/pedestrian wlk
1-6: stairways & T1-4 paths page 185
A-L: waypoints described page 186

Page 192

This Map

Page 68

	stairway	location: top / bottom	steps	
?	**Olive Hill**	A couple of park stairs up to the art ctr	145	
1	**Berendo**	4796 Bonvue Ave / 4803 Cromwell Ave	181	**A**

One of the top ten 10 in the city and it justly displays a cultural heritage plaque. Best known for the ornamental double entry at the bottom and the bench circle for repose near the middle. *(page 188)*

2	**Glencairn**	4811 Glencairn Rd / 4749 Bonvue Ave	70	**B**

Lovely and clean, it is easy to pass without noticing on the bottom and the arch over the top entry matches the home that is built along side it.

3	**Upper Glendowr**	2763 Glendower Ave / 4800 Bryn Mawr	133	**A**

There is a beloved "Public Walk" sign at the top and you really have a feel of walking out into the void from that end. Views towards Mt Washington.

4	**Lower Glendowr**	4800 Bryn Mawr / 2543 Glendower Ave	74	**A**

Much of this is built along a submerged water tank giving it a half circle shape. A wonderful mosaic was installed here in 2000 to decorate the stairs and combat a graffiti problem at the time. The $14,000 art project celebrates its location near the observatory. At risk youth from the Venice Community Housing Corp. were hired to install the tile pieces. Nice community effort! *(188)*

5	**Western Ave**	Near 2101 N. Western Avenue	173	**B**

A long sidewalk stairway on a paved path that runs adjacent to AFI, high on the slope above where Los Feliz Blvd ends at a curve into Western.

6	**St. Andrews**	5680 Tryon Rd / 1950 N. St. Andrews Pl	153	**B**

From Franklin to W. Live Oak is a prodigious climb, at which this striking stairway is at the center. Fitted with benches and balustrades, these stairs have not been treated kindly by the vandals. A wonderful improvement in 2013 is the addition of lights thanks to a campaign by The Oaks residents.

	pathway			

Griffith Park has 53 miles of official trails and maybe just as many miles of unofficial "use" paths. This book only represents 2 1/2 miles of trails that are on the south central part of the park and connect well to Los-Feliz.

T1 **Boy Scout Trail**   Climbs to the Observatory from Vista de Valley near Vermont. Total distance is 2/3 mile, 375' gain. Meets the Glendower Rd. trail on one-third mile, arrives the saddle trail junction at half a mile.

T2 **Glendower Road**   Just 600 feet from stairway #3, a 700 foot trail links a cull de sec to the Boy Scout Trail. Gate is unlocked sunrise-sunset. This has been the location of a GPS snafu leading drivers on a fruitless hunt for for an auto shortcut to the observatory.

T3 **Fern Dell - Observatory trails**

There are 2 parallel routes to make the highly popular 550' climb from Ferndale to the Observatory. From the Trails Café, "3a" stays on the near side of the creek and "3b" starts on the far side. "a" covers just over one mile to the observatory; "b" just under one mile.

T4 **Fern Dell creek**   The best of the walking in Ferndale is a 1/5 mile stretch beneath the surrounding road and trail surface. Find it at the bottom end by Black Oak Dr. On the top end, look for a gate just south of a cross over bridge - a bathroom building off to your left is a good landmark.

Los Feliz

The Los Feliz neighborhood consists of about 37,000 residents in 2.6 square miles and includes Franklin Hills which is mapped in a previous section of this book. It is situated largely on a slope above East Hollywood against Griffith Park and can be dramatically beautiful. From lovely period cottages on the lowlands to cliff-edge Mediterranean's to architectural exotics, the streets are full of character. A "Beverly Hills alternative" it is perhaps surprising that the Times cites Los Feliz for have much higher residential density and ethnic diversity than most of the rest of the city. Included in this section is southern Griffith Park and some of the Oaks neighborhood.

A	**Barnsdall Park**	36-acre Olive Hill was purchased in 1919 by oil heiress Aline Barnsdall who had a passion for leftist causes, experimental theater and the idea of a community arts facility. She brought Frank Lloyd Wright to LA to build a Hollyhock House and other buildings. She donated all to the city.
B	**Ennis House**	Frank Lloyd Wright built 1924 for a men's clothing store owner who loved Mayan art and architecture. One of 4 houses Wright built in LA using knit pre-formed concrete blocks (more than 30,000 blocks). 6000 Sqft 3 bedroom,3 baths-appeared in "Blade Runner" Now owned by Ron Burkle.
C	**Griffith Park**	6.75 square miles, 5 x's larger than Central Park in NY. Too large to cover in detail in the book, its 53 miles of trails would keep a walker very busy. Donated 1896 by controversial "Colonel" Griffith J. Griffith.
D	**Observatory**	The iconic crown of Los Angeles, it was built in classic WPA style during the Depression. Admission is always free thanks to a proviso in Col. Griffith's gift. Parking here is crazy: a great walking destination!
E	**Fern Dell**	Ah, Fern Dell: do we just laud it for the popular, cool green oasis it remains or do we focus on the extraordinary garden spot it was until the 1970's? Maybe both. Another product of the Depression, CCC crews built much of what remains. Locals used to fill their jugs with the spring water.
F	**AFI**	Film Institute's campus works towards conservation and education on this 8 acre campus. Immaculate Hearts College built here 1916. Its demise is an interesting story of Catholical political intrigue when post Ecumenical Council nuns rebelled against Cardinal McIntyre. They are not particularly welcoming to walkers but worth a glimpse.
G	**Casa Della Vista**	At 5608 Briar Cliff, built 1925, this was the home of historians Will & Ariel Durant from 1950 until they died in 1981.

H-K: 3 Lloyd Wright (son of FL) masterpieces in the area built 1922-26

H	**Taggart House**	2158 Live Oak E. but best seen from below on Black Oak. Fantastic blend of stucco and rust colored wood cantilevers set off by a memorable garden of agave.
J	**Samuels Navarro**	5609 Valley Oak - Pre-Columbian blend of pressed metal and textured blocks. Diane Keaton once owned this home
K	**Sowden House**	5121 Franklin - you need to stand right in front of it to see through the foliage. Mayan influence, known as "The Jaws House"
L	**The Casa Laguna**	5200 Franklin - beautiful courtyard apartment complex of 18 units. Spanish Andalusian and classically Hollywood.

Walk 15	LOS FELIZ, OBSERVATORY, FRANKLIN VILLAGE
6.7 miles to Franklin Village to link to walk 16 or 17	
8.3 miles including walking back to start point	
	Elevation gain: ++	6 stairways
Shorter walk option:	3 miles-transit back from Observatory
start:	Barnsdall Park - 4800 Hollywood Blvd - 90027
finish:	Franklin Village - 5929 Franklin Ave - 90028
Transit:	Metro Red Line: Vermont / Sunset station
Best time to walk	Always great unless it is really hot - Clear days are good as this is a "big view" walk. Gate into Griffith Pk closes at Sunset; Wednesday afternoon Farmers Market at Barnsdall complicates parking but could be a nice addition
Highlights	Wright architecture, Observatory & Park, Fern Dell
Break spots	Observatory, Fern Dell
Please read pg 12-15 for information common to each walk in this book	

This walk is designed to join with either walk 16 or 17 for an all day, 12-14 mile excursion. It is also a nice stand-alone walk. Start in the lower parking area of Barnsdall along Hollywood Blvd. This has both easy parking (except on Farmers Market day) and is transit friendly to the Red Line and 180/780 buses.

WALK BEGINS ON MAP PAGE 184

With your back to Olive Hill, walk out the pedestrian gate of the lot and cross Hollywood at a signal at New Hampshire. On the north side is your first enigma: a padlock collection.

The first mile and a quarter have no points of interest, just pretty blocks. Walk north on New Hampshire and cross Franklin in the crosswalk. Turn left on Franklin and right on Berendo. Turn left on Ambrose, left on Catalina and right on Finley. At Edgemont, turn right and follow up to Los Feliz, crossing the wide parkway at the signal. Turn right on Los Feliz and left on Catalina. Turn right on Cromwell and find monumental **stairway 1**, the Berendo Stairs.

Berendo stairs

At the top, turn right and watch carefully for the bottom of **stairway 2** at 4749. On top, turn and look how well concealed it is. I've always been partial to the steel skin home at 4835. Turn right on Catalina. At a "T" with Glendower turn right. Curve around until the "public walk" sign where you walk down **stairway 3**. At the cull de sec at the bottom, jog right and walk down **stairway 4** with the nice mosaic. Turn left at the bottom, again on Glendower. At 2567 is a 50's Schlinder with a green surround, on the right is a home with an exotic roofline and a witch weathervane, on the left two homes have switchback driveways.

Walk below the Ennis Home and then up to the front entrance

("B" Pg. 188). Leaving that, continue up Glendower Av. and watch for Glendower ROAD where you turn right. Look carefully near the end for a gateway into the park on the left. You have come 2.5 miles and now leave pavement.

Lower Glendower stairs

Frank Lloyd Wright's Ennis House (and a neighbor)   *page 186*

A ridge trail intersects with the Boy Scout trail (T1&2) where you turn left. Arriving at a saddle, take the trail headed right directly to the Observatory. ("D") This is the 3 mile mark and a good chance for bathrooms, water and exploration.

Leave the observatory as you came and walk down to that saddle again. On your right is a trail headed up, skip that but take the one next to it headed down with lots of walkers for company. In 900 feet, take the switchback on left and continue downhill. A mile from the Observatory is Fern Dell. ("E")

Amidst a myriad of paths, stay on the left side of the dry creek but closest to its edge. As you pass a bathroom building on your left, go past a foot bridge right but then pass through a gate to the creek path that goes under the roadway. This emerges at Black Oak Drive in about one fifth mile.

At Black Oak, look for the paved pathway continuing in the same direction as you were walking. You can see AFI on your right ("F") as you start down **stairway 5**. Turn right on Franklin and right on St. Andrews. Climb **stairway 6**, turn right on top and arrive at Tryon and Live Oak out of breath.

American Film Institute (originally Immaculate Heart College) page 186

Turn left and just a few more feet up hill is the ridgeline leaving Mocohuenga Canyon, entering Bronson Canyon. Follow Live Oak West as it turns to the right. In 450', stay right at the "Y" on to Mountain Oak. This street loops back to Live Oak W. where you quickly turn left, right on Hill Oak, bear left on Verde Oak. You won't miss the "2255" sign for the upslope side of Lloyd Wright's Samuels-Navarro House.

A little further down Verde Oak, turn right on Valley Oak (use

Lloyd Wright's Samuels Navarro house

the little stairway!) and walk a few hundred feet down and back to see the downslope side of the Wright house. ("J")

Turn right on Verde Oak, right on Briarcliff and look at Casa Della Villa on your left ("G")

Walk with care for the steep slope and the traffic down Briarcliff. Capitol Records building looms below you. Brad Pitt and Angelina Jolie own 5 linked parcels, 1.8 acres, out of view to your right in a gated community. Briarcliff bends left to end at Foothill and Van Ness. Turn right on Foothill, left in two blocks on Bronson, and arrive at Franklin Village.

This is another great place to walk to because parking here is impossible. There is an interesting array of shops and restaurants on the north side of the street and on the south side is Scientology's "Celebrity "Center" which once was the "Chateau Elysee", home at times to Clark Gable, Cary Grant, Charles Chaplin, George Burns and Edgar Rice Burroughs.

From here several choices: you can link up with walks 16 or 17 giving you an all-day Hollywood Hills excursion. You can walk west to Argyle and south to Hollywood Blvd to the Pantages Theater area and the Hollywood/Vine metro stop.

If you do that, you should get off at Vermont/Sunset and walk up and over Barnsdall to see the Hollyhock House and the view the great lawn (use the **"?" stairway,** map Pg. 184)

If you want to walk back to the start, head east on Franklin and watch for "K" – the Sowden House and "L" – The Casa Laguna (page 186). Then turn right on Edgemont and at Hollywood you will see where you started. That adds 1.6 miles after Franklin Village.

Beachwood-Bronson-Hollywood Dell

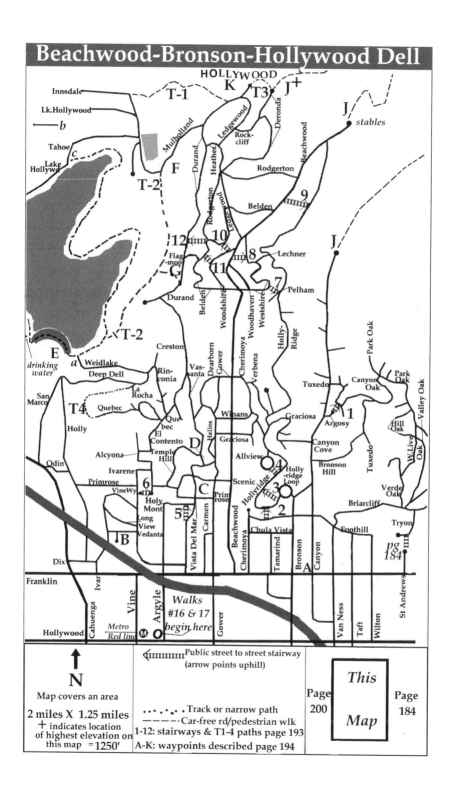

HOLLYWOOD

Innsdale
Lk.Hollywood
b
Tahoe
Lake
Hollywd
San
Marco
drinking
water

K T-1 T3 J+ J
stables
Mulholland Ledgewood Deronda Beachwood
Durand Heather Rock-cliff
Rodgerton T-2 F Rodgerton Belden 9
Rodgerton Ledgewood Lechner J
12 10 8
Flag-moor 11 7
G Belden Woodshire Pelham
Durand Woodhaven Westishire Holly-Ridge
E a Weidlake Creston Dearborn Cherimoya Park Oak
Deep Dell Rin-conia Vas-santa Gower Verbena Tuxedo Canyon Park
La Rocha Oak Oak
T4 Quebec Winans Graciosa Hill Valley Oak
Holly Que-bec Graciosa Argosy 1 Oak
Qdin El Contento D Allview Canyon Tuxedo
Alcyona Temple Hill Scenic Holly-ridge Cove Verde
Ivarene Holly-ridge Loop Bronson Oak
Primrose 6 Scenic 3 Hill Briarcliff
VineWy Holly Prim-rose 4 Tryon
Mont 5 C 2 pg
Long Vista Del Mar Carmen Chula Vista 184
View Beachwood Foothill
Vedanta Cherimoya Tamarind Bronson Canyon
B Dix A

Franklin
Hollywood Metro Walks #16 & 17 begin here
Cahuenga Ivar Vine Argyle Gower Van Ness Taft Wilton St Andrews
Red line M O

N

Map covers an area
2 miles X 1.25 miles
+ indicates location
of highest elevation on
this map = 1250'

⊲IIIIIIIIII Public street to street stairway
(arrow points uphill)

· · · · · · · Track or narrow path
– – – – – Car-free rd/pedestrian wlk
1-12: stairways & T1-4 paths page 193
A-K: waypoints described page 194

Page 200

This
Map

Page 184

	stairway	location: top / bottom	steps	
1	Argosy Way	5818 Tuxedo Terrace / 2424 Argosy Wy	51	B

A pretty, well-shaded stairway off on its own - kind of a transition from the Oaks neighborhood down to Bronson and further west

| 2 | Foothill | 2241 Hollyridge Dr / 5951 Foothill Dr | 61 | B |

The "blue bottle" stairway; adjoining garden has lots of cool glass in the design

| 3 | Hollyridge Loop | 2300 Hollyridge Dr / 2178 Hollyridge | 72 | B |

These stairs fall in the "drunken sailor" category, heaving starboard and port.

| 4 | Allview | acr fr 2332 Allview Terr / 2333 Hollyridge | 67 | B |

There's a gate at the top that I have never found to be locked; shade with a view

| 5 | Holly Mont | 6214 Holly Mont / 2071 Vista Del Mar | 61 | B |

Kind of a Hollywood grandee dame which now seems to be better looked after than when I made my first list in 2008. Wide at the bottom and top and separate, twin paths go either side of an island. On the edge of Krotona.

| 6 | Vine Way | 2100 Alcyona Dr / 6282 Vine Way | 47 | B |

A pleasing "S" curve in the Hollywood Dell

| 7 | Pelham | 2823 Pelham Place / 2744 Westshire | 149 | B |

A long way down or up, this one opens up in the middle.

| 8 | Westshire | 2935 Westshire Dr / 2810 Beachwood | 143 | A |

Just a beauty, the stonework is great and it has a cozy feel for being so long *(pg 196)*

| 9 | Hollyridge | 3057 Hollyridge Dr / 3020 Beachwood | 178 | B |

It's the longest of the Beachwood group but does not quite have the pizazz

| 10 | Woodshire double | 2950 Belden Dr / near 1815 Beachwood | 148 | A |

The cover girl of the LA stairs and of this book. The planters in the center once were cascading pools. I've heard that the noise of the frogs attracted to those pools was so annoying that the water was removed - maybe urban legend.

| 11 | Belden | 2872 Belden Dr / 2795 Woodshire Dr | 124 | B |

At the bottom there is a very imposing foundation wall of the characteristic Beachwood style, at the top you might walk right past it if your are not looking

| 12 | Durand | 2954 Durand / 2917 Belden | 118 | B |

The top of this one is even sneakier than #11 because the steps drop off parallel to the road. From either end, you cannot get a good idea how long it is.

	pathway			

T1 Innsdale Drive to Mulholland Highway

Half mile trail with no shade from Innsdale deadhead to 6201 Mulholland Hwy

T2 Mulholland Hwy One of the best short trails in the Hollywood Hills.

It is about 9/10 mile from where paved Mulholland Hwy meets Canyon Lake by Castillo del Lago to a gate next to the Lake Hollywood dam. Near the middle is a 500 ' trail exiting to Durand Dr next to Wolf's Lair. Be aware that road by the dam had rigid closing time and you cannot take a dog into the reservoir area.

T3 Mulholland Highway to Deronda Drive

Mulholland Hwy ends for drivers at a barrier but the road is walkable another 3/10 mile until it comes to the end of Deronda with a confusing gate arrangement.

T4 La Rocha -Quebec This quarter mile is more likely to take you out of your way than to be shortcut but it has great views and a nice bench along the way.

Beachwood - Bronson - Hollywood Dell

These are three finger canyons leading south of the Santa Monica Mountains that best personify the image most folks have of the Hollywood Hills. Bronson Canyon is a thicket of secluded streets including the classic Oaks Neighborhood and the avenue penetrates into Griffith Park. Hollywood Dell at its best is historic cottages on lanes tucked out of sight but also includes busy ridges of gaudy view homes. Beachwood is a wonderful village with the wildest collection of chateaus, domes, castellated walls, and watch towers in the city – and the best 6-pak of stairways.

A	**Franklin Village**	A commercial district at the foot of the canyon roads

with a quirky set of shops and cafes. Across the street is "Chateau Elysee", now Scientology's Celebrity Center, which was a residence hotel for old Hollywood

B	**Vedanta Temple**	An Italian villa-style convent that was once home to

actress Jeanette MacDonald, is now a welcoming center for worship, meditation and vespers services. Nice bookshop, closed Wednesdays

C	**Krotona**	A Theosophical colony was established here in 1912

and maintained a spiritual, intellectual and agrarian presence over many acres of lower Beachwood before moving on to Ojai 12 years later, partly to escape the onslaught of the vulgar film industry. An exotic "Eastern" theme is found in many remaining buildings all over the area but centered on what is now the Krotona Hotel on Vista Del Mar.

D	**Moorcrest**	At Vasanta and Temple Hill, it was built by architect

and theosophy devotee Marie Russak Hotchener in 1921. Charlie Chaplin was a tenant but the home was long owned by the family of actress Mary Astor. It is a fascinating story and the walker should check out Hope Anderson's blog, "Under the Hollywood Sign" for the whole scoop on much of the canyon lore. A lot of what I enjoy and know here, I only know from Ms. Anderson.

E	**Hollywood Reservoir**	It was built 1924 and can be 180 feet deep - a plan to cover the water surface was beaten back and now 2

huge tanks hold the drinking water at north end. Walking around the lake is a very popular exercise and DWP reopened the west (and best) walkway 2013. It is closed by sunset and dogs are not permitted. 3 access points are noted on the map; distance a-b: 1.2 miles; b-c: 2/3 mile(path along active motorway); c-a: 1.5 miles. There are potable toilets at a & b and drinking water as shown.

F	**Castillo del Lago**	Residence of Bugsy Siegel in the 1930s and Madonna in the 90's. John DeLario's 1926 Andalusian masterpiece

G	**Wolf's Lair**	Milton Wolf, a 1920's art director and Hollywoodland

developer, built this Norman castle -eight-bedroom, six-bath. Purchased for in 2008 by electronic music wizard, Richard Melville Hall, aka Moby. He has been a tremendous friend to Los Angeles arts and architecture.

J	**Griffith Park trails**	Mapping most of the Griffith Park trails is beyond scope of this book but "J" indicates where trails leave

residential areas and will inter-connect in the park to make a walking loop

K	**The sign**	A location you MAY NOT walk to. Built 1924 reading

HOLLYWOODLAND. The city tried to tear the sign down in 1949. Then partially refurbished without "LAND". Major refurbishment in '78 cost $27K per letter.

WALK 16	HOLLYWOOD & VINE TO BEACHWOOD	
7.1 miles	elevation gain: ++	10 stairways
Shorter walk option: 4 miles - take Dash bus back from middle		
start / finish:	Pantages Theater - 6233 Hollywood Blvd 90028	
Transit:	Metro Red Line - Hollywood - Vine station	
Best time to walk	always a great walk but a clear day will add to the view over the Hollywood Reservoir - bail out Dash bus does not operate on Sundays	
Highlights	Classic stairways, Beachwood Canyon homes, nearness to Hollywood sign, view over Hollywood Reservoir	
Break spots	Beachwood Market and Beachwood Café - at 4 mile mark No other amenities - watch for portable toilets	
Please read pg 12-15 for information common to each walk in this book		

The end point of walk 15 and the start points of walk 16 and 17 are near each other and designed to link any two of those three walks together to make a longer day. The Pantages is across the street from the Hollywood/Vine Red Line station.

ENTIRE WALK ON MAP PAGE 192

Facing the W Hotel from the Pantages, turn left and walk east on Hollywood Blvd. to Gower and turn left. Pass huge Hollywood Pres which was the largest Presbyterian church in the world in the 1960's. At Franklin, cross to the north side of the street and turn right. Turn left on Cherimoya and just before it dead ends, turn right on Foothill. Climb **stairway #2** by the blue bottles. On top, turn right on Hollyridge and dip down to address "2178" where you climb **stairway #3**. Turn right on top and walk a short distance to "2333" and turn up **stairway #4** on your left. Turn right on circular Allview Terrace.

Westshire stairs
Ying Chen photo

You are on the ridge that separates Bronson Canyon on your right from Beachwood Canyon to your left. Streets are very confusing around here.Make a right turn at the end of the loop, and then bear left on Hollyridge and watch the street numbers get larger. Come to a fork with Graciosa and bear right, staying on Hollyridge. The next "Y" is for Graciosa headed right (the only driving street that connects the 2 canyons). Ignore that, bear left. Then another "Y", ignore Verbena to the left, stay on Hollyridge. There is an "s" curve and then the last of the mind-numbing series of "Y"'s. Ignore Rutherford on the left, stay on Hollyridge on the right. Now you can relax on your junctions for a while. Around the 2800 block, watch for a view towards the Bronson quarry. Opened in 1903, it was important source of rock for road building and ballast for the trolley lines. In this area (out of sight from Hollyridge) is the tunnel that will always be known as the "Bat Cave", thanks to 1960's television.

At Pelham on your left, you've come just about two miles and are ready to tackle the upper Beachwood stairs. Go down **stairway #7**. Turn left at the bottom on Westshire and the market comes into view.

King's mouth   Carol Hoffstedt photo

That can wait a bit; turn right on Woodhaven. Watch for the comical expression on the castellated house on your right. Woodshire ends at Beachwood where you turn right and walk just 100 feet to find the bottom of **stairway #8**. Climb these and turn right on top. At the junction, take little Lechner Place on your left, arriving way back up on Hollyridge. Turn left. At 3057 you'll locate dizzying **stairway #9** headed back to Beachwood. Turn left at the bottom and walk a quarter mile down Beachwood past Belden & Ledgewood on right.

At Woodhaven, find the bottom of the famous **stairway #10** (on the cover of this book). It's worth doing twice so climb up to the top and notice the steel nuts on a rod that looks like an abacus; it is a lap counter. We follow the example of the first Big Parade in 2009: the line of participants climbed up staying right, then came down staying right. The Big Paraders high-fived each other across the middle of the stairway. Turn right (on Beachwood, not Woodshire) at the bottom and walk 250 yards to the village center and market.

This is the mid-walk break – you have come about 4 miles. Buy something at the store or the restaurant to get permission to use their bathroom. If you have to leave the walk now, the DASH bus leaves from the gates any day but Sunday to take you back to Hollywood and Argyll.

Rested, facing the market, turn right and walk up Belden. Take the first right on Woodshire and locate **stairway #11** at 2795. On top turn right and look for the last of the Beachwood **stairs, #12**, at 2917 Belden. Turn right at top on Durand which you follow for half a mile to Mulholland Highway.

Castillo del Lago with stripes in the Madonna days

The nearer you get to Mulholland, the more you need to be aware of crazed motorists searching for the Hollywood sign.

Take the first left which looks to be just a private driveway for Castillo del Lago. You will see a dirt path/road continuing beyond the gate to the villa. Follow this, enjoying views of the reservoir for less than half mile. You'll see a distinct trail (actually called Wetonia Drive) up to the left. Walk up this 500' to the castle of Wolf's Lair ("G").

Mulholland Dam and Lake Hollywood from Mulholland Hwy trail

At Wolf's Lair, leave the trail and turn right on Durand. Durand ends soon at a "T" at Creston; turn left starting downhill. At the next "Y", bear left on Vasanta as Creston goes right. Vasanta ends at a "T" at Temple Hill, next to Moorcrest on your left ("D"). Turn left on Temple Hill, then quickly right on Vista Del Mar. After you curve downhill and come to the corner with Primrose, you are at ground zero of the old Krotona colony ("C"). Keep going straight on Vista del Mar. Make the first right after Primrose onto Holly Mont.

On your right at 6215 is an oddity that had a pretty chilling ghost story attached to it from the 70's (search Don Jolly house). Now it features a pretty hideous collection of statuary. One internet report identified the owner as "an international concert pianist, former child prodigy, spiritual recluse, and ping pong enthusiast". Look across from that for **stairway #5.** Go down stairs and continue straight down Vista del Mar. Turn right on Franklin, left on Argyll, back to the Pantages.

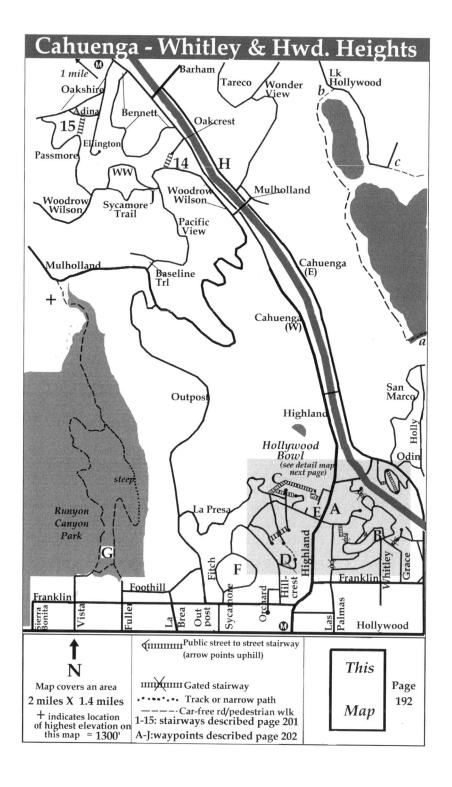

Cahuenga - Whitley & Hwd. Heights

1 mile

Oakshire
Adina
15
Ellington
Passmore
Bennett
Barham
Tareco
Wonder View
Lk Hollywood
Oakcrest
WW
14 **H**
Woodrow Wilson
Mulholland
Woodrow Wilson
Sycamore Trail
J
Pacific View
Mulholland
Baseline Trl
Cahuenga (E)
Cahuenga (W)
+
Outpost
Highland
San Marco
Hollywood Bowl
(see detail map next page)
Holly
steep
Odin
Runyon Canyon Park
La Presa
C
E **A**
G
B
Fitch
F
D
Highland
Whitley
Grace
Franklin
Franklin
Sierra Bonita
Vista
Fuller
La Brea
Out post
Sycamore
Orchard
Hill-crest
Las Palmas
Hollywood

N

Map covers an area
2 miles X 1.4 miles
+ indicates location
of highest elevation on
this map = 1300'

◁〈▥▥▥▥▥▥ Public street to street stairway
(arrow points uphill)
▥▥▥╳▥▥▥ Gated stairway
•·••·•· Track or narrow path
–––– Car-free rd/pedestrian wlk
1-15: stairways described page 201
A-J:waypoints described page 202

This
Map

Page
192

	stairway	location: top / bottom	steps	
1	Iris Place	6825 Iris Circle / 6831 Iris Drive	44	B
	Steps split a pretty oval block; this one has seen a terrific recent cleanup job			
2	Whitley / Iris Circle	6813 Iris Circle / 6814 Whitley Terrace	27	B
	Easy to overlook; a nice companion to stairway #1			
Stairways in Whitley Heights that have a combination lock				
3	Holly Hill	1970 N. Grace Ave / 2010 Holly Hill Terr.	31	gates
4	Wedgwood Place	6754 Wedgewood / 2133 Fairfield Av	69	gates
5	Las Palmas	6684 Bonair Place / 6689 Emmett Terr.	53	gates
6	Mary Jackson	2044 Grace Ave / near 6687 Whitley Terr	25	B
	You need to pay attention at either end to find this; it even has a plaque.			
7	Whitley Terrace	6666 Whitley Terr / 6640 Milner Road	160	A
	One of the city's prize stairways, it is long, full of turns, has great distant views and discreet near view. You get a feeling of how lovingly refurbished these are.			
8	Alta Loma Place	2186 Broadview Ter / 6836 Alta Loma Pl	89	A
	A local treasure, about 900 feet of steps & paved pathway are an artery that connect 30 soulful properties. Likely to be locked at the bottom on Bowl nights			
9	Broadview Terr	2187 Broadview Terr / 6889 Yeager Place	136	A
	This one that takes past the High Tower elevator. It connects to stairway #11 on the way up and then to stairway #8 at the top. No where else in LA like this			
10	Los Altos East	2164 Rockledge Rd / 2112 High Tower Dr.	10	C
11	Los Altos West	2067 Broadview Terr / 2131 High Tower Dr	23	B
	Two short stairs that spread right and left from High Tower, West is more useful			
12	Lower Paramount	2032 Glencoe Way / 2033 High Tower Dr	103	B
13	Upper Paramount	2030 Paramount Dr / 2039 Glencoe Way	110	B
	One of the best stairway pairs in the city, these give you 130' elevation gain (seems like more). Lower is wooded & shady, upper has the view to Griffith Pk.			
14	Oakcrest Drive	7001 Woodrow Wilson / 3113 Oakcrest Dr	83	B
	#14 & 15 are included in a nice little walk called "Happy Trails" in *Secret Stairs*			
15	Adina-Passmore	3012 Passmore Dr / 3335 Adina Drive	136	B
	Long, leafy, claustrophobic and distant from any other stairway but one.			

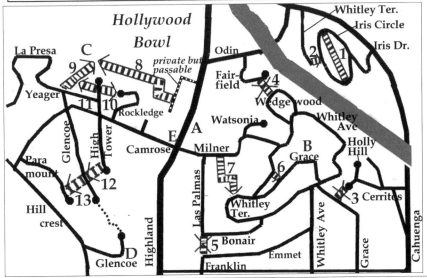

Cahuenga - Whitley and Hollywood Heights

This section covers another amalgamation of micro-neighborhoods that the LA Times mapping project would throw into their "Hollywood Hills" or "Hollywood Hills west" delineations. Whitley Heights and Hollywood Heights are each historic zones that are magical to discover on foot and they each have a nice cluster of stairways. Runyon Canyon is one of most famous walking areas in the city. Also in this section near Universal City is a quiet neighborhood with 2 stairways and a maze of sinuous streets with back alleys referred to as "trails" All of this area abuts the most heavily visited parts of Hollywood: the Bowl and the area around Hollywood and Highland.

A	**Hollywood Heritage Museum**	100 years ago Jesse Lasky and Cecil B. DeMille moved into this barn (then at a different location) to begin producing movies. The site is now a museum open Weds-Sunday, noon-4pm. Here you get a notion of Los Angeles movie making as a cottage industry, not mega-business of today. This location has been friendly to passing walking groups needing to use their bathrooms, so I hope that many future walkers will reward themselves and thank the museum by way of the $7 adult admit.
B	**Whitley Heights**	Founded in 1920's and listed on the National Register of Historic Places. It was completely severed in 1951 by the Hollywood Fwy; the top of one hill was lopped off. Once home to Lombard & Powell, WC Fields, Valentino, Gloria Swanson, Harlow, Garland, Dietrich etc. The Heights found themselves under siege in the 1970's by wayward drug users up from the boulevard and autos looking to park on Bowl nights. Guards now ward off the cars during events and three stairways that were entry zones on the south, north and east sides now have gates with combination locks. The combination is known to some of the walkers but it would not be productive to publish it. They lost a lawsuit filed by "Citizens against gated enclaves" in 1994 when they tried to withdraw their streets from general city usage. That has been a landmark case to challenge other such proposals.
C	**High Tower**	The High Tower is a 1920's Bolognaise folly framed on either side by 1930's streamline moderne. Considered together with the district of exceptional walkways, stairways and homes unapproachable by motor around it and you have a unique, stand-along destination that will never fail to wow a visitor. Walk it quietly, respectful of the residents.
D	**F L Wright**	The Freeman House built 1924 is a textile block construction with a "tulip" motif. It has a spectacular living room overlooking Hollywood-owned by USC-undergoing renovation see: sphericalphotos.com
E	**Highland-Camrose**	A colony of seven bungalows a century-old have been adapted for various uses related to the adjacent Bowl. They are the survivors of a battle to save 14 such houses in the 1990's. It is a cute park setting cultivated for Bowl picnickers that can be accessed from Camrose when the gates facing Highland are locked.
F	**Yamashiro**	Built by the Bernheimer brothers in 1914 as a hilltop mansion to house their collection of Asian treasures. Hundreds of skilled craftsmen came from the Orient to create a replica of a Kyoto palace.

G	Runyon Canyon	A place of veneration from the dog walkers and fitness seekers, Runyon can be also be a great asset to the cross-town walker. The trails offer scenic and direct walkers-only passage from Hollywood to the ridge of the Santa Monica Mountains at Mulholland Dr. Considering the park's popularity with all the parking restrictions around it and this is a destination that increasingly is accessible only to the walker or the transit user.

trail description: A main trail that starts closer to the Vista gate climbs 660 feet elevation on old pavement and reaches Mulholland Dr. in 1.6 miles. One mile up, it meets the east trail. The east trail begins closer to Fuller gate first going up the canyon bottom then switch backing on dirt that gets very steep climbing up a series of anti-erosion steps before it meets the main trail. It is 9/10 mile up the east trail to its junction with the main trail. The very steep bit over the steps climbs a challenging 340 feet in one third mile.

H	Cahuenga Pass	When the Los Angeles walking crowd laments how some vital spots have been completely given over to the motorist, this historic and natural saddle will likely be part of the conversation. Cahuenga West is too dangerous to walk. Cahuenga East is dicey but doable so long as you are ready to dive into the weeds to avoid wayward autos and you are preferably facing south. Bicyclists have also had this zone on their radar as an area that must get improved; walkers might reap some benefit if bike lanes are created.

J	Ehling tile house	A tour-de-force of LA expressionism, this 45 year labor of mosaic love seems a world away geographically but linked culturally with Rodia's towers. Only six hundred feet from the Oakcrest stairs, this location stops walkers in their tracks as cars might race past. Creator George Ehling is a former studio craftsman, one time wrestler and self-proclaimed madman.

The High Tower & Broadview Terrace
Howard Petersen photo

WALK 17	WHITLEY HEIGHTS & HOLLYWOOD HTS	
5.2 miles		elevation gain: +	9 stairways
Shorter walk option: 4 miles, leaving at Hollywood Heritage Museum		
start	Pantages Theater - 6233 Hollywood Blvd 90028	
finish	Hollywood & Highland Entertainment Center	
Transit:	Metro Red Line: Hollywood+Vine & Hollywood+Sunset	
Best time to walk	Wednesday through Sunday mid-day to early afternoon to make the noon-4pm opening time of the museum. Better to avoid Hollywood Bowl event time.	
Highlights	Hollywood Dell, historic Whitley Heights, High Tower area, Yamashiro vicinity, Hollywood&Highland finish	
Break spots	coffee at Franklin & Cahuenga, 3 1/2 mile break at Hollywood Heritage Museum	
Please read pg 12-15 for information common to each walk in this book		

The end point of walk 15 and the start points of walk 16 and 17 are near each other and designed to link any two of those three walks together to make a longer day. The Pantages is across the street from the Hollywood/Vine Red Line station.
WALK BEGINS ON MAP PAGE 192

Facing the W Hotel from the Pantages, turn left and walk to the corner and turn left on Argyle. Walking under the 101 freeway, pass Franklin and pass an on-ramp, then turn left on Vine-Dix. You are entering the Hollywood Hills and soon turn left on Vedanta. In the middle of the block on the left visit the Vedanta Temple (turn your phones off please and remove your shows if you go into the temple). Leave the temple walking down their front steps, turn right and left again on Vedanta. Turn right on Ivar. As you turn right on Longview, enjoy a faux Norman castle built 1926. Take Longview to Vine. Before you turn left, go across the street and slightly right and peer into the courtyard of a 1918 hacienda at 2030 Vine that MAY have been the home of William Boyd aka Hopalong

Cassady. Take Vine north a block and turn right on Vine Way to go up **Stairway #6** (page 192).

From the top of the stairs, you are well into the Hollywood Dell. Turn left on Alcyona. Pass Primrose on the right and make a left on Ivarene. Turn left on Vine and right on Primrose. Turn right on Holly, then left on Odin. Climb steeply out of the dell up to Cahuenga. Turn right and walk to the signal to cross.
You've left the Dell and are entering Whitley Heights.
REST OF WALK ON MAP Pg. 200 & DETAIL MAP Pg. 201.
After crossing, turn back left on Cahuenga and make a right on Whitley Terrace. At the end of the street, look left and take **Stairway #2** up to Iris Circle. Turn left and follow the oval and watch on the right for a sign post and the pretty Iris Pl. sign which marks **Stairway#1**. Follow steps and path back to street and turn left. Make a right at the "Y" and return to Cahuenga. Turn right, pass under freeway, then get further from the traffic by crossing right to Wilcox. Follow this to Franklin.
This is a bit over 2 miles from the start and another 1.5 miles to a break spot that is only open Weds-Sun noon to 4. So you might consider a coffee break now across Franklin at Solar de Cahuenga.
Turn right on Franklin and take the next right on Grace as you climb Whitley Heights. A First World War era mansion at Franklin and Grace is the lone holdout in a sea of apartments.
Near 1970 Grace notice the gate to the Holly Hill stairs that is not included on this walk. Pass the historic district sign ("B") and the transition from apartments to lovely 90-year old homes is abrupt. Continue up Grace to a complicated intersection with Whitley Terrace and Whitley Avenue. Bend right, and then continue straight on Grace. Grace curves to the left and near 2044 you find little wood **Stairway #6** on the

Whitley Terrace steps *Ying Chen photo*

right. Go down these. Turn right on Whitley Terrace and make a very sharp left on Milner.

Duck down and back on Watsonia Terrace to look at a secluded enclave of residences with old time Hollywood connections including Villa Vallambrosa at 2074.

Returning to Milner, turn right and look on your left for the signed entrance to the Whitley Terrace **stairway #7**. On top, consider the story of Barbara Lamarr who lived 2 doors left at 6672. An actress and screenwriter of the silent film age, she was celebrated at "the girl too beautiful", married five times and died before her 30th birthday. Head right or counter-clockwise on the Whitley Terrace circle. Turn right on Bonair. Where Bonair ends at Las Palmas, notice locked Stairway 5 on your left. Follow Las Palmas to Milner, turn left and when you come up to Highland, turn right into the park area where the Hollywood Heritage Museum is located in the barn ("A").

Here is the rest point in the walk after 3.5 miles.

Return to the corner and walk across Highland at the cross-walk. The route goes right on Highland but first walk up Camrose (Milner has changed names) about 100 feet to look inside the restored group of bungalows that are now Bowl related offices. ("E")

Turn around and return to Highland. Walk north towards the Hollywood Bowl but just beyond the end of the picnic area turn left into Alta Loma Terrace which will have an open gate unless the Bowl is having an event.

The string of little garages is a tip-off that this is as far as an auto is allowed to enter. There's a gap between garages where you find the arched entry to the pedestrian zone of Alta Loma Place. You head up a few stairs and turn right then left as the signs direct to stay on Alta Loma **(Stairway #8).** Then more stairs lead to a very long paved path.

At the top, follow the sign that tells you to turn left for Broadview Terr. Take the steps **(Stairway #9)** under the bridge that heads to the elevator door. You will find Los Altos - **Stairway #11** intersects on the left so take those instead of following Broadview to the bottom. You wind up on High Tower Dr. looking back up at the tower elevator.

Turn right. Cross busy Camrose carefully and continue on High Tower until it dead ends with **Stairway #12** on your right. At the top, **Stairway #13** awaits you across Glencoe.

At the top of that turn right on Paramount and left when you get to Camrose. You arrive at a summit crossroads. You want to take Sycamore to the right. This will make a big curve downward and point towards Yamashiro ("F"). The road curves on either side, you should stay left. Approaching Franklin, you are on the back side of the 1909 Chateauesque mansion that is the Magic Castle. Turn left at Franklin and cross to the south side of the street at Orange. Still going east on Franklin, turn right on Orchid and enter the Hollywood Highland complex through the service corridor.

You will find the Red Line at the corner of Hollywood and Highland for one stop back to the start. You could enjoy walk the 8/10's mile back to the start enjoying Hollywood Blvd.

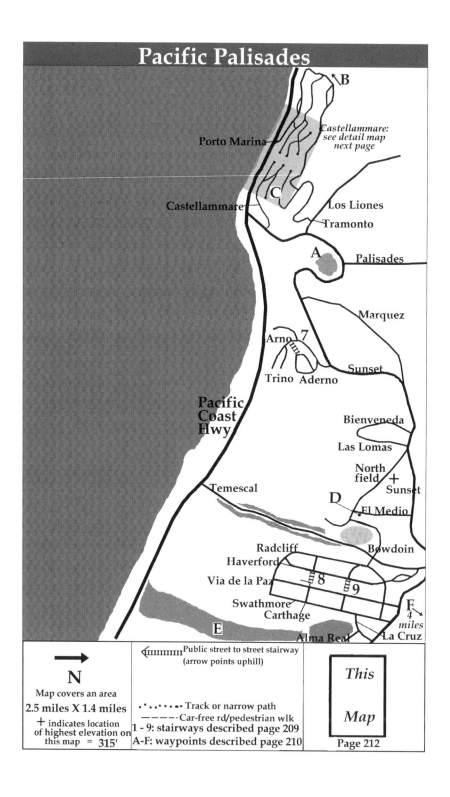

Pacific Palisades

B

Porto Marina

Castellammare:
see detail map
next page

Castellammare

C

Los Liones

Tramonto

A

Palisades

Marquez

Arno 7

Trino Aderno

Sunset

Pacific
Coast
Hwy

Bienveneda

Las Lomas

North
field

Sunset

Temescal

D

El Medio

Radcliff

Bowdoin

Haverford

Via de la Paz

8

9

Swathmore
Carthage

F
4
miles

E

Alma Real

La Cruz

→

N

Map covers an area

2.5 miles X 1.4 miles

+ indicates location
of highest elevation on
this map = 315'

◁ⅢⅢⅢⅢⅢPublic street to street stairway
(arrow points uphill)

•••••••• Track or narrow path

————· Car-free rd/pedestrian wlk

1 - 9: stairways described page 209

A-F: waypoints described page 210

This

Map

Page 212

	stairway	location: top / bottom	steps	
1	Revello	17804 Castellammare / 17737 Porto Marina	86	B
2	Breve Way	17718 Revello / 17703 Castellammare	91	B
		So often you walk the neighborhoods with sea views and there is no shade as the locals obliterate any vegetation that interferes with the view. Come to stairways one and two for deep shade under thick oleander cover. No sea views at all!		
3	Lower Breve	top: across fr 17711 Porto Marina	37	C
		bottom: north of 17575 Pacific Coast Hwy		
		Needs to be listed because it is here, but PCH is too dangerous to walk at bottom.		
?	Revello dead-end	Revello Drive at Posetano Road		
		The area's most noticeable stairs go nowhere; a relic of the pre-landslide days		
4	Lower Castellammare	17575 Castellammare / 17580 P.C.H.	75	A
5	Upper Castellammare	top: 17606 Posetano	69	B
		bottom: across from 17560 Castellammare *(page 211)*		
?	Posetano-Revello	17603 Posetano		
		A wonderful pair of stairs today that would have been a magnificent trio during before landslides and rezoning knocked out the top. These stairs are always going to be mentioned together with the 1935 mysterious death of actress Thelma Todd Her "Sidewalk Café" is the building on PCH by the overpass; she walked up the steps to Roland West's home before being found dead in the garage the next morning.		
6	Posetano	17496 Revello / 17445 Posetano	122	A
		Long and open along one side for great views over the ocean. Revello on top is a truncated end of a street that looks like it is connected to life support . *(page 211)*		
7	Arno Way	242 Aderno Way / 300 Arno Way	117	B
		Reminiscent of the Cumberlain/Clayton stairs in Franklin Hills: a dogleg in the middle conceals how long these are. Nice glimpse of the Pacific through foliage.		
8	Carthage Street	677 Via de la Paz / 670 Haverford	61	B
9	Bowdoin Street	773 Via de la Paz / 800 Haverford	59	B
		A matched pair of short stairs 800 feet apart climb up to Via de la Paz. Each is a hard to find the top; Carthage is at the end of an alley, Bowdoin is on a parking lot		
T-1	Posetano trail	Bridges the landslide chasm; a vital passage for the walker		

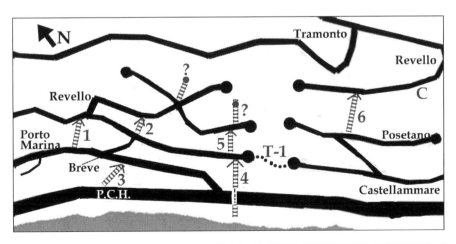

Pacific Palisades

The Palisades is a huge neighborhood; at 23 square miles, it is half the size of San Francisco. It is the one of the wealthiest neighborhoods in the city and is the whitest. While it would not be expected to have much of a walkability score, Pacific Palisades does have a nice cluster of public stairways in its Castellammare district plus three more between there and the neighborhood center of Palisades village. This book section addresses a very selective group of blocks in a small section of the Palisades between Sunset and the Pacific. Castellammare surprisingly is a great area to walk both because of the stairs and because the devastating landslide activity through the years has made it a particularly difficult area to navigate by automobile.

A	**The Lake Shrine**	If you have ever observed the stressful car jockeying to get into and park here on a pleasant afternoon, you can understand how ideal the shrine can be as a walking destination. It can be as beautiful and tranquil as any cultivated landscape in the city. Paramahansa Yoganada and the Self Realization Fellowship purchased the site in the late 1940's from an oil company exec who was planning to build a hotel complex on the ten acres. The site became an unintentional lake during irregular development in the 20's & 30's and a film studio construction VP dreamed up some of the setting we enjoy today. SRF added their own signature including a memorial with some of Gandhi's ashes. The site is open daily except for Mondays. Please turn off your phones. Unless there is an event, they now seem amenable to walkers who enter nearer to Castellammare near the lake and exit up top via the stairs to the temple - a good option for a through walker headed for the other stairs.
B	**Getty Villa**	This famous and sublime destination is just one half mile from the bottom of the Castellammare stairs and as much as I would like to say it is a natural tie-in, the Villa forbids entry to walk up visitors-poor form!
C	**Pierre Koenig**	Best known for his Case Study projects, this important architect built the Beagles House at 17446 Revello, a few hundred feet from the top of the Posetano stairs. From the street, it appears as a sliver of cold steel and glass. It expands downslope as an ocean view masterpiece.
D	**Eric Owen Moss**	Now best know for his memorable buildings at the Hayden Tract in Culver City, the now 30-year old modifications he made to a ranch house at 708 El Medio are a fun, rare display of Palisades eclecticism.
E	**Portrero Canyon**	We will have to wait until at least 2015 but this area is now being rehabilitated into a passive park that will some day offer a direct, car-free walker's route from Palisades Village to the sea.
F	**Murphy Ranch**	Sometimes known as the "Nazi stairs" because of an urban legend about a spy network that may have been here in WWII. These now are some of the most famous stairways anywhere (512 steps!) but they just do not fit the profile of what this book is about. Read yelp or the excellent narrative written by Charles Fleming in *Secret Stairs* walk 42.

Posetano stairs

Upper Castellammare stairs

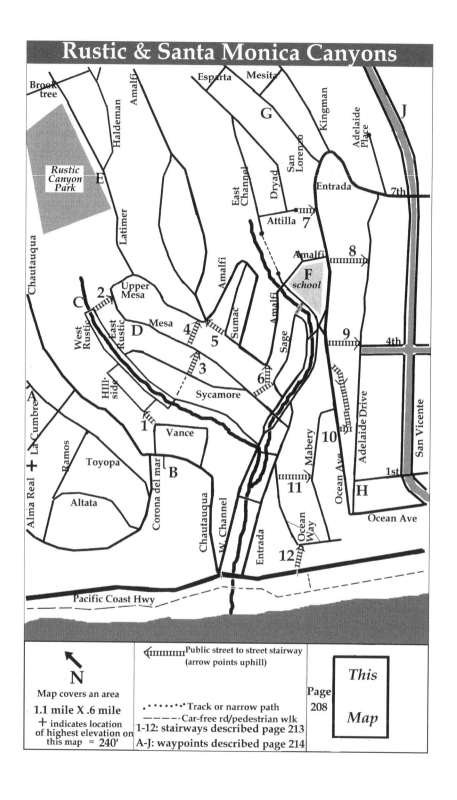

Rustic & Santa Monica Canyons

Brooktree
Amalfi
Esparta Mesita
Haldeman
Kingman
Adelaide Place
J
G
Rustic Canyon Park
E
San Lorenzo
Dryad
7th
Latimer
East Channel
Entrada
Attilla 7
Amalfi 8
Chautauqua
Amalfi
F school
Upper Mesa
C 2
West Rustic
East Rustic
D Mesa 4
Sumac
5
Sage
9 4th
Hillside
3
Sycamore
6
San Vicente
LaCumbre
A
1
Vance
Adelaide Drive
Ramos
Toyopa
Corona del mar
B
Mabery
10
Alma Real
Altata
Chautauqua
W. Channel
Ocean Ave
1st H
11
Ocean Way
Entrada
12
Ocean Ave

Pacific Coast Hwy

N

Map covers an area
1.1 mile X .6 mile
+ indicates location of highest elevation on this map = 240'

⟨ⅢⅢⅢⅢ Public street to street stairway
(arrow points uphill)

• • • • • • • Track or narrow path
– – – – - Car-free rd/pedestrian wlk
1-12: stairways described page 213
A-J: waypoints described page 214

Page 208

This
Map

	stairway	location: top / bottom	steps
1	Hillside Lane	390 Vance / 419 Hillside	88
			B
Serves like a secret passage in and out of Rustic Canyon. Enjoy the tile and glass on the home at the top			
2	E.Rustic-Mesa	491 Mesa / 544 E. Rustic	61
			B
A "use caution" sign on top is correct: these stairs are irregular. The bottom is not at all apparent.			
3	Sycamore-Mesa	401 Mesa / 400 Sycamore	48
			B
These stairs are a diminutive relation to their companion, #4. Bottom of these is behind a privacy hedge.			
4	Upper Mesa	407 Upper Mesa/404 Mesa	201
			A
One of LA's great stairways, these get overlooked by the crowds on Adelaide. From bottom or top, they just seem to go on forever into the greenery. No handrail!			
5	Sumac Lane	309 Amalfi / 323 Sumac Ln.	124
			B
I like how the top of these stairs is just 70 feet from the top of #4 yet they go down to different canyons			
6	Sage Lane	top: 271 Amalfi Dr.	124
		Two bottoms: 320 Mesa or 333 West Channel	B
A "privacy" hedge hides the top; the bottom goes 2 ways.			
7	Attilla Road	460 Entrada / 14100 Attilla	88
			C
Inconsequential - easy to go right by the top			
8	Adelaide Wood	526 Adelaide / 421 Entrada	166
			A
Other than the Bunker Hill stairs, these & #9 are the most frequently used in LA, mostly by the fitness crowd			
9	4th Street	406 Adelaide / 350 Entrada	189
			A
The metal inserts on the narrow treads indicate how much use these get; You will never be alone here.			
10	Ocean Avenue	Between 262&350 Ocean Av	79
			B
Long secret pathway, easily overlooked			
11	Mabery	249 Mabery / 278 Entrada	79
			B
Nice tree cover; lonely compared to #8 and #9			
12	Ocean Way	99 Ocean Way / 14700 PCH	48
			B
Combines with a PCH underpass for a beach route			
13	Montana Ave	top: Palisades Pk / Montana	166
		bottom: 723 Palisades Bch	A
Memorable eroded bluffs and switchback stair- trail			
14	Calif. Incline	top: Palisades Pk / Idaho	47
		bottom: 1200 Palisades Bch	B
A odd group of ramps that are unified by stairs			
15	Arizona Ave	top: Palisades Pk/Arizona	111
		bottom: near 1268 P.C.H.	B
Switchback stairs to pedway overpass to stairs to PCH			
16	Santa Monica	top near 1415 Ocean Ave	85
		bottom: near 1425 P.C.H.	B
Lovely "S" curve stairs to pedway overpass to PCH			*(pg 216)*

Santa Monica Palisades

Adelaide

San

Vicente

Georgia

Marg-

uerita

Alta

Pali-

sades

Montana

13

Idaho

14

Pacific Coast Hwy

Wash-

ington

Calif-

ornia

Ocean Avenue

Wil-

shire

15

Arizona

Santa

Monica

16

Broad

-way

N

Map covers 1.6 mi X 3/10 mi.

Colorado

Santa Monica and Rustic Canyon

The City of Santa Monica needs its own book to describe its many merits for walkers. This guide considers only that part of Santa Monica where the cliff stairways join Ocean Ave. to PCH. This chapter primarily treats a splendid section of Los Angeles in Rustic and Santa Monica canyons that is near the beach and just north of Santa Monica. Here is a zone of natural and built beauty laced with a network of public stairways. The down home funk and blight found in many stairway adjacent districts covered in preceding sections is absent here. It's a restful place to walk.

A	**Olmsted legacy**	Unless you are creating a walk that joins the Palisades section with this chapter (which I heartily recommend) you might miss the artful planning of the streets in the Huntington Palisades. The design comes from the Olmstead Brothers who also proposed for Los Angeles a massive network of parks and green spaces in 1930. Those plans were disregarded.
B	**Eames House**	The home and studio built for the Case Study program Walk up the private drive marked 201-205 off Chautauqua to see it in its pristine canyon setting. Do not stray beyond the sign unless you have pre-arranged for the $10 tour, an investment that would enhance any walk here.
C	**Rustic Canyon**	Even if there were no stairs, this would still be one of most sublime residential districts in the city to explore on foot. The homes are in scale with street and canyon showing none of the excesses you might expect from such a wealthy district. The creek has water almost year-round.
D	**Entenza House**	At 475 Mesa is the always eye-catching home that Harwell Harris built for John Entenza who, as editor of Arts and Architecture Magazine, was a pivotal foster to the modernist architecture movement.
E	**Uplifter's Ranch**	The park history is notable in two regards. An early 20th century experimental forestry station here promoted the local introduction of the eucalyptus tree. In the 20's, prominent LA businessmen built their ranch here for the Uplifter's Club. It was a rustic retreat full of hijinks and avoidance of Prohibition enforcement. Their lodge & playhouse are now the Rec Center.
F	**Canyon School**	Notice the landmark 1894 one room schoolhouse
G	**Marquez cemetery**	An extraordinary remnant of local history hemmed in by 2 to 4 million dollar homes. The Californiano Marquez family once owned the surrounding land and established a family plot here in 1840. Your visit is limited a sidewalk view; it is an evocative and moving experience nevertheless.
H	**Adelaide Drive**	The character of this truly beautiful Santa Monica street is now much about the fitness crowd here for the stairs but take time to look at the wonderful 90-100 year old homes, particularly between 1st and 4th.
J	**San Vicente**	"Rails to Trails" in the Westside. A center median that was once covered by trolley tracks is a popular walking/running greenway protected from autos for 3.4 miles from Montana to Palisades Park.
	Palisades Park	This 1.6 mile bluff top park has seen promenading visitors for 120 years and there is a wonderful catalog of period historical and art objects throughout the park. Rampant use of the park for fitness classes has driven Santa Monica city to discourage them with new fees.

WALK 18	SANTA MONICA AND RUSTIC CANYON		
8.5 miles		elevation gain: +	15 stairways
Shorter walk option: 6.2 miles - take bus back to beginning			
Shorter walk option 2: stripped down version 7 miles			
start / finish:	Ocean Avenue at Santa Monica Blvd- Santa Monica		
Transit:	from Los Angeles: Metro line 704, Big Blue Bus line 10		
Best time	Excellent any day or season		
to walk	Rustic Canyon Park is closed Sundays		
Highlights	Rustic Canyon, Eames Home, Marquez Cemetery, many beautiful stairways, Palisades Park		
Break spots	Rustic Canyon Park; Mini-mart on PCH, Palisades Park		
Please read pg 12-15 for information common to each walk in this book			

One of the most scenic walks in the book with pretty, up-scale canyon homes and bluff top views of Santa Monica Bay. If needed, you can shorten the walk at the ¾ mark by boarding a frequent local bus. The route also has three interesting appendages that you can slice off. This option is good if you are rushed or are repeating and don't need the frills.

Beginning on Santa Monica Palisades map page 213

From Santa Monica and Ocean facing the ocean, walk to the path along the bluff and turn south towards the pier. Across from the cannon, go down **Stairway 16** and take the pedway overpass across PCH. This ends in a parking lot; go straight for the ocean front walk and turn right. You don't stay long on this path. After passing a group of ocean front buildings, turn right when you get to another parking lot and head back towards PCH. You find a second pedway with steps leading up to it. Take this (**Stairway 15**) back up to Palisades Park. Turn left on top and saunter on grass or trail four blocks passing a century old craftsman pergola and a stone archway with Batchelder tile. At the edge of the bluff from that archway take a ramp down to PCH that walks over a double pedway with **Stairway 14** and a spiral ramp.

On Pacific Coast Hwy, stay near the road instead of the beach as that first pedway north is your next task.

Santa Monica stairs and pedestrian overpass

Go up another spiral, cross over PCH and take the long **Stairway 13** back up to the palisade. Turn left continuing to walk north through the park. At San Vicente, exit the park and take the cross walk to the other side of Ocean Av. Continue going up Ocean and where it begins to curve right, take Adelaide directly right.

Now on Map, page 212

Enjoy views and homes along this fabulous street. Across from 4th St., go down **Stairway 9**. Turn left at the bottom. Almost immediately, find **Stairway 10** headed left of the sidewalk. Go up 45 steps then walk along a concealed path that gets high above the street. When you see 34 steps headed down to your right, take those even though the path seems to continue. Down to sometimes busy Ocean Ave, leave the stairway carefully as there is no sidewalk on your side. Cross to other side of street and turn right headed downhill. Turn left on Mabury and watch for **Stairway 11** on right near 249.

Turn left at the bottom on Entrada then take a diagonal left onto Ocean Way.

Climbing slightly up, this street bends left as you take **Stairway 12** towards the ocean straight ahead. At the bottom you see an underpass for the beach. Today, turn right towards the Chevron station. This is the 3-mile mark. If you are doing this walk on Sunday, the next break will be in 4 miles.

Leaving, walk up PCH past Entrada and turn right on West Channel. Back into the canyon, pass Rustic and Mesa. Stay to the left of the channel at Mesa. Turn left on Sage which looks to be a one way alley. As Sage curves right, look for the short stairway on your left. Turn from this onto **Stairway 6** headed up to the right. At the top, go around a hedge and turn left on Amalfi. Amalfi turns full right while you keep going straight on Sumac. As that starts turning right you take **Stairway 5** climbing steeply in the shade. On top, it is 70 feet across two driveways to the start of **Stairway 4** headed down on the left. The top is not obvious. It's a long way down, take your time.

At the bottom, turn left. Turn right beyond the speed bump to go down **Stairway 3**. Straight across from the bottom of these stairs is a passage with no stairs along a fence that takes you to East Rustic. You are facing the creek and bridge across it to West Rustic. Take that turning right then left on Hillside Lane. Here the first of two "out and back" forays from the route. This one will return to where you are standing after 4/10 mile. Go up the discreet cement and brick **Stairway 1** to the right of a white garage door in the corner where Hillside curves right.

If you are doing the abbreviated walk, skip stairway 1 and take Hillside back to West Rustic.

Stairway 1 comes up to a curve in Vance Street. Turn right at the top and follow to Chautauqua. Cross very carefully in the crosswalk to the other side of the street. Turn left on Chautauqua and soon find a private driveway reading "201,203,205". Turn right on this, mindful that you have left public streets. At the end of this short drive find a

sign and chain for Charles and Ray Eames Case Study House.

Unless you have made prior reservations for a $10 tour to go along with your walk (which would be an excellent idea), please respect the wishes of the Eames Foundation: do not go beyond the boundary; enjoy a quick look of this very important work of local architecture, turn around and depart. Cross Chautauqua again and head back down the stairs.

Turn right on Hillside and walk back to West Rustic and turn left walking with the creek on your right. Cross the bridge. Just as you begin to curve right on East Rustic, find the sidewalk entry to **Stairway 2** to the right of the 550 address.
On top, the abbreviated walk turns right on Mesa; the full walk returns here after a half mile loop.
Turn to the left on top of the stairs and follow the loop of Mesa Road until you meet Latimer Road on the left. Take that and find the park on the left. ("E") Imagine the hijinks of a wealthy men's social club that escaped here from their Pasadena and Hancock Park homes in the 1920's. This is about the 4 ½ mile mark of the walk and a pretty spot to get water, use bathrooms or sit with a snack you have been carrying. The center is closed on Sundays. You can still picnic here and find water but no open bathrooms. Explore beyond the clubhouse perhaps but take Latimer and Mesa back to stairway 2.

Marquez family cemetery   *page 214*

Now head south on Mesa. Pass the Entenza House on your right ("D"). Just beyond where Sycamore has joined Mesa on your right, take the stairs on the left. This is actually the alternative bottom to stairway 6 which you have already climbed. This time, ignore the main part of that stairway on your left and keep going straight to come down on Sage Rd. Go straight ahead on Sage (not right). Sage intersects West Channel; go over a little foot bridge. Facing the Canyon School grounds ("F") turn left on East Channel. In two blocks, walk through two car barriers. *The abbreviated walk turns right on Atillia and goes up Stairway 7 to join Entrada and turn right.*

The full walk follows East Channel almost another third mile after the car barriers before turning right on Esparta and quickly right on San Lorenzo. Look for the Marquez burial ground on your right beyond Mesita. (G)

Leave here, walking the same direction and turn right from San Lorenzo to Entrada.

The walk still has 2 ½ miles back to the start. You could catch Big Blue Bus route 9 across the street by Stassi Lane to get within two blocks of the start. Otherwise, remain on the right side of Entrada passing on short stairway 7 on your right. Cross Entrada in a crosswalk by the school and follow the crowd up **Stairway 8**.

On top, turn right on Adelaide, left on 4th and right on San Vicente. Walk the median path. At Ocean, find bathrooms on your right as needed. Turn left on Ocean. Most of the 1.4 miles back to Santa Monica and Ocean is repeat but there is enough beauty and options along Palisades Park to keep it fresh.

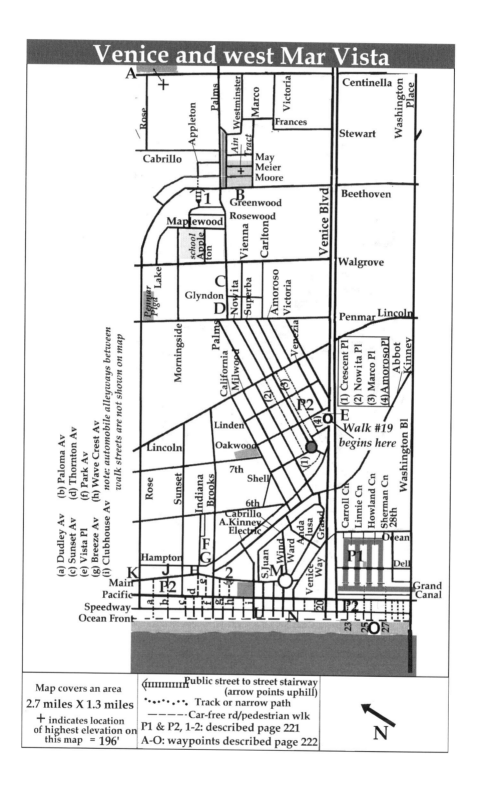

Venice and west Mar Vista

A

Rose
Appleton
Palms
Westminster
Marco
Victoria
Frances

Centinella
Washington Place

Stewart

Ain tract

Cabrillo
May
Meier
Moore

B 1
Greenwood
Rosewood

Beethoven

Maplewood
Apple ton
school
Vienna
Carlton

Venice Blvd

Walgrove

Pennar High Lake
Glyndon
C
D
Nowita
Superba
Amoroso
Victoria

Penmar   Lincoln

Morningside
Palms
California
Milwood
Venezia

(1) Crescent Pl
(2) Nowita Pl
(3) Marco Pl
(4)Amoroso Pl
Abbot Kinney

note: automobile alleyways between
walk streets are not shown on map

Linden
Oakwood

(3)
(2)
P2
(4)
O E
*Walk #19
begins here*

Washington Bl

Lincoln

Rose
Sunset
Indiana
Brooks
7th
Shell

(1)

6th
Cabrillo
A.Kinney
Electric

Carroll Cn
Linnie Cn
Howland Cn
Sherman Cn
28th

Ocean

(a) Dudley Av   (b) Paloma Av
(c) Sunset Av   (d) Thornton Av
(e) Vista Pl   (f) Park Av
(g) Breeze Av   (h) Wave Crest Av
(i) Clubhouse Av

Hampton
F
G

S.Juan
Wind
Ward
Anda
Jusa
Grand

P1

Dell

K   J
Main
Pacific
Speedway
Ocean Front
P2
a b c d e f g h i
2
M
Venice Way
20
P2
23 25 O 27

Grand
Canal

N

Map covers an area **2.7 miles X 1.3 miles** **+** indicates location of highest elevation on this map = 196'	◁▥▥▥▥ Public street to street stairway (arrow points uphill) •••••••• Track or narrow path – – – – Car-free rd/pedestrian wlk P1 & P2, 1-2: described page 221 A-O: waypoints described page 222

N

Venice and west Mar Vista

Venice is one of most popular places to visit within Los Angeles and is also a wonderful place to walk. Some of the best walking in Venice can be on streets and pathways that throngs of sunny day visitors overlook. Beneath the layer of transient day users, Venice has a village aspect that many of its 39,000 residents fight to maintain. The clash between long standing cultural norms and the influx of so much affluence plays out daily. A recent rejection of overnight parking zones was a victory for the old time Venetians. The great walks that an outsider will find in this area owe much both to the fiercely defiant arts culture here and to the affluence that helps to sustain and enhance it. Abbot Kinney's Venice included miles of wide canals and was first envisioned as an attraction attending to the intellectual, artistic and spiritual improvement of its visitors. He turned to amusements when business languished.

| P1 | Canal Paths | The 5 canals of Venice have 9 foot bridges and 2 3/4 |

miles of paths that welcome a walker to wander freely. The waterside blend of early 20th century cottages and massive 21st century additions provides visual interest as it also demonstrates the typical Venice conflict between the historical and the wealth-driven artistic addition. Actually these were not part of the Kinney canal scheme which was built roughly in the triangle formed by Venice Bl, Pacific Ave, & Abbot Kinney Bl. I thank local historian Glen Howell for pointing out that the canals we enjoy today were built by the Short Line Beach Company. In the 1920's all of the canals suffered from cave ins, mosquitoes, flooding and sewage leaks. The Kinney canals in the main business district got the funding to be filled in. The canals south of Venice Blvd were a less affluent residential area and never "enhanced" by having them filled in. They remained problematic until a 1990's restoration that brought them to what we enjoy today but saw many tenant residents pushed out.

| P2 | Walk streets | Venice has about 2 dozen streets built for non-motor |

use with a total length of about 3 miles. Homes are built oriented to the walkable lane with motor access alleys at their rear. This provides a beguiling intimacy between home, front yard and walk street and creates a walking experience found nowhere else in the city except for the homes built along the stairways. These originated in the original Venice of America design but were never canals. Three of these streets inland between Shell and Lincoln are especially fine because their length, their narrow width and their feel.

	stairway	location: top / bottom	steps	
1	Appleton Way	3428 Beethoven / 12900 Appleton Way	30	B

An attractive short but wide stairway across Beethoven from a pedestrian passage to Moore Street. A good walkable companion to the Ain Tract nearby *(224)*

	stairway	location: top / bottom	steps	
2	Wave Crest Ave	Wave Crest pathway / 1101 Main	10	C

Barely meets the minimum step count to get listed - at the end of a walkstreet

	Venice and west Mar Vista	
A	**Ocean View Farm**	A worthy walking destination not really near anything else. The views from these 200 foot "heights" are great and you will find a spectacular community garden that is very enjoyable seen from its perimeter.
B	**Ain Tract**	Prominent modernist architect Gregory Ain built this colony of 54 "Modernique" homes in 1948 as a demonstration of how LA's booming housing needs might be addressed. Designed around a 1060 sq foot template, they had floating interior walls in the design to customize a home for an individual family. First marketed at $12k when nearby standard was $5000.
C	**W 3 architects**	At 1337 Palms, an award winning design of two 1100 square foot studios with a high sustainability pedigree.
D	**Ed Moses studio**	At 1233 Palms the barn structure was built by Steven Ehrlich in 1987 for legendary LA experimental painter, Ed Moses.
E	**SPARC**	Social Public Art Resource Center is located in a 1929 era Art Deco/Egyptian Revival building, once the Venice Police Station. The current mission mainly concerns murals. The facility is an arts center that produces, preserves and conducts educational programs about community based public art works. Open daily except Sunday and next to free parking!
F	**Indiana Ave Hses**	At 326 Indiana, Frank Gehry designed three 1500 sq ft. studios each based on a theme and using different exterior materials.
G	**Hopper House**	at 330 Indiana architect Brian Murphy's corrugated metal façade with a wave roofline was home and gallery for actor Dennis Hopper.
H	**Tasty Spuds**	Once a potato processing plant, artist Charles Arnoldi turned this colorful muraled industrial building into a working studio.
J	**Chiat-Day Bldg.**	At 330 Main, a famous collaboration in 1980's post-modernism from Frank Gehry, Claes Oldenburg and Coosje van Bruggen.
K	**Rose and Main**	Wonderful Venice contrast: northeast corner is the historic 1909 firehouse; north west corner is the 1989 Renaissance Bldg. reimagining historic Kinney era elements with the Ballerina Clown sculpture.
L	**Mural tradition**	The public mural tradition is an essential element of the Venice vernacular executed by many artists. Rip Cronk has produced many of the most famous examples like the Jim Morrison by 18th and Speedway and "Venice Beach" on Ocean Front Walk south of Club House. Walkers should get hold of the Venice Chamber of Commerce's printout of a self-guided mural and public art walking tour for much more detail than this book could provide.
M	**Windward Circle**	Even historical photos make it hard to appreciate how this was once the lagoon and the streets fanning out from the circle were canals. What stands here now is the privately owned post office building concealing a wonderful WPA mural of Venice and also three buildings from architect Steven Ehrlich. Each of these three late 1980's buildings around the circle carries playful symbolism for what stood here a century ago.
N	**Venice arcades**	Windward at Speedway reveals the symbols the tourists come to find: the signage, the murals on St. Charles Hotel and the colonnaded buildings with capitals designed by an Italian sculptor in 1904.
O	**Norton House**	Frank Gehry's beach house with a study modeled after a lifeguard station; in all its flamboyant glory at 2509 Ocean Front Walk (1983)

WALK 19	VENICE AND WEST MAR VISTA	
8 .25 miles	elevation gain: +	2 stairways

Shorter walk option: 5.5 miles (cutting off section east of Lincoln)	
start / finish:	SPARC: 685 Venice Blvd. 90291
Transit:	Metro Expo Line to Culver City station; then Metro 33 bus 4 1/2 miles west to stop id 12429
Best time to walk	Excellent any day or season; SPARC is closed Sundays crowds on hot weekends or holidays will impact the walk
Highlights	Walk streets and canal paths of Venice; significant and eclectic architecture, Venice boardwalk, murals
Break spots	café opportunities mid-walk, bathrooms along boardwalk
Please read pg 12-15 for information common to each walk in this book	

This walk is a fat loop heading east, then west, then north, then south before turning east to where it began. An option shortens the distance by a third, chopping off the eastern loop – not recommended but there if needed.

SPARC is advantageous location to begin a walk. You'll find a free parking lot, engaging exhibitions that will inspire the day's activity and a bathroom opportunity. SPARC is closed Sundays (the parking is still available).

ENTIRE WALK ON MAP PAGE 220

Facing the Venice Jail, aka SPARC, side entrance from the parking lot, turn right in the alley then right into a 2nd alley that leads you to Oakwood. Turn left. Notice but pass the openings to Amoroso Place walkstreet left and right. Walk to Marco Place, beyond Marco Court, and turn right. This is the first of ten walk streets you'll utilize today so begin to appreciate their beauty and subtle differences. Reaching a cross-street, Linden, turn right and then left from Linden into Amoroso Pl.

Exiting at Lincoln, if bathrooms were missed at SPARC, maybe find one in a business now.

The shorter option turns left on Lincoln then after 700 feet turns left into Nowita Place walk street.

Turn right and cross Lincoln in the crosswalk proceeding east on Amoroso Place (now an automobile street). Jog left then right at Penmar to pickup Carlton Way.

Amoroso Place

In two blocks turn left on Glyndon Ave (not Court) and turn right on Vienna. Arriving at busy Walgrove, you are passing from Venice to Mar Vista. Turn left and crossover to the east side of Walgrove at Palms. Continue another block north and turn right by the school at Appleton. Next block turn left on Maplewood and right to get back on Appleton which will curve right. **Stairway #1** comes in view to your left at the end of the cull de sac. Go up these and cross Beethoven. Straight ahead, take a shady foot passage across an alley and come out on Moore St. Turn right. Moore drops down to Palms Ave where you see a median with white fence. Cross the street when safe and walk down the median left of the fence.

Appleton stairs

You are entering the Ain Tract ("B"). Get familiar some of the 54 little houses – each similar and unique both.

Walk straight ahead on Moore; turn right on Marco and right on Beethoven. Turn left on Palms and perhaps stop in at the cozy neighborhood market – you have done 2.3 miles.

Come back west towards Venice on Palms. After crossing Walgrove, residential character heightens: notice on your right the W 3 architects studios at 1337 and the barn that architect Steven Ehrlich built for painter Ed Moses at 1233. At Penmar, turn left then right on Norwita. Back at Lincoln, turn left towards the crosswalk allowing you to cross Lincoln. Turn right and watch for the entrance to the Nowita Place walkstreet (after Nowita Court).

Rejoin the short option here

Enjoy this for 3 blocks until you exit at Shell Avenue. Turn right. Shell ends at California, but across the street is entry to an alley called San Clara Court and you bear left on that. This exits out to 6th Avenue where you turn right. Walk 10 half-blocks (counting the alleys) now in the Oakwood section of Venice. Turn left past the "Pueblo Chucho" mural from Francisco Letelier and Mary Fama into Indiana Court. Take this alley down to 5th Avenue.

"Pueblo Chucho" mural in Oakwood

Turn right then left on Indiana Ave. Stop to enjoy on your left glimpses of Frank Gehry's 3 studios built at 326.

"Tasty Spuds" Arnoldi studio

Immediately right of that find a factory corrugated front and wave roof line on a home that Brian Murphy built for Dennis Hopper. This house had a living area room built just for his motorcycles ("F"&"G")

Across Hampton you cannot miss the murals on an old potato processing plant that Charles Arnoldi has made into a studio.

Turn left on Hampton. You have come 4.8 miles and Brickhouse Kitchen is the first of several intriguing break spots you will pass in the next mile. A bit complicated here: from Brickhouse, cross Hampton, and angle left on Brooks. Turn right on Abbott Kinney. At the corner of Main, cross in the crosswalk to the left, cross Main towards Christian Science and turn right crossing Brooks to head north on Main.

In 200 feet, turn left into a pretty walk street, Park Place. At Pacific, cross carefully, jog right and duck left into Park Ave. This walkstreet has a particularly fine collection of old homes.

At Speedway, turn right and in 200 feet turn right into Thornton Ave, another walk street. Turn left when you hit Pacific. The massive POW-MIA wall reflects that the LA Times says more than 800 Vietnam vets live in Venice. Cross to north side of the street at the Sunset Av. crosswalk and continue north on Pacific.

Turn right into Paloma Court walk street. As you exit and turn left on Main, you are across from the Binoculars Building (J).Continue to the corner of Rose where you find the old firehouse and the ballerina clown on the Renaissance Bldg.

Come towards the beach on Rose, turn left onto the west side of Pacific and right into Dudley Av. walkstreet. Take this right out to Ocean Front Walk. Now stroll south on the misnamed boardwalk about a third of a mile until you see R Cronk's "Homage to Starry Knight" mural. You'll be turning left on Wave Crest but before doing so, walk a bit more more to look up and enjoy Cronk's trompe l'oeil "Venice Beach" high on the south wall of the Beach House.

Thornton Avenue

Go inland on Wave Crest Ave. At Speedway it becomes an ok walk street. Cross Pacific carefully, go left a bit and right into another section of Wave Crest Avenue that is super.

Drop down **Stairway 2** (10 steps or more counts in my book) and turn right on Main. Cross to the east side of the street at Westminster and continue south on Main. The long Luna Garcia building at San Juan has an interesting history besides being a great pottery gallery. When San Juan was a canal, canal boats were stored here. In the 70's the "Eagles" had their uproarious first gig here and Thom Mayne of Morphosis had an apartment and a gallery dedicated to architecture here.

Keep walking on Main to Windward Circle and imagine it as the great lagoon of Venice of America. Three Steven Ehrlich buildings hold symbols to the Abbot Kinney days. Across from you, "Race through the clouds" hints at a roller coaster of the same name here a century ago. The building on your left has design elements that mirror Hotel Antler which stood here. The building on your right makes a whimsical nod to the dredging machines of 1905 Venice. This is 6 ½ miles.

Turn right and pick up that stretch of Windward that has all the visual symbols people come to see: the colonnaded arches, the Venice sign, the one-time St. Charles Hotel with murals on three sides including a mysterious lady in the window, the glimpse of Jim Morrison looking south on Speedway and the path back to the crazy boardwalk.

Turn left follow the boardwalk beyond Venice Blvd and past 25th Ave. to see Frank Gehry's Norton beach house at 2509 with a study in the guise of a life guard tower.

Frank Gehry's beach house

Turn left after that on 26th Avenue which becomes a walk street. Turn right on Pacific, use a crosswalk at 26th and pick up the 27th Ave. walk street to arrive on the south side of the Grand Canal facing a footbridge.

You are on the southwest corner of the canals and you want to come out on the northeast corner. You could wander here for hours. One direct way out is cross the footbridge over Grand Canal and turn left on the path. Walk around the corner to the right and cross the footbridge over Sherman canal. Continue straight across on the roadway to the footbridge over Howland canal. Cross that and turn left taking the path along the edge. Coming up on Linnie canal, go over the footbridge and turn right following the path that will eventually have to turn left on the east end. Take the footbridge across that slip and turn left.

Now passing the head of Carroll canal on your left, turn right on the street that will cross Eastern Ct. Turn left on Ocean. Turn right on Venice and the Venice Jail-SPARC is a half mile up on the other side of the street – just past "Beyond Baroque". Cross Venice at Abbot Kinney.

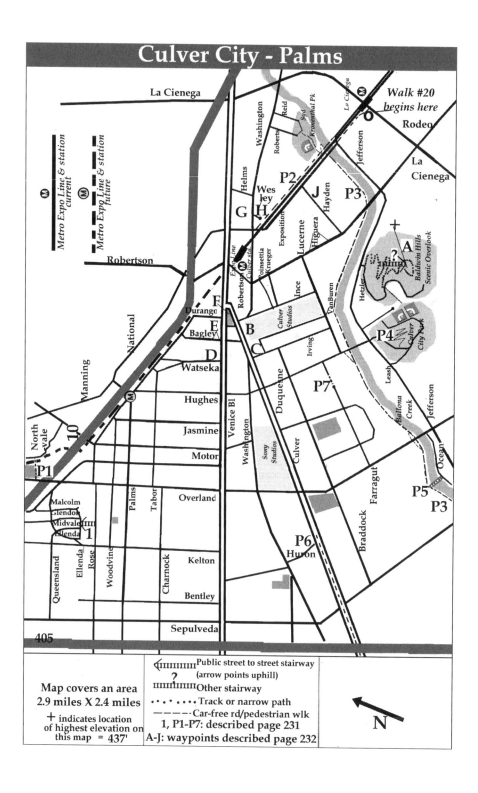

Culver City - Palms

La Cienega

Metro Expo Line & station current

Metro Expo Line & station future

Robertson

Walk #20 begins here

Rodeo

La Cienega

Washington

Reid

Kronenthal Pk

La Cienega

Syd

Roberts

Jefferson

Helms

P2

Wes ley

J

Hayden

P3

G

H

Higuera

Lucerne

A

Baldwin Hills Scenic Overlook

?

animal

Exposition

Poinsettia

Krueger

Robertson

Expo Line

Culver stn

Hetzler

National

Manning

F

Durango

E

Bagley

B

Vince

VanBuren

Culver Studios

P4

Culver City Park

Leash

D

Watseka

C

Irving

Hughes

P7

Jefferson

Jasmine

Venice Bl

Duquesne

Ballona Creek

North vale

Motor

Washington

Culver

Ocean

P1

10

Sony Studios

Farragut

P5

P3

Overland

Palms

Tabor

Malcolm

Glendon

Midvale

Glenda

1

Braddock

P6

Huron

Queensland

Ellenda

Rose

Woodbine

Charnock

Kelton

Bentley

Sepulveda

405

	stairway	location: top / bottom	steps	
1	**Palms stairs**	10830 Kingsland / 10825 Rose	73	**B**

A good transitional stairway joins the apartment zone to Westside Heights above

	stairway	location: top / bottom	steps	
?	**Baldwin Hills overlook stairs**	Bottom - near entrance 6050 Jefferson top: overlook plaza near 6300 Hetzler	282	

There is no secret about this location anymore; it is highly popular particularly because the stairs are so demanding. Built with recycled broken concrete placed in a straight line, the steps come as a shock to the uninitiated partially because they are so irregular and partially because some step ups are extremely long. I can only think this was originally someone's pet project as a throw in to the development of the overlook park in the early 2000's. Now they rival the great views as to what visitors associate with this park. They are only open 8am to sunset and dogs are not permitted. These are an aberration that we don't include on "the list" of street to street public stairways. However, it would be silly of the author to pretend that they are not there; a sensational stair climbing experience!

other pedestrian assets

P1 Dunleer bridge Palms Recreation Center to 10464 Northvale

A pretty and useful conveyance that will soon find the Expo Line trains humming beneath it. It has a "ward off the barbarians" type gate locked during night hours by security hired by a Cheviot Hills homeowners association.

P2 Expo Line Bike path From Venice Expo Station to National & Washington
This does not go far, only about 4/5's mile, but it gives a walker or cyclist the opportunity to link to the Ballona Creek path or many of the side streets. It is nicely "architecturally adjacent' as it passes Eric Owen Moss's Hayden Tract and also the Morphosis offices.

P3 Ballona Creek Bike path Runs from Syd Kronenthal Park in Culver City for 6.7 miles to Marina Del Rey where it connects to the coastal bike path south another 8+ miles. Only a third of this path is reflected on the map. The entire path has limited access with thirteen entry points.

P4 Culver City park boardwalk Built onto a 300 foot slope is a connected series of wood ramps that extend into a path of more than one quarter mile. A walker's folly, this location is a both a location for moderate fitness training and for family fun. It is remarkable that two jurisdictions (city and State) have each invented such joyous and well used resources for walkers so near to each other as this boardwalk and the Baldwin Hills steps. Note: no dogs.

P5 Ballona Creek footbridge Near 10811 Ocean Drive connecting to Ballona bike path
A simple & graceful asset for cyclists, walkers & neighbors

P6 Culver Boulevard Median bicycle path

There is a paved trail for cyclists and a semi-soft parallel trail next to it for walkers. It runs 2.1 miles along a former rail right of way. The map only reflects a quarter of its length from Huron Avenue on the northeast to McConnell Blvd southwest.

P7 Farragut path Just a 200' gap on Farragut Drive usable only to those on but it is the type of asset to bring a smile to the author's face.

Culver City and Palms

Culver City finds itself in a good place these days. Forty years ago it was a bland bedroom community sliced by busy roads taking people somewhere else. Landmarks MGM and Helms sat derelict. Now it enjoys Westside cache and has leafy residential blocks that have resisted apartments, a new light rail station, dynamic revitalization with some good adaptive reuse and a thriving community of architects. Ballona Creek and the Baldwin Hills were Culver City barriers; now they are assets. Culver City is an independent city of about 40,000 founded by promoter extraordinaire Harry Culver in 1913. In 1930's & 40's half of all US movie production was done here. Palms has a highly diverse and dense population of 44,000. Founded in 1886 it is the oldest independent community annexed by Los Angeles (in 1915). There is much to discover on foot in both communities.

A	**Baldwin Hills Overlook Park**	Besides the stairs (page 231) there is a serpentine trail, an interpretive center open Fri-Saturday and a stunning vista. The $6 parking has done wonders to get people out of their cars to walk up.
B	**Culver Studios**	Founded by Thomas Ince in 1918 and subsequently owed by Cecil B DeMille, RKO (studio exec Joseph Kennedy),Howard Hughes, Pathe, Selznick, Desilu etc. The famous white mansion façade is a prominent feature.
C	**Culver Hotel**	was a "skyscraper" when built in 1924 by Culver City founder Harry Culver and Charlie Chaplin. Legend is that Chaplin sold it to John Wayne for $1 in a poker game. Further legend is that the Black Panthers sought to buy the hotel from Wayne and were rebuked. It was site of many hijinks by the the "little people" staying there while cast as Munchkins during the 1939 filming of Wizard of Oz. Seven stories in a flat iron shape that anchors great Town Plaza.
D	**Iskon Krishna Temple**	An interesting walkers stop: their temple is interesting inside and they have a vegetarian buffet restaurant.
E	**Museum of Jurassic Technology**	Witty, esoteric, offbeat, peculiar; this museum defies explanation. An $8 adult admission when open Thurs-Sun afternoons is all that keeps you from exploring LA's most unusual collection.
F	**Ivy Substation**	Now home to a 99 seat theater, this 1907 building converted AC current to DC to power the Los Angeles Pacific Railway trains. Last used for power in 1953, renovated 1993. Home of "The Actor's Gang"
G	**Helms Bakery**	Helms was an LA area institution for four decades ending with the 60's. Their bakery was here and, rather than sell through markets, they sold direct off their fleet of yellow and blue, square trucks. The plant has been adapted to a huge complex of furniture markets, restaurants and galleries. Don't miss the mixed media piece facing Washington illustrating Helms truck and town.
H	**Morphosis**	This firm and principal Thom Mayne are among the most important architects based in the LA area. They moved into Culver City in 2012 into what is the largest energy net-zero building in Los Angeles. 3440 Wesley
J	**Hayden Tract**	Owners Frederick and Laurie Samitaur Smith have turned a warehouse district into a phenomenal creative colony working with local architect Eric Owen Moss. The buildings are audacious. These blocks were never really "walking scale" but the Expo Line bike path might entice you in.

Ballona Creek footbridge at Ocean Drive

WALK 20	CULVER CITY - BALDWIN HILLS	
5.5 miles	elevation gain: +	2 stairways
Shorter walk option: 4.1 miles (board Expo Line at Culver City Sta.)		
start / finish:	Metro Expo La Cienega/Jefferson Station	
	3400 S. La Cienega Los Angeles 90016	
start / finish: (alternative)	Syd Kronenthal Park	
	3459 McManus Culver City 90232	
Transit:	Metro Expo Line - La Cienega/Jefferson station	
Best time to walk	Anytime; best to avoid peak of rush hour and Baldwin Hills scenic park is open 8am to sunset	
note:	dogs are not allowed in two parks along much of walk	
Highlights	Baldwin Hills Scenic overlook and stairs, Culver City arts, Downtown Culver City and Helms Bakery complex	
Break spots	Baldwin Hills State Park; downtown Culver City	
Please read pg 12-15 for information common to each walk in this book		

This walk blends some of the best of Culver City's share of the Baldwin Hills with some of the best of downtown Culver City. There is a particular emphasis on the trove of outdoor public art that the city offers and cultivates.

ENTIRE WALK ON MAP PAGE 230

From the bottom of the escalator on the west side of the La Cienega, look left (south) to see the start of a bike path. Take this and in about one third mile, the bike path crosses Jefferson where you angle diagonally right to stay on it. Notice the relic bridge of the railroad days. Passing under the light rail tracks, leave the main bike path turning right on to an extension that veers down towards Ballona Creek. Make a U-turn where the ramp meets bike path heading downstream.

If you parked at Syd Kronendahl then walk to the far left corner past a ball diamond and find the bike path into Ballona Creek.

Walk along the bike path for 1.4 miles careful of passing bike riders. You can look way up to the left to see the people on the Baldwin Hills stairs where you soon will be. The next exit is yours - the ramp doubles back to Duquesne Ave. Turn right on top. The water jug sculpture is called "Cross Currants", artist Don Merkt. At Jefferson, cross twice so that you are diagonally across. Head east on Jefferson for about a quarter mile.

Cross Hetzler in the crosswalk and you will see a trail start on your right behind the wall with the State Park sign – open 8am to sunset and no dogs allowed. You won't be alone! Start up the trail which switches back right and comes to the bottom of the Baldwin Hills Scenic Overlook stairs. Be careful going up them; this is not your typical stairway. Also know that the trail you are leaving will criss-cross the stairs 3 more times in case you want to take that much lengthier option.

Departing the stairway on top, you have climbed 380 feet from the Ballona Creek bike path. Look for the visitor center along a path to the right. The displays might be closed except for Friday- Saturday but the bathrooms will be open. You have come 2 ¼ miles.

Leaving the visitor center, the route is a bit counter-intuitive. Walk out through the gap between bathrooms and interpretive center, find the trail and turn left. Stay left at a "Y" with the right option going down.

Your path will cross the stairs at that circle with the "375'" elevation you passed before. Stay on the trail as it snakes down the hill through about 8 turns. Finally, the trail comes to a "T" and you go left. A bit more trail and you **come** to the access road for the park.

Take the crosswalk and go straight across onto a service road. Soon you go under a nice Brett Goldstone gate that indicates you have left the State Park and are entering the city park. Walk in the gap between two baseball diamonds to a park building. If the Little League is going that day, perhaps buy a freshly grilled hot dog here. Turn right and walk towards field 3 in the corner. Opposite that is a stairway down to the next terrace. After 37 steps, aim straight across to the sundial sculpture. ("Homage to La Ballona Creek, 1994 by Lucy Blake-Elahi)

The boardwalk in Culver City Park

Here, start down the boardwalk (pg. 231 P4). Enjoy every joyous step for more than a quarter mile. You pass a ropes course/climbing wall that concessionaire Fulcrum Adventures opens month. At the bottom of the boardwalk, turn right on Duquesne St. running downhill out of the park.

Reach the corner with Jefferson, cross diagonally again but this time you want to be on the north east corner. Cross over Ballona Creek and make first right on Lucerne. Take the 3rd left on Van Buren. The massive Culver Studio buildings are to your right (B). Van Buren ends at "A" St. But you walk ahead through a passage next to the movie theater.

Here you reach the outstanding Town Plaza framed by the 1924 Culver Hotel (C). There is a fun bronze lion sculpture/fountain on your left and a couple life size bronze figures to the right of the hotel. This is the 3 ½ mile mark and there are lots of possibilities for a break around here. Walk to your right to see the Colonial Mansion façade of Culver Studios, best known as the backdrop to the end titles of "Gone with the Wind"

From Culver Studio gates, go left on Washington towards and past Trader Joes. Cross Culver into the green space and look at the intriguing Ivy Substation, a 1907 trolley power transformer building now renewed into a popular dramatic theater. Reaching Venice turn right and walk a loud half mile. At Robertson you start passing the Helms Bakery design center complex. Turn right into Helms Avenue and walk ahead to Washington.

The route will go right but go a few feet to your left to see the funny mix-media "Helms Coach gone a Rye" (2002 - Architect Andrea Cohen Gehring, muralist Art Mortimer, and fabricator Global Entertainment Industry). Also look inside the amazing Arcana store of art books here.

You cross Washington at Helms in the cross walk and turn right. Turn left into Wesley. At the end of the block on the left is the Morphosis Architects offices. They are completely decked out with solar collectors and feature an artistic entryway titled "Nueva" and done by Tom Farrage.

Exit Wesley onto the Expo Line bike path and turn left. From here it is three quarters of a mile on the bike path back to the La Cienega Expo station (passing the path to Syd Kronendahl on the way. Looking right three blocks from Morphosis, you get an idea of the huge architectural campus that Eric Owen Moss has built on the Hayden Tract called Conjunctive Points. The Samitaur Tower will impress, amaze and confound you as you pass.

Offices of Morphosis Architects

Palos Verdes - Malaga Cove

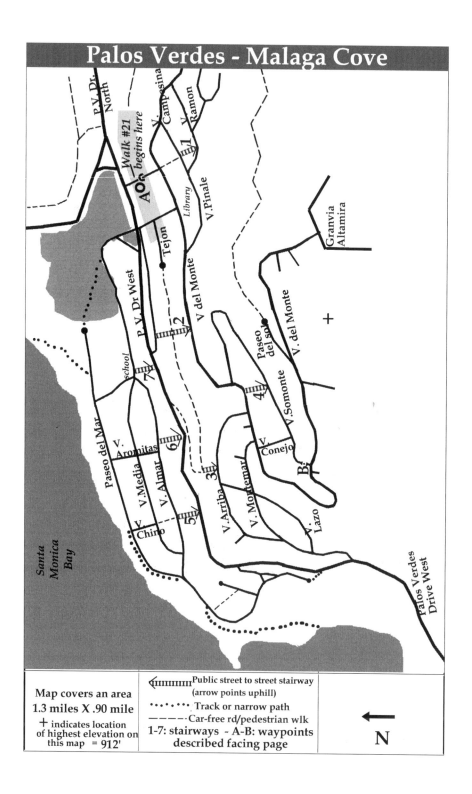

P.V. Dr. North

V. Campesina

V. Ramon

Walk #21 begins here

A

Library

V. Pinale

Granvia Altamira

Tejon

P. V. Dr West

V. del Monte

Paseo del sol

V. del Monte

+

school

V. Aronitas

Paseo del Mar

V. Somonte

V. Conejo

B

V. Media

V. Almar

V. Arriba

V. Mortemar

Lazo

V. Chino

Santa Monica Bay

Palos Verdes Drive West

Palos Verdes - Malaga Cove

Palos Verdes is huge: 25 square miles not including San Pedro which shares the peninsula. This book maps less than a quarter of that area in two sections with admittedly selective content; carved to illustrate the 17 street to street stairways. I write of PV as a bit of a poseur. There are so many parks, trails and secrets here, I just don't have the knowledge to treat it in depth. The new stairs and trails found here remind me (ironically) of Berkeley and their Path Wanderers Association; it is nice to see them crop up rather than disappear. Malaga Cove is the one part of Frank Vanderlip's 16,000 acre empire where the pre World War One concept of a rigidly planned Mediterranean-themed millionaires colony came to fruition. Three other such villages dreamed for Lunada Bay, Valmonte and Miraleste never went beyond the planning stages.

	stairway	location: top / bottom	steps	
1	Chico Path	2501 Via Ramon / 2500 Via Pinale	28	B

New stairway built in an easement – path from Campesina to Pinale; steps from Pinale to Ramon. Google Maps shows they continue as Chico Trail that climbs high into the woods south. We will have to wait for that to be reality.

	stairway	location: top / bottom	steps	
2	Buena Path	601 Via del Monte / 396 Palos V Dr West	125	B

An impressively long stairway split exactly in half as it is intersected by the upper fire station trail. The junction of stairs and trail has superlative views north.

	stairway	location: top / bottom	steps	
3	Ariba Path	1701 Via Arriba / trail junction	141	B

Another new one: the two fire station trails converge at the base of this stairway.

	stairway	location: top / bottom	steps	
4	Somonte Trail	Across fr 824 V.Somonte/708 V.del Monte	87	B

All the new wood or concrete stairs in this area are great but enjoy Somonte for its beautiful stonework – this one has some age to it. Nice wooded setting *(pg 242)*

	stairway	location: top / bottom	steps	
5	Chino Path	549 PV Dr West / 552 Via Almar	26	B
6	Aromitas Path	501 Palos V Dr West / 452 Via Almar	20	C
7	Arroyo Path	415-445 Palos V Dr W / 440 Via Almar	35	B

Stairways 5-7 are each short easement steps that connect the same two streets. Arroyo by the school looks to have been around a while but Arromitas is new and Chino is still getting built as this book is written.

	waypoints			
A	Malaga Cove Plaza	This district was cohesively planned and built in the 1920's with the earnest contribution of the Olmsted Brothers to		

the landscape design and Myron Hunt and Walter Webber and others to the architecture. 90 years later, it is an enduring treasure to enjoy. For better and for worse, this is not the sort of unified design we are used to in Los Angeles. The Mediterranean theme is represented in the commercial buildings, civic center, library and school and it carries to many of the surrounding residences.

	waypoints			
B	La Venta Inn	Built 1923 as a clubhouse for realtors and their millionaire		

clients, this was the singular Palos Verdes landmark for decades. It has so far resisted notions to tear it down in favor of more view homes. Brother architects Pierpont & Walter Swindell Davis had interesting local resumes besides their PV work. They participated in building Aliso Village and Ramona Gardens, General Hospital and several Hollywood area villas. The unusual tower is 50 foot tall.

WALK 21	PALOS VERDES - MALAGA COVE		
4.4 miles		elevation gain: +	7 stairways
Shorter walk option: none			
start / finish:	Malaga Cove Plaza		
	Via Chico at Palos Verdes Dr. West, Palos Verdes Est. 90274		
Transit:	none		
Best time to walk	A great walk anytime		
Highlights	Ocean views, classic Malaga cove,		
Break spots	Short walk - enjoy a break before and after		
Please read pg 12-15 for information common to each walk in this book			

This is a good intro to Palos Verdes offering some nice stairs and great beauty in less than five miles. Malaga Cove Plaza has a deli/market and restaurants which you should visit before or after your walk to warrant use of the easy parking.

ENTIRE WALK ON MAP PAGE 238

On the east end of the plaza ("A") walk through the arch. Architectural historian Robert Winter identifies this as a "sally port" which is an archaic name for a double secured passage to a fortification. Directly in front of you is "Chico Path" which starts as a path and after crossing one street, becomes **Stairway #1**. Turn right on top on Via Ramon which blends back into Via Pinale. From this junction find a route down path and park steps to the left of the library. Turn left on the next road, Via Del Monte and walk to address 601 and turn right down **Stairway 2**. This is a long one but we save the bottom half for the end of the walk. Turn left on the dirt pathway. This is a great 4/10's of walking with views over the south bay. You come to well-made new **Stairway 3 – Arriba Path.** Turn left on top, walk to Via Del Monte and turn left.

Shortly by address 708 turn right and enjoy the lovely stonework on **Stairway 4**, Somonte Canyon Path. Turn right on top on Via Somonte. Walk past signs meant for cars that indicate a dead end ahead. Pass a chain barrier and you arrive at La Venta Inn on your right (read "B", page 239).

Turn right on Via Del Monte – there is no sidewalk so walk carefully in the bike lane. You make a sweeping right curve. At Via Montemar turn left. This will lead to Palos Verdes Dr. West after a quarter mile of walking since La Venta. Watch for traffic and cross to the other side of PV Dr. West. Turn right. Walk along the side of PV Dr. West about 500 feet until you see where you can cut down a trail to get to the cull de sac of Paseo Del Mar. Follow this as it curves left towards the coast.

Enjoy the views and notice (but pass unless you are adding to your walk) the start of the popular Bluff Cove trail. Make the 2nd right turn on Via Chino. Take this until it ends at Via Media. Straight ahead is a slender and steep trail up the easement to Via Almar. Here the easement has the start of a short new **Stairway #5** (Chino Path)to help get you up to Palos Verdes Dr. W. Turn left, walking carefully in the edge of the bike lane. At 501 take another easement **Stairway#6** (Aromitas Path) down to Via Almar and turn right. Across from the distinctive school tower turn right on **Stairway 7** (Arroyo Path) headed back up to Palos Verdes Drive West. Turn left and look for an opportunity to cross to the south side of the street. Make a right turn on an unnamed street that curves above you. As you get to the first home on the right, you see and ascend the bottom half of **Stairway 2**. Turn left on the trail. This takes you straight back into Malaga Cove Plaza.

Somonte Canyon Path

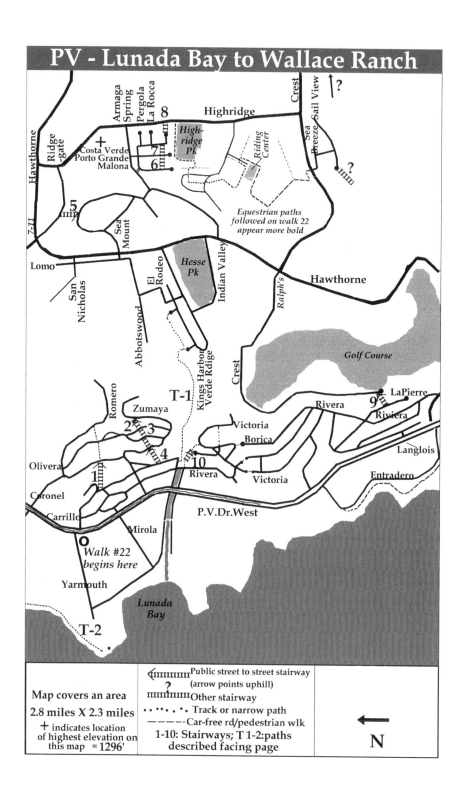

PV - Lunada Bay to Wallace Ranch

Armaga Spring
Pergola
La Rocca
8
Highridge
Crest
Sea Breeze Sail View
?

Hawthorne
Ridge -gate
Z-11
+ Costa Verde
Porto Grande
Malona
7
6
High- ridge Pk
Riding Center
?

5
Sea Mount
Equestrian paths
followed on walk 22
appear more bold

Lomo
San Nicholas
El Rodeo
Hesse Pk
Indian Valley
Ralph's
Hawthorne

Abbotswood
Kings Harbor
Verde Rdige
Crest
Golf Course

Romero
T-1
Zumaya
Rivera
9
LaPierre
Riviera

Olivera
2
3
4
10
Victoria
Borica
Langlois

1
Rivera
Victoria
Entradero

Coronel
Carrillo
P.V.Dr.West

Mirola
O
Walk #22
begins here

Yarmouth
Lunada Bay

T-2

Map covers an area
2.8 miles X 2.3 miles
+ indicates location
of highest elevation on
this map = 1296'

ꝏꞪꞪꞪꞪꞪPublic street to street stairway
? (arrow points uphill)
ꞪꞪꞪꞪꞪꞪOther stairway
· · ·· · · ·· Track or narrow path
— — — -Car-free rd/pedestrian wlk
1-10: Stairways; T 1-2:paths
described facing page

N

Palos Verdes: Lunada Bay to Wallace Ranch

My comments on page 239 about Palos Verdes apply here also. The area detailed on the map is contrived to illustrate the street to street stairways and a long walk that will take them all in. There is much more to discover here, someone should write a book!

	stairway	location: top / bottom	steps	
1	Via Romero Strs	Nr 1201 V. Romero / nr 1001 V.Ventana	87	B

This fine stairway is a good example of rusticity of some Palos Verdes stairways. Steps alternate with trail in this wide park area. The views down to Lunada Bay are fantastic. Above Via Romero, there is path, no steps, reaching the next 2 streets.

2	Valdez-Zumaya	1325 Via Zumaya / 2640 Via Valdez	38	B
3	Olivera-Valdez	2633 Via Valdez / 2648 Via Olivera	10	B
4	Carrillo-Zumaya	1136 Via Zumaya / 2624 Via Carrillo	55	B

A stack of five streets is connected in succession by a series of four easements with stairs. The connection between Via Olivera and Via Zumaya is there to walk but only has 7 steps so is not listed. The bottom section above Via Carrillo is particularly enchanting with pine woods and a tree house.

5	Ridgegate	Nr 28223 Covecrest/near 6238 Ridgegate	34	B

A slipway of 150 feet connects two points where an auto would need 1.1 miles.

6	Via Malona	47 V.Porto Grande / 50 Via Malona	34	B
7	Via Porto Grande	48 Via Costa Verde / 46 Via Porto Grande	25	B
8	Via Costa Verde	75 Via Costa Verde / near 28632 Highridge	31	B

Who knew? This Wallace Ranch tract of about 70 homes that now are valued in the $1.75 to 2 million range was built in 1990 with....3 stairways. They have distinctive portals at each end and two go up and back down. The map also shows access stairs with less than 10 steps to this tract off Armaga Spring Road.

9	Pt Vicente Pthwy	30621 Calle d Suenos/30724 Rue d l Pierre	217	A

The finest stairway on the Palos Verdes Peninsula and one of the best in the LA basin. Google says it is a 3.9 mile drive from the top to the bottom. Partially hidden in the woods; mostly visible from a distance on the open slope. Someone must have taken the beware of rattlesnake signs but that's good advice in summer.

10	Lunada Canyon	2801 Via Buena / near 2700 Via Rivera	114	A

A new one found by a path from Via Rivera walking to the right of the storm drain. Look down from the top and appreciate the curving line; this was built by a craftsman.

	Other stairs	PV has other stairway curiosities that can be sought out that	

are beyond what this guide is written for. They are not built to connect streets or neighborhoods; they often culminate in a gully where you would just turn around and walk back out. Those who climb stairs purely for fitness might be fine with this and I suspect they will ask with frustration why I list a 10 step stairway and disregard something mighty. The Sail View stair location is one example and shown on the map. The famous one in the area is normally called the Del Cerro Stairs found near a park of that name and a mile off the southeastern edge of this map – 273 steps!

T1	Lunada Cny Trail	About one mile long from Via Carrillo up to Posey Way.

1200 feet is very steep and would be a difficult descent without walking sticks.

T2	Shipwreck trail	The Dominator wrecked here in 1961 and many take the

"Drainpipe" trail to get to it - off edge of map where V.Colonel/Cloyden Rd ends.

WALK 22	PALOS VERDES		
	LUNADA BAY TO WALLACE RANCH		
11 1/2 miles		elevation gain:+++	10 stairways
Shorter walk option: none			
start / finish:	Lunada Bay Plaza		
	2201 Palos Verdes Drive West 90274		
Transit:	none		
Best time to walk	Some of this walk would be impassible when muddy from recent rains; otherwise a good walk for any time		
Highlights	great coastal views, pretty bridal trails, the challenge		
Break spots	at one third mark: 7/11 store or Valero gas station		
	at two third mark: Ralphs Grocery store		
Please read pg 12-15 for information common to each walk in this book			

This is a rewarding but lengthy walk. An uphill section of the Lunada Canyon trail is steeper than anything else in the 23 walks in this guide. A mile and a half of this walk is on pretty equestrian paths so maybe leave the dog at home. The spots providing food water or bathrooms are at markets or gas stations so prepare in advance. Typically you will get coastal breezes but not much shade.

ALL ON MAP PAGE 242

Walk straight towards P.V. Dr. West from in front of Chase Bank in the plaza and take the crosswalk across and go up Via Carrillo. This will curve right and shortly after passing Via Ventura on your left, enter the park trail that soon turns to **Stairway #1**. When you reach the street above continue on the trail directly across the street. Reaching the next street, you will see that the trail continues up another round. Disregard that and turn right on Via Olivera.

After crossing the open space of Zumaya Canyon, you come to a Y and bear left on Via Valdez. Look for **Stairway #2** on your left by 2640. On top turn right and make a loop back to Valdez. Turn left going down an easement and **Stairway #3** at

2633. Proceed directly across through the next easement which has only 7 steps. Again at the next street, continue straight across and down **Stairway #4,** the longest and nicest of this string. Turn left at the bottom which again is Via Carrillo.

You reach impressive Lunada Canyon and the start of the obvious trail going up it just after Carrillo curves right. The trail is about a mile long with a fifth of that very steep hiking. The trail crosses to the right side and comes to the first street exit point. Follow signs pointing left to stay on the trail a bit further until it exits on Posey Way. It is not so steep now that you are pavement but the climb continues. Turn left on Kings Harbor, quickly left on El Rodeo, left on Trailriders and right on Abbotswood. This curves into Lomo as the route flattens out. Walk 5 blocks and turn right on San Nichols. Turn left onto Hawthorne and soon pause at gas station or 7/11 store. *Here is 3.9 miles and 800 feet higher than the start.*

Cross Hawthorne at the signal and walk up Ridgegate Dr. On the right in a little park find the bottom of short **Stairway #5.** Turn left on top onto Covecrest. On a typical day, your elevation and southwest angle gives a good glimpse of Catalina Island. Turn left on Indian Valley and then quickly left on Armaga Spring. Just past Meadowmist on left, there are steps on right down into the Wallace Ranch development. Walk straight ahead on Via Malona and look near "50" for a portal to **Stairway #6**. This goes up and down and, after crossing the next street, flows into **Stairway #7**. Turn right when leaving and curves to the left ending in **Stairway #8.** This leaves the tract and goes onto Highridge Rd. Turn right.

Now comes the bridal paths. Turn right into Highridge trail at the edge of a playing field. Follow this as it curves left and then right at the far end of the park. In 100 yards you come to a "T" and go right and in just 100 feet your path turns left. Cross a little road and curve left then go straight. Coming to another little road, cross it on a jog to the left and enter the path signed Horseshoe Trail. This gets pretty and you become aware of a canyon opening up on your right.

After a long stretch and a curve left you find the impressive Peninsula Riding Club on your right. The route goes around this by crossing the parking lot to a path on the other side signed Clear Vista trail. Turn right so you are passing the other side of the riding center again on your right. The route walks along a canyon edge, turns left by a tennis court and left again, away from the canyon, at another tennis court. Again a long and lovely stretch. Meeting another path, bear right were the sign says Northrop trail. You come to a fence laced with pink roses and go left then right leaving the paths to go right on Crest Rd.

Now a mile on autopilot down Crest until you can go no further. Perhaps stop in at:
Ralphs Market where you are   7 ¼ miles done and 3 ¼ to go.

Crest turns into Calle de Suenos at some point but you won't notice it. Ending at a gated community, on your right is the start of **Stairway #9**, the wonderful Point Vicente pathway.
Turn right at the bottom and follow La Pierre to the school and turn right on Rivera. Take the 2nd left onto Victoria. After Rue Godbout, it will seem that you have dead ended, but this

is one of three municipal boundaries (two more uphill from you) where cars are blocked but there is a discreet pass-through for walkers. Cross Riviera, stay on Victoria and at a "Y" bear left on Via Buena. At the end, go down **Stairway #10.** Take the trail at the bottom out to Via Rivera. Cross and walk down the grassy median of Paseo Lunado. You could save a half mile by turning right on P.V.Dr. West and going directly back to Lunada Plaza. The recommended route continues down the median to bear right on Paseo del Mar walking above the sea. Turn right on Yarmouth and walk up to where you started.

Point Vicente Path   *Liz Thomas photo*

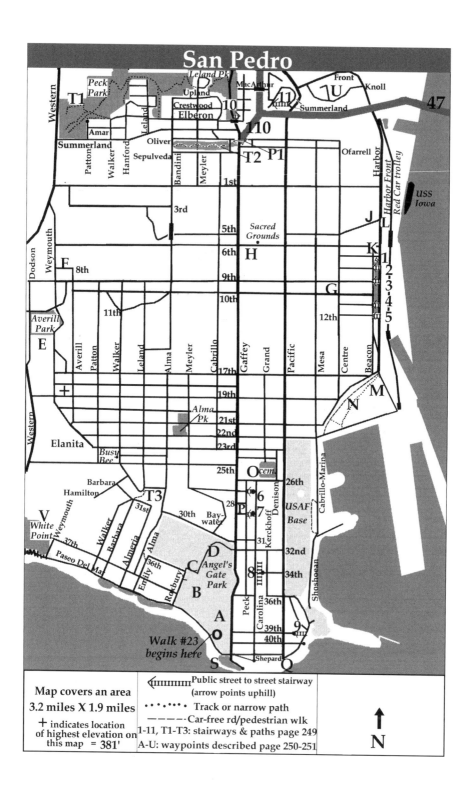

San Pedro

Peck Park
Leland Pk
T1
Upland
Crestwood
MacArthur
Front
Knoll
U
47
Elberon
10
11
Summerland
Amar
Summerland
Oliver
110
Patton
Walker
Hanford
Sepulveda
Bandini
Meyler
T2
P1
Ofarrell
Western
Leland

USS
Iowa
1st
3rd
Harbor
Harbor Front
Red Car trolley
5th
Sacred
Grounds
J
Dodson
Weymouth
F
8th
6th
H
K
1
9th
2
3
Averill
Park
E
10th
G
4
11th
12th
5
Averill
Patton
Walker
Leland
Alma
Meyler
Cabrillo
Gaffey
Grand
Pacific
Mesa
Centre
Beacon
17th
+
19th
Alma
Pk
21st
N
M
22nd
N
Western
Elanita
Busy
Bee
23rd
25th
O
cem.
26th
Cabrillo-Marina
Barbara
Hamilton
T3
31st
30th
Bay-
water
28th
6
7
Denison
Kerckhoff
USAF
Base
V
White
Point
Weymouth
Walker
Barbara
Almeria
Alma
37th
36th
Emily
Rockury
P
31st
32nd
Shoshonean
Paseo Del Mar
D
Angel's
Gate
Park
C
B
8
34th
Peck
Carolina
36th
A
O
9
39th
40th
Walk #23
begins here
S
Shepard
Q

Map covers an area	Public street to street stairway (arrow points uphill)
3.2 miles X 1.9 miles	•••••• Track or narrow path
+ indicates location of highest elevation on this map = **381'**	– – – – Car-free rd/pedestrian wlk
	1-11, T1-T3: stairways & paths page 249
	A-U: waypoints described page 250-251

N

	stairway	location: top / bottom	steps	grade
1	7th & Harbor	150 W. 7th Street	11	C

Short corner stairs that relate to the Plaza Park and stairways #2-5.

	stairway	location: top / bottom	steps	grade
2	8th Street	800 S. Beacon / 801 S. Harbor	52	B
3	9th Street	900 S. Beacon / 901 S. Harbor	50	B
4	11th Street	1100 S. Beacon / 1101 S. Harbor	53	B
5	12th Street	1200 S. Beacon / 1101 S. Harbor	50	B

Each of these was closed for some time during restoration work that may disrupt disrupt them again. Harbor Blvd below is not very walkable so the stairs might stay mostly unused except for exercisers or stair collectors.

Beacon St. above with the string of palms and great view over Port's o Call into the main channel is a great place to stroll. Part of the charm of San Pedro is that elsewhere; this might be lined with restaurants and shops. Here, it is wonderfully homey with highlights like the Post Office Building, the old Army-Navy YMCA building and Den Norske Sjomannskirke (test yourself on the Scandinavian flags).

6	27th Street	2702 Peck / 674 W. 27th	36	B

One of the best of the San Pedro stairways. It splits into a double stair and is nicely planted including a pepper tree that dominates the top.

7	29th Street	2910 Peck / 670 W. 29th	27	B

Not much to this one but fits well with stairway #7 and steep 28th Street.

8	Carolina sidewalk	3311 Carolina / 3337 Carolina	30	B

A sidewalk stair next to the school which ties into a path to 34th Street

9	39th Street	430 West 39th / 3906 S. Bluff	56	B

Very nice spot with fine homes at bottom and top, the stairs are oriented for a view to Angel's Gate Lighthouse. A "300" might begin or end here.

10	Elberon	Near 717 Elberon/Gaffey St by overpass	40	B

An 80-year old bridge carries Elberon over Gaffey in north San Pedro and this stairway is found on the northeast corner of that overcrossing.

11	Upland Ave	457 Elber on / Upland 160' west of Pacific	122	B

A long stairway behind the Occupational Center gives access to a remote island of San Pedro. It is hemmed in by the 110 Fwy and the Vincent Thomas bridge ramps.

	paths			
T1	Peck Canyon			

31 acres of Peck and Leland Park were improved 2-4 years ago with new trail building costing $5mill. The result is an outstanding city asset. Adjacent Peck and Leland Parks cover a narrow roadless area that extends .85 mile from Western to Gaffey. From the parks southwest corner, two trails begin and later join going east. The trail network passes through a wooded area and crosses some foot bridges in a deep canyon. The main trail is 1.25 miles long from near Western and Summerland to an exit at Lois and Meyler. There are access trails on the south at Walker, at Hanford and at the 1000 block of Elberton. After a bit of paved Herbert Ave., another trail goes 1000 feet further to Gaffey.

T2	Bandini Pk path	Simple winding path in a newly reclaimed canyon	

linear park. It runs for about a third of a mile & is an unexpected gift to the feet.

T3	Hamilton Trail	Like a "secret stair" from 31st+Barbara to 2749 Walker
P1	Oliver over pass	This has two elaborate ramps that look like wings.

The overpass is a steep walk too. Nice view towards Bandini Park

San Pedro

San Pedro is such a joy and offers so many treasures, I fear that they will start charging admission. It is a beach town that does not act it. It's a village of multi-generational depth that was an independent town between the 1880's and 1906 and still shows it. Unusual for Los Angeles, it possesses discernable immigrant communities of European origins. Like parts of San Francisco, it has a rigid street grid hammered onto topography of some very steep hills. It has stairways, it has paths, it has some of the jewels of the LA park system, and it has history and good period architecture. Even if they were to remain entirely on the sidewalks, the walker would be happy here.

A	Korean Bell	A gift from Korea for the 1976 Bicentennial. 17 tons of copper & tin modeled after a 7th C. bell in Korea. Rung 5 times annually.
B	Harbor artillery	On the decommissioned upper reservation of Fort MacArthur. The Battery Osgood-Farley was World War One era technology and was obsolete by the mid 1920's. It is listed on the National Register of Historic Places. Disappearing carriage guns could send a ¾ ton shell 14 miles.
C	Marine Mammals	A hospital for ill, injured and orphaned marine mammals. Primary work is the treatment and release of rescued seals & sea lions. The center is open and welcoming daylight hours. You may walk near to the recovering animals behind a fence and perhaps get information from the staff. No dogs.
D	Angel's Gate Pk	After 94 years as an Army installation, Fort MacArthur was turned over to the city in 1982. The transition to Angel's Gate Park has come slowly and it would seem without the benefit of a master plan. It makes no provision for walkers but is a pleasant place to go anyway. On top of the hill, the Marine Exchange has the best view in town as it serves as sort of a sea traffic control for the harbor. Behind that is a cluster of old base building adapted to new uses (like a cultural center) However that road is one way in and one way out- not walker friendly. Open daylight hours: gates near Korean Bell & at Gaffey & 32nd.
E	Averill Park	A sprawling and hilly green place that is as fine as any other Los Angeles park. You will never be here on a bright weekend without seeing a wedding or Quinceanera party being photographed. The gazebo is iconic and the creek area a delight for kids of all ages. Appreciate how the perimeter of this park flows from and back to the homes that ring it. Walk up here and picnic.
F	Weymouth Corner	Centered on the 1400 block of 8th St. a micro retail and business district in a scale reminiscent of 1900's America. Completely natural and non-self-conscious; urban planners sweat and spend on projects that never nail the result a nicely as this location does.
G	Vinegar Hill	There is an Historic Preservation Overlay Zone (HPOZ) centered on 9th & 10th between Centre and Palos Verdes Streets. More blocks of interesting 1880's-1920's period homes extend beyond that. Highlights include the 1885 Queen Anne "Danish Castle" home on 10th west of Centre. Also of note is the 1918 board-and-batten YWCA building on 9th near Mesa built by Julia Morgan. Morgan is best known for the design of Hearst Castle.

H	6th Street	From Pacific down to the waterfront, here shows the

best of the San Pedro revitalization. The 1936 Warner Grand is moderne art deco and worth a return visit to see the lavish detailing inside. Across the street, the Arcade Building is a beautiful interior courtyard of shops built in 1924. Duck into the hobby shop, get coffee at Sacred Grounds. San Pedro Brewing is 2 blocks east.

J	Liberty Hill	The hill has been leveled but a monument remains for

the 1923 IWW harbor workers strike. Upton Sinclair was arrested here for reading from the first 10 amendments of the US Constitution. He was jailed under the nefarious criminal syndicalism acts. Other references nearby to this era in labor history include a handsome bronze bust of the ILWU's Harry Bridges along Harbor and a plaque remembering Bloody Thursday (July 5, 1934) near 6th Street.

K	Beacon Hill	West and upslope from Harbor are three large interesting

period buildings. The Municipal Bldg between 6th & 7th is a 1928 Beaux Arts Cube. Look for an old cast iron water fountain and look inside the fire station when open The Post Office Building a block south is pure WPA Moderne 1936. Look inside the post office for a wonderful mural and beautiful detailing in the floor and work desks. A block further south, the former Army Navy YMCA, 1926, has been reborn as Harbor View House, a board and care facility for mental health rehabilitation.

L	Harbor front	Spend too long here and your walk won't get too far.

The Merchant Marine Museum at 6th is where the ferry boats once crossed to Terminal Island. In front is a number of memorials. The must see is the US Merchant Marine Memorial designed by local sculptor Jasper D'Ambrosi and completed by his sons. The Iowa is open daily on an $18 ticket. 6th St. is one of four stops on a fun restored Red Car that can take you up and down the waterfront for one all day ticket. The stop north is a fountain area near the cruise terminal.

M	Crafted in S.P.	Just getting off the ground in 1940's era warehouses. An

artist's marketplace that a walker can enter one end and continue out the other

N	22nd St Park	18 acre Union Oil tank farm reclaimed for new park
O	Harbor View	An odd blend of historic cemetery opened in the 1880's

with interesting grave monuments and a park. Open 7am to 2pm and has NO view.

P	28th St	600' of 28th St is 33.33% grade, which makes it steeper

than Eldred, Baxter or Fargo. Just west of Peck. Often debated, see what you think.

Q	"Sunken City"	A 1929 "slump" caused earth movement up to 11"/day.

Several blocks were lost but most houses moved in time. It is best viewed from the end of Pacific Ave. Has been a popular spot for extra-legal adventuring and graffiti art; check Google images. "Sunken City" Trail" on Google maps is pure fiction.

S	Point Fermin	Historic recreational location. Of interest is the biker's

hangout Walker's Café, A 1874 "stick style" lighthouse, a charming small stage and the promenade at the edge. Monarch butterfly winter migration passes here.

U	Knoll Hill	The locals have saved this for open space at least for now.

Great gritty view of the harbor and bridge; recall "To Live and Die in LA"

V	White Point	Nature preserve with 102 acres of restored coastal sage

scrub habitat; walking trails. Paseo del Mar now closed by landslide-walkable.

WALK 23	SAN PEDRO	
11.5 miles	elevation gain: +	9 stairways

Shorter walk options: 6 or 7 miles (taking bus back to beginning)	
start / finish:	Joan Milke Flores Park
	(signs read Battery Osgood Farley)
	834 W. Paseo del Mar, 90731
Transit:	Metro Line 246 (not very convenient but available)
Best time to walk	An excellent walk any time during daylight hours
	Normally a good alternative when central LA is hot
Highlights	Great coastal and harbor views, local history, period architecture, isolated village feel
Break spots	Averill Park (3.5 miles; Sacred Grounds (6.5 miles)
	Crafted in San Pedro (8.1 mi) Pt Firmin Mkt (10.7 miles)
Please read pg 12-15 for information common to each walk in this book	

A great walk with a lot of variety in a loop shaped like an hourglass. Metro Line 246 operates at 15 minute weekend intervals along Pacific Avenue which the center line of this loop. You can cut loose and take that bus back to Paseo del Mar and Gaffey at numerous locations.

ENTIRE WALK ON MAP PAGE 248

Begin in the parking lot inside a gated area. Facing the gate and Paseo del Mar, look on your left for a thin dirt track that climbs up to the Korean Friendship Bell; this is the steepest and least obvious part of today's entire route. As you reach the top of the little hill, spend some time at the bell ("A" Pg. 250). Walk through the parking lot and towards a singular basketball court. The bathrooms on your right might be the last for about 3 miles. Past the court is a small pedestrian gate you pass through. Meet a trail here across an open field but bear left to go around the first bunker. You are in the Ft. MacArthur Museum Battery Osgood-Farley ("B"). Walk carefully to the near side of the second bunker and go down stairs built into the concrete construction. At the bottom are some displays. Walk to left of the camouflage building.

Osgood Farley Battery
(Korean Friendship Bell rear)

Look slightly left along the boundary fence with the neighborhood and pass through a semi-concealed gate. Turn right on Roxbury St. which curves left into 36th. Enter the gate on your right which gives access to several facilities including the Marine Mammal Care Center on the distant right ("C") which you want to visit. Walk back across the parking lot aiming for an old chapel. Turn left in front of that and left on the base road that goes over the hill. The Army in the 1970's deemed this as surplus property and eventually transferred it to the city in 1982 for Angel's Gate Park ("D"). Just stay on the main road as it climbs and curves right for a third mile. Exit on to Gaffey and turn left and soon turn left on 30th.

Take the first right on Baywater, the first left on 29th and the first right on Emily. Turn left at a "Tee" onto Hamilton, right on Alma, left on 26th, right on Leland. Cross busy 25th.
On the left side of Leland beyond 25th notice 5 little cottages. Each was built in 1923 and is 411 square feet. Turn left on 24th.
Walk 24th St. west to Walker Avenue.
Busy Bee Market (closed Sundays) at the corner is a San Pedro tradition for sandwiches and the best option if you are going to buy food for a picnic in Averill Park one mile away.

At Walker turn right to go three blocks to 21st and turn left. Take 21st two blocks to Averill and turn right. The multi-story home at 21st and Patton that looks like an old Victorian is a bit of a ruse. Walking near it, you see that it is one of the newest homes in the area; built 1981 – 4500 sq. ft. Here in the uplands of San Pedro are found an assemblage of well-kept homes, many from the 1920's.

On the whole, these homes still maintain their wonderful relationship and scale to the street and have not been reworked solely for the resident's possession of a view. Turn left on 20th, right on Elanita, right on 19th, left on Averill. Turn left on 17th and right on Weymouth which leads into Averill Park. Walk straight towards the gazebo. Averill Park ("E") is about the 3.4 mile mark of the walk.

From the gazebo, walk left down the pathway to the restroom. Then take the grassy slope or pathways diagonally right to follow a walkway left of the creek. At the head of the creek turn right then right again, now walking "downstream" as you follow a path that climbs away from the creek uphill to Averill Park Drive. Reaching the corner of Weymouth and Averill Park Drive, cross the street to walk past the "Do not enter" sign and walk up Harbor View Ave. Turn left on 9th, go up to the signal and cross to go right on Weymouth.

The little business district here along 8th is called Weymouth Corner. ("F")It is a good example of the unique patterns of use you find in San Pedro. A folksy little block of independent businesses is a wonderful discovery on foot. Go down 8th street one block and turn right on Averill.
Be VERY careful crossing busy 9th St and continue along Averill one more block to 10th, then turn left. Then take 11th St on the right. Wavy 11th is a refreshing variation from the rigid grid.

It's lined with attractive homes. Follow 11th St until it merges again with 10th.

At Pacific, the route has covered 5 miles. A bus stopping at 11th St. to your right would return you south to the start. In one more mile and there is another bus option.

Weymouth corner signage

Walk 5 more blocks on 10th to Pacific. That impressive building at 10th and Cabrillo was once a Christian Science Church. Continue on 10th past Pacific. Follow 10th east two long blocks to Centre. This is the Vinegar Hill district which is partially protected under an HPOZ. ("G") The landmark house on 10th before Centre is the 1888 Lindholme house, sometimes called the Danish Castle.

Turn left on Centre, walk 3 blocks to 7th. As you turn left on 7th, notice the "Mojo" interactive sculpture on the northeast corner by artist Christian Moeller. 7th is lined with many original storefronts. Turn right on Mesa

Take Mesa to 6th St. and turn left. This block is ground zero for the architectural renaissance of San Pedro. The 1931 Art Deco theater barely escaped the wrecking ball to be lovingly restored. Across the street the 1924 Arcade Building is typically open except on Sunday and is a surprising treat. Duck into the hobby shop.
This could be the mid walk break with Sacred Grounds coffee house here and San Pedro Brewing down the street at 331 6th. Again, if you are looking to leave, take 6th past the Warner Grand to Pacific and turn right to 5th and Pacific to catch the Metro 246 bus south back to the start.

Leaving here, walk 3 blocks down 6th to Palos Verdes St. and turn left. At 5th street, cross twice to reach the northeast corner. The Liberty Hill monument is in middle of block. ("J")
Keep going east on 5th; cross Harbor at the signal and turn right, walking south on the parkway, west of the tracks

This stretch of the San Pedro has enough attractions to keep you busy for a whole day or more with the Battleship Iowa, the Maritime Museum, the pinkish barn housing the fireboat and a museum in old Fire Station #36 which is open Saturdays in the municipal building. Walk south on Harbor in front of the municipal building.

WPA mural inside 1936 San Pedro Post Office

At 7th St. take tiny **Stairway #1** up to 7th and Beacon. Beyond 8th is the Federal Building with the post office, which you must go in to see if they are open (read "K").

The next bit of gymnastics on the route is for stair collectors; you can remain on Beacon and miss all the fun. From the post office go down **Stairway #2** at 8th St, go up **Stairway #3** to 9th, turn left on Beacon and go down **Stairway #4** in front of the Norwegian Seaman's Church. Return up **Stairway #15** to 13th and Beacon and turn left going south. At 14th, follow Gulch Rd diagonally down on your left to Harbor and turn right.

Where Harbor goes right, continue straight on Miner and enter the yellow warehouse "Crafted in San Pedro" through the walk-in gate on your right.

Fishing boat harbor from Beacon Street

Admission is free, open Friday thru Sunday 11am to 6pm. ("M") Walk through the warehouse space of artisan exhibits. At the far end is a welcome bathroom and water. Exit on that side, turn right then left to head out the southwest entrance.

If Crafted is closed or you want to pass, you would turn right on to the dirt trail next the Bike path at that Harbor Blvd/Miner St. "Y" we just past. You can meet the route, far end of 22nd Street Park.

From the southwest Crafted gate, walk on paths between 22nd St. Park ("N") on your right and a parking lot on your left. Past the end of the parking lot a path heads to a stairway back up to Crescent Ave. Go up this pretty park stairway (not on the list).

From the top of stairs, go west on 21st, turn left on Grand beyond Pacific. Grand ends at Harbor View cemetery ("O") which is interesting but closes at 2pm. Turn in succession: left on 24th, right on Dennison, right on 26th and left on Carolina. Turn right on 27th and go up **Stairway #6.** On top turn left on Peck. Consider the first 600' of **28th Street** on your right which are said to be steeper than Eldred or Fargo. ("P") Walk up and back that short stretch to test it out. Then take Peck to 29th and turn left down **Stairway #7.**

Turn right on Carolina and pass some unusually small 25' wide lots. Past 32nd on the left, **Stairway #8** is a sidewalk stairs. Find a path off of them going left that joins 34th, Turn right on Kerkhoff, left on 36th, right on Pacific. At 39th is a chance for refreshment at the market or restaurant. Crossing Pacific, go left on 39th and down **Stairway #9.** Turn right at the bottom and come back up Bluff. At 40th St. is a great view of the harbor breakwater and Angel's Gate. Bluff ends at Pacific where there is a little plaza area with a view of the "Sunken City" (Q). Immediately turn left on Sheppard, and then left on Gaffey into Point Fermin Park. Take some time to enjoy the look of Walker's Café on your left, the old community outdoor stage, the rescued 1874 lighthouse (*thank you, John Olguin!*) The start point is just slightly west across Paseo del Mar.

Other isolated stairways

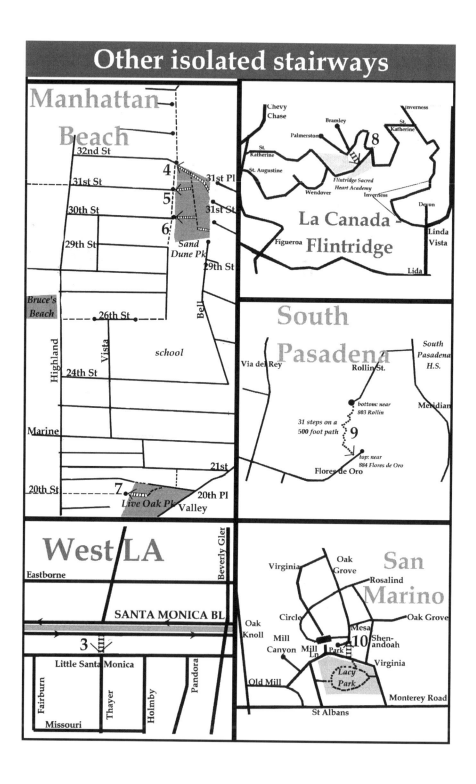

Manhattan Beach

32nd St
31st St
30th St
29th St
26th St
24th St
Marine
20th St

31st Pl
31st St
29th St

4
5
6

Sand Dune Pk

Bruce's Beach
Highland
Vista
school
Bell

7

Live Oak Pk Valley
21st
20th Pl

La Canada - Flintridge

Chevy Chase
Inverness
Bramley
St. Katherine
Palmerston
St. Katherine
St. Augustine

8

Flintridge Sacred Heart Academy
Wendover
Inverness
Devon
Figueroa
Linda Vista
Lida

South Pasadena

Via del Rey
Rollin St.
South Pasadena H.S.
Meridian

bottom: near 803 Rollin

31 steps on a 500 foot path

9

top: near 884 Flores de Oro
Flores de Oro

West LA

Eastborne
Beverly Glen
SANTA MONICA BL

3

Little Santa Monica
Fairburn
Thayer
Holmby
Pandora
Missouri

San Marino

Virginia
Oak Grove
Rosalind
Circle
Oak Knoll
Oak Grove
Mesa
Mill
Shenandoah
Canyon
Mill Ln
Park
10
Virginia
Old Mill
Lacy Park
Monterey Road
St Albans

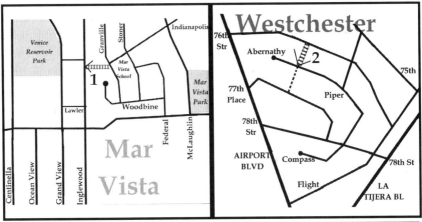

	stairway	location: top / bottom	steps	
1	Mar Vista	3296 Indianapolis / 3297 Granville	97	A

These are very tidy with a surprising good view on top. They are well used by the up & down & up fitness types but the mood remains pretty mellow. They have even become wards of a local Girl Scout troop. Check out the mosaics and WPA era graphics on the elementary school while you are here.

| 2 | Westchester | 5915 Abernathy / 5868 W. 76th St. | 40 | B |

Unexpected; has a path up one side and short stairs and long path down other.

| 3 | Holmby Hills | 10506 Little Sta Monica/10495 Sta Monica | 39 | C |

Half way between Century City and the LDS Temple; steps up the embankment between main line Santa Monica and Little Santa Monica

4	32nd street	476 32nd Street / near 553 31st Place	208	B
5	31st street	477 31st St / Sand Dune Park ramp	53	B
6	30th Street	476 30th St / near 563 29th Street	162	B

Each of these three stairways are actually built within a park and they test our general rule to leave park stairs off the list. Each begins at a cull de sac on top and adjoins streets on the bottom. They are the only means for a walker to get through the escarpment. If you lived on top and needed to walk to work or school on the bottom these stairs would be how you would get there. Each is pretty in the trees with low wood risers and wide treads.

| 7 | 20th Street | 429 20th Street / near 502 20th Street | 42 | B |

Another Manhattan Beach stairway in a park leads down from a walk street. The case for this stairway to be on the list is weaker but it ties well with #4-6.

| 8 | Flintridge | near 440 St Katherine / 525 Palmerstone | 107 | B |

Elevation 1600' and it is a pretty short walk from here to Angeles National Forest. If you were to walk the "Inman 300" chances are you would begin or finish with this nice stairway.

| 9 | Flores de Oro | 884 Flores de Oro / 803 Rollin | 31 | B |

A passage with steps through an easement that is mostly zigzag trail

| 10 | Lacy Park | 1401 Park Place / 1407 Virginia Road | 86 | B |

As you would expect from the rest of San Marino, very pretty and immaculate.

The "Inman 300" and the idea of a walkers route across Los Angeles

"Imagine, if you can, an elongated park extending from the Angeles National Forest to the Pacific Ocean…..All that remains to be done to give this park reality is to acquire a few small links in the chain of parts, give it a name, and begin to promote its use". *Footprints in the Parks* by George Hjelte, (1977). These words were written long ago by a city bureaucrat, the General Manager of LA Recreation and Parks. George Hjelte was my father's boss and I recall his deep voice asking my Dad to come to the phone. His words indicate that what we endeavor for today is not new and that perhaps the dream is further from attainment now than it was then.

I know that I am not alone to speak for the purity and the value of a non-automotive path across our great and vast city.

The sons of Frederick Law Olmsted were engaged by the LA Chamber of Commerce in 1927 and they created a plan for reservations and parkways that would have benefited non-motor travel across the city. The plan was disregarded. The Backbone trail of the Santa Monica Mountains was a hard fought and noble crusade yet it begins its trek to the sea from West LA. Extending it east to connect to Griffith Park proved to be beyond the pale.

Yes the *Big Parade* is about stairways; but it is just as much about creating a single ribbon of travel that connects for the enthusiast the neighborhoods from Pershing Square to the Hollywood sign. The Great Walk Los Angeles each November sticks to major streets but plays on the attraction of crossing the city on foot, learning neighborhoods from central LA to the ocean. "GWLA" attracted their biggest participation ever in 2013. No other installment of CicLAvia had so much resonance as when traffic lanes were closed to automobile use from Downtown to Venice.

Perhaps the allure of passing by foot across the breadth of the city is that it just seems so improbable; the territory is so large and so antagonistic to walkers. The media would also like you to believe that the crossing is so fraught with peril to be akin to some sort of thrill sport.

We do not have an established trail across Los Angeles. Our best option is to weave together the walker's amenities described in this book. Carve a footpath across the metropolis staying as much as possible on stairways, dirt trails, walkstreets and pedways. Check them off as you flow through the city as if you were walking the Camino de Santiago and each was stamped on your *credencial.* "The Way" of the stairs across Los Angeles has a name. As much as modesty causes the author to gag, it is called by some the "Inman 300".

In May 2012, I was asked to create and conduct a cross city hike visiting every stairway that we knew in LA and its surrounding communities. It was the idea of my friends and patrons of LA stairwalking, Andrew Lichtman and Ying Chen. The three of us walked 185 miles inside of ten days. We visited 315 stairways. We carried our clothing, our beds and our necessities on our backs. We stayed at friend's homes or cheap lodging. Our odd journey attracted some media notice.

Ying Chen on "The 300" - Tillie Street

We believed then and now that "doing" every stairway from Flintridge to Pacific Palisades to San Pedro was a nobler cause than say seeing every firehouse or every old air raid siren (as cool as those endeavors might be). Using the stairs as our checkpoints, we were all about the walkable Los Angeles and we were drawn into the enduring soul of our vibrant city. Our route as walked was:

Day	miles	neighborhoods	stairways
1	12.2	Flintridge, Pasadena, Eagle Rock (Friday night 6 hours)	19
2	24	Verdugo Vly, Glassell Pk, Mt Washington, Highland Park	31
3	23.6	York Valley, Gravanza, Hermon, Montecito & Lincoln Hts.	40
4	23.6	El Sereno, East LA, Downtown, Westlake, Temple-Beaudy	28
5	21.2	Solano Cyn, Elysian Hts, Echo Park, Silverlake south&east	54
6	20.6	Glendale-Allesandro, Silver Lake East, Franklin Hills	61
7	18.1	Los Feliz, Beachwood-Bronson, Whitley-Hollywood Hts	36
8	20	Palms, Marvista, Palisades, Santa Monica, Rustic Canyon	28
9	16.9	Palos Verdes Peninsula	12
10	4.8	San Pedro (Sunday morning 3 hours)	6

During that trek and after came the conversation. Could this become an established route that others might follow?

Including every stairway on your foot-venture across the city from mountain to sea is hardly efficient. The stairways indexed in this book (20 more than what we knew or considered in 2012) are scattered in 34 zip codes. A non-stairway, all sidewalk route touching each of those zones would take many fewer than the 185 miles we required. All the "misdirection" created by following the stairs is a big part of why you do it. An interesting comparison is a stairway cross city route that Joshua Bobcat Stacy created for San Francisco that was partly inspired by the "300". In that much smaller city, his effort to cover 370 of the listed 675 stairways took 110 miles to walk and generated 65 pages of maps and directions. Following the way of the stairs requires a much higher level of attention to turns then putting one foot in front of the other on a foot trail.

As the first urban thru-hike, it becomes important to define what the "Inman 300" is so that a new participant can complete the same tasks, even if done in an entirely new sequence. People are interested in how long it took to complete in the past. Some will endeavor to set a new FKT – fastest known time.

We asked ourselves, how much dependence on transit is allowable to connect the dull flat spots between stair clusters? We chose to use some buses because our window of days was limited. When I do the route again, I would like to remain on foot. Some individual stairs are really out of the way. May a "full" completion of the route permit bypassing a few insignificant stairways? Our group walks eschew backtracking, particularly taking a single stairway both up and down. Again because of time, we broke that rule reluctantly on "The 300". How about establishing some sort of "green way" which would make the route longer and might drop a few flatland stairs for greater adherence to a network of trails to avoid streets? Dan Koeppel has been working this angle. Andrew was the visionary who was certain that others would follow our lead on this trek doing it faster and smarter. I had my doubts.

The author & Andrew Lichtman on "The 300"   Ying Chen photos

April 2013 our route (plus a few more stairs) was completed by Liz "Snorkel" Thomas in just over 5 days. Thomas is a an ultra-light backpacker who has completed the PCT, the Continental Divide Trail and holds the speed record for an unsupported woman on the Appalachian Trail. Her effort added serious credibility to the "Inman 300" as she attracted good media attention. Dan Koeppel wrote a story for *Backpacker* magazine about her achievement. Liz did not treat the route merely as a climbing wall to check off a list and move on. She embraced the fun and beauty of the stairways and city and the enthusiasm of our walking community.

Another accomplished wilderness fastpacker, Ryan "Dirtmonger" Sylva, came for much of the "Inman 300" six months later. His inspired approach was to walk off a flight at LAX and tred north then east then north. He did the Westside stairs, traversed a Santa Monica Mountain trail, did one hundred more stairs and slipped up into the Angeles Forest to join the Silver Moccasin Trail. Others will follow!

Liz "Snorkel" Thomas on "The 300"   *Gilbert Garcia photo*

"Dirtmonger" on the 300   *Ryan Sylva photo*

Acknowledgments

Much of what I know and share about the city and its stairways and paths has been gained from conversation with enthusiasts on our walks. I consider my role producing this book in many cases to be as much as an editor than as an author. The following are cited for special thanks:

Andrew Lichtman and Ying Chen, my "300" companions, have been friends and patrons to the stair walking community. They were my compass for the destination of this book as I kept adding content.

Dan Koeppel has been a collaborator and soul mate as we each have put our own take on stairway listing, pedestrianism, route planning, local culture and walk leading.

Adah Bakalinsky, Larry Gordon, Erin Mahoney Harris, Virginia Comer and Charles Fleming have each made contributions to the literature about exploring the city and the stairways. I have learned much from them and have endeavored to pilot my labors around their work.

Dr. Robert Winter reinforced a notion this one time Occidental College freshman had that Los Angeles truly is "magnificent". His architectural guidebooks, co-authored with the late David Gebhard, have been at my fingertip for 45 years. The structure of my guide is so completely modeled on their books that you might say I totally ripped them off!

The Eastsider and Jesus Sanchez in Echo Park have been kind to stairways and to me over the years. I read it three times a week and always find that they have written or directed me to some item that makes interesting sharing when leading a walk.

My Occidental friends: Dave and Sally Schnitger have provided faithful encouragement. Dave found an archaic but useful city stairway inventory for me six years ago that was the nucleus to my indexing. George Waddell was walking with me on that momentous day in 2004 when I first visited the Loma Vista Place, Earl and Edendale stairs. He walks with me still.

Dave Ptach is a gentle soul who tirelessly runs Tomato Pie, organizes cleanups and brings us together through LA Stairstreet Advocates.

Steve Matsuda, Carl Encke, Gilbert Garcia, Carol Hoffstedt, Liz Thomas, Ryan Sylva, Ying Chen and Jinjer Hundley were kind to allow me to use photographs of walks we have taken together or that they have done on their own. Howard Peterson's artful portraits of some of the stairs were a key contribution. Being able to include photos from my father was a singular pleasure in this work. Clarence was a long time photographer for Los Angeles Recreation and Parks.

Not already mentioned, Dave "Rocket" Rowley, Jacques Monier and Dean Okrand have been instrumental to my learning of new stairways, walker's amenities and city lore. They have proved to be thoughtful, instructive companions. I often kid Jacques that this book would have been done months ago if he just would have stopped giving me new stuff.

Special thanks to Doug Beyerlein, Friends of Public Stairs, Alissa Walker, Los Angeles Walks, Jeremy Raub & Eagle Rock Brewing, TERA, ERVHS, SPARC, LA Conservancy, Highland Park Heritage Trust, Louisa Van Leer, Pasadena Heritage, Kalee Thompson, Berkeley Path Wanderers Association, Echo Park Historical Association, Kyle Bilowitz & the Verdugo Bar, Joe Linton, Friends of the Los Angeles River, Tuck Newport, David Ryan, Hope Anderson, Zach Behrens, Diane Edwardson and others whom I am sorry to have forgotten to mention here.

Much gratitude to all those people who come on LA walks led by me, by Dan, by Dave, by Tuck, by Charles, by Michael and by others. You come with a smile, energy, curiosity and passion for the city. You know who you are. This book is my meager gift to reward your interest.

Finally, of course, thanks with love for the patience, enthusiasm and encouragement from Barbara and Leah. They endured a husband/dad who just could not stop drawing maps.

INDEX

#	page	stairway	location: top / bottom	zip	steps	grade
1	34	Loma Vista Pl	2384 L.V.Place/2220 Allesandro	90039	348	A
2	146	Heidleman Road	near 4948 O'Sullivan/5010 Williams PL	90032	234	A
3	46	Baxter	2101 Park Drive / near 1501 Baxter Street	90026	231	A
4	34	Earl	2104 Roselin / Silver Lake Court	90039	218	A
5	242	Pt Vicente Pthwy	30621 Calle d Suenos/30724 Rue d l Pierre	90275	217	A
6	258	32nd street	476 32nd Street / near 553 31st Place	90266	208	B
7	68	Udell Major	2040 Mayview / 3838 Udell Court	90027	206	B
8	212	Upper Mesa	407 Upper Mesa/404 Mesa	90402	201	A
9	40	Cove Allesandro	2265 Lake Shore / 2117 Loma Vista	90039	198	B
10	98	Eldred	708 Cross / 4864 Eldred	90042	196	A
11	46	Avalon east	1893 Lucretia / 1550 Avalon	90026	192	A
12	136	Upper Tourmaline	near 4404 W.Rose Hill/2929 Pyrites	90032	191	B
13	212	4th Street	406 Adelaide / 350 Entrada	90402	189	A
14	40	LomaVista Alles	2265 Lake Shore / 2117 Loma Vista	90039	182	A
15	184	Berendo	4796 Bonvue Ave / 4803 Cromwell Ave	90027	181	A
16	192	Hollyridge	3057 Hollyridge Dr / 3020 Beachwood	90068	178	B
17	26	Angelus Avenue	1482 Angelus / 1456 Angelus	90026	177	A
18	184	Western Ave	Near 2101 N. Western Avenue	90068	173	A
19	68	Prospect walk (U)	3814 Franklin / 1800 Holly Vista	90027	167	A
20	212	Adelaide Wood	526 Adelaide / 421 Entrada	90402	166	A
21	212	Montana Ave	Montana+Ocean / 723 Palisades Beach	90402	166	A
22	26	Mattachine(Cove)	2331 Cove Ave / 2335 Cove Ave	90039	164	A
23	40	Fellowship Park	1831 Cerro Gordo / 2365 Fellowship Pk	90039	162	A
24	258	30th Street	476 30th St / near 563 29th Street	90266	162	B
25	200	Whitley Terrace	6666 Whitley Terr / 6640 Milner Road	90068	160	A
26	26	Ivan Hill upper	2605 Ivanhoe Dr / 2626 Ivan Hill Terr	90039	156	B
27	18	Landa-Edgewood	3541 Landa / 3633 Landa	90039	155	A
28	98	Clermont	438 Avenue 43 / 375 Canon Crest	90065	153	A
29	184	St. Andrews	5680 Tryon Rd / 1950 N. St. Andrews Pl	90068	153	B
30	192	Pelham	2823 Pelham Place / 2744 Westshire	90068	149	B
31	192	Woodshire double	2950 Belden Dr / near 1815 Beachwood	90068	148	A
32	34	Edendale	2248 Edendale / 2258 Fair Oak View Terr	90039	147	B
33	40	Landa-Wolcott	1926 Walcott / 2359 Landa	90026	146	B
34	46	Donaldson east	across fr 2202 Princeton / 2174 Echo Park	90026	143	B
35	192	Westshire	2935 Westshire Dr / 2810 Beachwood	90068	143	A
36	238	Ariba Path	1701 Via Arriba / trail junction	90274	141	B
37	106	Pullman	Pullman pathway / 5401 Monterey Road	90042	140	B
38	60	Descanso	3365 Descanso / 3200 Larissa	90026	139	B
39	68	Scotland Street	2232 Lyric / 2301 Hyperion	90027	137	B
40	200	Broadview Terr	2187 Broadview Terr / 6889 Yeager Place	90068	136	A
41	200	Adina-Passmore	3012 Passmore Dr / 3335 Adina Drive	90068	136	B
42	90	Tillie Street	1804 Kilbourn / 1811 Kemper	90065	135	A
43	34	Corralitas	across fr 2611 Corralitas / 2463 Corralitas	90039	133	B
44	60	Music Box	3278 Descanso / 935 Vendome	90026	133	B
45	60	Marathon	3278 Descanso / 935 Vendome	90026	133	B
46	90	Kilbourn	1645 Kilbourn / 3180 Future	90065	133	B
47	154	"The 100 steps"	3958 Dwiggins / 1243 Bonnie Beach	90063	133	B
48	184	Upper Glendowr	2763 Glendower Ave / 4800 Bryn Mawr	90027	133	A
49	82	Banbury Place	2669 Medlow Avenue / 2686 Cunard St	90065	132	B
50	90	Oneonta-Olancha	across fr 1105 Olancha / nr 1085 Oneonta	90065	132	A
51	106	Salient	5027 Montezuma / 701 Avenue 50	90042	132	C
52	46	Curran	1540 Curran / 2403 Valentine	90026	130	A
53	40	Ewing west	2004 Alvarado / 2003 Ewing	90039	129	B
54	146	Academy Street	4762 Academy/4765 Huntington Dr N.	90032	129	B
55	106	Granada	5322 Granada / 420 Avenue 54	90042	127	A
56	68	Cumberland Ave	3884 Clayton Av / 3953 Cumberland	90027	126	B

#	page	stairway	location: top / bottom	zip	steps	grade
57	68	Radio Walk (U)	3860 Franklin / 1848 Holly Vista	90027	126	B
58	106	Upper Bushnell	Pullman Pathway / 5417 Bushnell	90042	126	A
59	126	Hough	760 Avenue 66 / 6635 Hough	90042	126	A
60	46	Avalon west	1902 Lemoyne / 1907 Vestal	90026	125	A
61	46	Delta	1600 Lucretia / 1620 Delta	90026	125	B
62	238	Buena Path	601 Via del Monte / 396 Palos V Dr West	90274	125	B
63	192	Belden	2872 Belden Dr / 2795 Woodshire Dr	90068	124	B
64	212	Sumac Lane	309 Amalfi / 323 Sumac Ln.	90402	124	B
65	212	Sage Lane	271 Amalfi / 320 Mesa	90402	124	B
66	136	Mallard - Onyx	2602 Onyx / 2539 Mallard	90032	123	B
67	208	Posetano	17496 Revello / 17445 Posetano	90272	122	A
68	248	Upland Ave	457 Elber on / Upland 160' west of Pacific	90731	122	B
69	164	Angels Flight	351 S. Hill St. / 350 S. Olive Street	90013	121	B
70	192	Durand	2954 Durand / 2917 Belden	90068	118	B
71	208	Arno Way	242 Aderno Way / 300 Arno Way	90272	117	B
72	40	Peru	2378 Peru / 2366 Peru	90026	114	B
73	112	Myosotis	6203 Saylin / 6179 Kirby	90042	114	B
74	242	Lunada Canyon	2801 Via Buena / Lunada Canyon trail	90274	114	A
75	18	Tesla Avenue	2358 Moreno Dr / 2421 Kennilworth	90039	111	B
76	212	Arizona Ave	Arizona+Ocean / 1268 PCH	90401	111	B
77	18	Middle Swan	1784 Rotary / 1760 Redesdale	90026	110	B
78	68	Radio Walk East	2342 Lyric / 2413 Claremont	90027	110	B
79	200	Upper Paramount	2030 Paramount Dr / 2039 Glencoe Way	90068	110	B
80	60	Lwr Micheltorena	3315 Larissa / 3324 Sunset	90026	109	B
81	26	Easterly-Fanning	1771 Fanning / across fr 1809 Easterly	90026	108	B
82	258	Flintridge	near 440 St Katherine / 525 Palmerstone	91011	107	B
83	90	Hines-Brilliant	3726 Brilliant / 2400 Hines	90065	106	B
84	90	Arthur-Yorkshire	2359 Yorkshire / 2333 Arthur	90065	106	B
85	136	Galena Street	4521 East Rose Hill / 3420 Galena	90032	106	B
86	26	Silverwood N.(U)	1613 Silverwood / across fr 1601 Easterly	90026	103	B
87	136	Browne-Florizel	4534 Florizel St / 4537 Browne Ave	90032	103	B
88	154	Sunol Street	north:4030 CesarChavez/south:332 Sunol	90063	103	B
89	200	Lower Paramount	2032 Glencoe Way / 2033 High Tower Dr	90068	103	B
90	18	Elevado Street	1435 Elevado St / 3103 Hamilton Way	90026	102	B
91	98	Canyon Vista	331 Canyon Vista / 326 Avenue 43	90065	102	B
92	26	Lower Effie	1692 Mohawk / 2219 Effie	90026	101	B
93	54	Court Street	236 Lake Shore Terr / Glendale+Court	90026	101	B
94	54	Toluca	across fr 255 Emerald / 244 Toluca	90026	101	B
95	164	Bunker Hill	400 S. Hope / across from 630 W. 5th	90071	101	A
96	18	Upper Swan	1748 Webster / across fr 1784 Rotary	90026	100	B
97	54	Innis	804 E.Kensington Rd / 1302 Sunset Blvd	90026	100	B
98	126	Redwood-Tamarac	365 Tamarac Dr / 390 Redwood Dr	91105	99	A
99	126	Glenullen-Cherry	351 Cherry Dr / 360 Glenullen Dr	91105	99	A
100	146	Lower Phelps	2736 Lynnfield / 2852 Phelps	90032	99	B
101	34	Roselin	2104 Roselin / Silver Lake Court	90039	98	C
102	126	Elmwood-Redwood	395 Redwood Dr / 420 Elmwood Dr	91105	98	A
103	68	Radio Walk (L)	1849 Holly Vista / 1856 Deloz	90027	97	B
104	259	Mar Vista	3296 Indianapolis / 3297 Granville	90066	97	A
105	60	Upr Micheltorena	1330 Micheltorena / 3316 Larissa	90026	96	B
106	136	Coral Street	2351 Coral St / near 3830 Broadway	90031	96	B
107	40	El Moran	near 2032 El Moran / 2066 El Moran	90026	95	B
108	146	Upper Beagle	4419 Cato St / 4418 Beagle St	90032	95	B
109	146	Upper Far Place	2779 Chadwick Cr/2815 Lynfield Cir	90032	95	B
110	18	Meadow Valley	Acr fr 3328 Fernwood / 2009 Meadow Vly	90039	93	B
111	90	Crestmore Place	2640 Crestmoore Place / 2714 Crestmoore	90065	93	B
112	18	Landa-Lucille	3701 Landa / near 1843 Lucille	90039	92	B
113	60	Bellev-Coronado	side of 626 Coronado / 2416 Bellevue	90026	92	B

#	page	stairway	location: top / bottom	zip	steps	grade
114	208	Breve Way	17718 Revello / 17703 Castellammare	90272	91	B
115	18	Cicero Drive	1637 Cicero Dr / 1632 Redcliff St	90026	90	B
116	18	Hamilton Way	3324 Hamilton Way / 3329 Sunset Blvd	90026	90	C
117	126	Tamarac-Glenullen	362 Tamarac Dr / 363 Glenullen Dr	91105	90	A
118	26	Silverwood S.(U)	1525 Silverwood / 1480 Easterly	90026	89	B
119	200	Alta Loma Place	2186 Broadview Ter / 6836 Alta Loma Pl	90068	89	A
120	54	Clinton	across fr 617 Belmont / 700 block Glendale	90026	88	B
121	212	Hillside Lane	390 Vance / 419 Hillside	90402	88	B
122	212	Attilla Road	460 Entrada / 14100 Attilla	90402	88	C
123	60	Bellev-Alvarado	2132 Bellevue / 2112 Bellevue	90026	87	B
124	154	Miller-Van Pelt	1179 Van Pelt / 1174 Miller	90063	87	B
125	238	Somonte Trail	Across fr 824 V.Somonte/708 V.del Monte	90274	87	B
126	242	Via Romero Strs	Nr 1201 V. Romero / nr 1001 V.Ventana	90274	87	B
127	208	Revello	17804 Castellammare / 17737 Porto Marina	90272	86	B
128	258	Lacy Park	1401 Park Place / 1407 Virginia Road	91108	86	B
129	54	Crosby	1002 Crosby / 867 Laguna	90026	85	B
130	68	Shakespeare Bdg	3970 Franklin / 2056 Sanborn	90027	85	B
131	212	Santa Monica	1415 Ocean / nr 1425 P.C.H.	90401	85	B
132	18	Landa-Redesdale	3031 Landa / 2026 Redesdale	90039	84	B
133	146	Upper Phelps	2746 Chadwick Cir/2735 Lynnfield Cir	90032	83	B
134	200	Oakcrest Drive	7001 Woodrow Wilson / 3113 Oakcrest Dr	90068	83	B
135	18	Effie-Redesdale	1724 Rotary / 1705 Redesdale	90039	82	B
136	26	Silverwood S.(L)	1483 Easterly / Across fr 1433 Occidental	90026	82	B
137	34	Hidalgo	2470 Hidalgo / 2221 Electric	90039	82	B
138	106	Avenue 58	147 Avenue 58 / 200 Avenue 58	90042	80	B
139	120	Nolden	1961 Nolden / 1983 Nolden	90041	79	C
140	212	Mabury	249 Mabury / 278 Entrada	90402	79	B
141	212	Ocean Avenue	Between 262&350 Ocean Av	90402	79	B
142	18	Lower Swan	1760 Redesdale / 2958 Swan	90026	78	B
143	120	Arbor Dell	1100 Arbor Dell/ 1371 Hill Drive	90041	78	B
144	136	Montecito Street	near 3029 Johnston / 2817 Montecito	90031	78	B
145	34	Silver Lk Av(U)	2484 Silver Ridge / 2501 Lake View	90039	77	B
146	146	Lower Beagle	4418 Beagle/4388 Huntington Dr. So.	90032	77	B
147	26	Silverwood N.(M)	1601 Easterly / near 1606 Occidental	90026	75	B
148	146	Edison Walk	5246 Almont / 5253 Huntington Dr N.	90032	75	B
149	208	Lw Castellammare	17575 Castellammare / 17580 P.C.H.	90272	75	A
150	54	McDuff	1332 Laveta / behind 1501 Sunset	90026	74	C
151	184	Lower Glendowr	4800 Bryn Mawr / 2543 Glendower Ave	90027	74	A
152	18	Moreno Drive	2200 Moreno / 2201 W.Silver Lake Blvd	90039	73	B
153	146	Lower Far Place	2815 Lynnfield Cr/2763 Ballard St	90032	73	B
154	230	Palms	10830 Kingsland / 10825 Rose	90034	73	B
155	192	Hollyridge Loop	2300 Hollyridge Dr / 2178 Hollyridge	90068	72	B
156	68	Prospect walk (M)	1801 Holly Vista / 1740 Deloz	90027	71	A
157	98	Mavis	340 Mavis / 4567 Starling	90065	71	B
158	184	Glencairn	4811 Glencairn Rd / 4749 Bonvue Ave	90027	70	B
159	200	Wedgwood Place	6754 Wedgewood / 2133 Fairfield Av	90068	69	gated
160	208	Up Castellammare	top: 17606 Posetano	90272	69	B
161	154	East 6th Street	2755 E. 6th / 2728 E. 6th	90033	67	B
162	192	Allview	acr fr 2332 Allview Terr / 2333 Hollyridge	90068	67	B
163	54	Kent	1728 Kent / 700 block Glendale Blvd	90026	66	B
164	60	Robinson	832 Robinson / 827 Dillon	90026	66	B
165	60	Reno	511 Reno / 3001 London	90026	66	B
166	90	Cleland-Frieda	4832 Frieda / 4841 Cleland	90065	66	B
167	112	Sterling Walk	271 LaFollette/6155 Mt Angelus Drive	90042	66	B
168	54	Laveta Terrace	1349 Laveta / 1322 Laveta	90026	65	A
169	34	Red Car Viaduct	Red car path / near 2500 Riverside	90039	64	B
170	46	Lucretia	1546 Lucretia / 1701 Grafton	90026	64	C

#	page	stairway	location: top / bottom	zip	steps	grade
171	120	Tai chi	1007 Glen Arbor / across fr 7149 Figueroa	90041	64	B
172	126	Grace Walk	88 Grace Terrace / 54 Grace Walk	91105	63	B
173	136	Homer-Griffin	4433 Griffin Ave / 4426 Homer	90031	63	B
174	136	Avenue 41	4103 Griffin / 4102 Homer	90031	63	B
175	82	Hyper-Riverside	3101 Waverly/3100 Riverside	90039	62	B
176	106	Lower Bushnell	403 Wheeling Way / 5571 Via Mirasol	90042	62	B
177	106	Avenue 64	139 Avenue 64 / 201 Avenue 64	90042	61	B
178	192	Foothill	2241 Hollyridge Dr / 5951 Foothill Dr	90068	61	B
179	192	Holly Mont	6214 Holly Mont / 2071 Vista Del Mar	90068	61	B
180	208	Carthage Street	677 Via de la Paz / 670 Haverford	90272	61	B
181	212	East Rustic-Mesa	491 Mesa / 544 E. Rustic	90402	61	B
182	82	Avenue 37	3700 Roderick Road / 3637 Fletcher Drive	90065	60	B
183	98	Lynn	4932 Lynn / 4922 Lynn	90042	60	B
184	120	Saginaw	1301 Linda Rosa / 1450 Holbrook	90041	60	B
185	126	Sycamore Glen	240 Redwood Dr / 252 Sycamore Glen	91105	60	B
186	136	Griffin-Berenice	4507 Montecito Dr / 4430 Griffin Av	90031	60	B
187	54	Wallace	1100 West Edgeware / 1484 Wallace	90026	59	C
188	208	Bowdoin Street	773 Via de la Paz / 800 Haverford	90272	59	B
189	40	Oak Glen	2225 Lake Shore / 2034 Oak Glen	90039	58	B
190	40	Ewing sidewalk	2137 Ewing / 2161 Ewing	90039	58	C
191	98	Glenalbyn Way	4600 Glenalbyn / 4601 Marmion	90065	58	B
192	68	Prospect walk (L)	1811 Deloz / near 3976 Prospect	90027	57	A
193	26	Ivan Hill lower	2615 Ivan Hill Terr / 2617 Glendale Blvd	90039	56	B
194	90	Danforth Drive	776 Danforth / 4018 Marchena	90065	56	B
195	106	Abbott Place	429 Avenue 51 / 432 Avenue 52	90042	56	C
196	248	39th Street	430 West 39th / 3906 S. Bluff	90731	56	B
197	54	Glend-Bellevue	602 Belmont / corner Bellevue+Glendale	90026	55	C
198	106	Glen Mary Arch	Top: 4733 Figueroa	90065	55	B
199	164	Acadia Street	near 400 N. Hill / near 401 N. Broadway	90012	55	B
200	242	Carrillo-Zumaya	1136 Via Zumaya / 2624 Via Carrillo	90274	55	B
201	82	Hilda Avenue	1359 Romulus Dr / 1360 Hilda Av	91205	54	B
202	146	Beatie Place	2221 Lafler Rd / 5140 Bohlig Rd	90032	54	B
203	18	Murray Drive	1551 Murray Dr / 3359 Hamilton Way	90026	53	B
204	126	Upper Cherry Dr	437 Cherry Drive / Cherry Alley	91105	53	B
205	154	4th St Bridge Wst	SW bridge deck / near 500 S. Mateo	90033	53	C
206	200	Las Palmas	6684 Bonair Place / 6689 Emmett Terr.	90068	53	gated
207	248	11th Street	1100 S. Beacon / 1101 S. Harbor	90731	53	B
208	258	31st street	477 31st St / Sand Dune Park ramp	90266	53	B
209	248	8th Street	800 S. Beacon / 801 S. Harbor	90731	52	B
210	18	Lanterman Terr	2423 Lanterman / 2366 Panorama Terr	90039	51	B
211	154	4th St Bridge East	SE Bridge deck / near 401 S. Anderson	90033	51	C
212	192	Argosy Way	5818 Tuxedo Terrace / 2424 Argosy Wy	90068	51	B
213	126	Rosewood Terrace	1102 Lantana / 1113 Avenue 64	90042	50	B
214	248	9th Street	900 S. Beacon / 901 S. Harbor	90731	50	B
215	248	12th Street	1200 S. Beacon / 1101 S. Harbor	90731	50	B
216	164	110 Spiral Stairs	Southbound side/Northbound side	90012	49	B
217	112	Mt. Angelus	6218 Mt.Angelus Pl / 6171 Piedmont	90042	48	gated
218	212	Sycamore-Mesa	401 Mesa / 400 Sycamore	90402	48	B
219	212	Ocean Way	99 Ocean Way / 14700 PCH	90402	48	B
220	54	Sunset sidewalk	west: 1472 Sunset, east: 1428 Sunset	90026	47	B
221	120	Neola	near 4827 Neola Pl / 1321 Neola St	90041	47	C
222	164	1st St/Figueroa	near 900 W. 1st / near 100 N. Figueroa	90012	47	C
223	192	Vine Way	2100 Alcyona Dr / 6282 Vine Way	90068	47	B
224	212	Calif. Incline	Idaho+Ocean / 1200 Palisades Beach	90403	47	B
225	112	Andes Walk	244 Lamont / 6134 Garrison	90042	46	gated
226	154	4th Lorena east	NE bridge deck / across fr 321 Lorena	90063	46	B

#	page	stairway	location: top / bottom	zip	steps	grade
227	164	110 Solano Strs	110 pedestrian route / near 545 Solano	90012	46	C
228	34	Waverly Drive	2601 Waverly Dr/ Red car path	90039	45	B
229	106	Figueroa Walk N.	Top: 4733 Figueroa	90065	45	C
230	112	Grimke Walk	242 Wayland / corner Outlook+Lamont	90042	45	B
231	126	Evergreen Dr	610 Evergreen Dr / 1560 La Loma Rd	91105	45	C
232	164	San Fernando/110	110 pedestrian route / 4575 Sn Fernando	90031	45	C
233	126	Avon Avenue	1428 Capinero Dr / 1437 Cheviotdale	91105	44	B
234	154	1st Street Bridge	NW bridge deck / 132 Center	90033	44	B
235	200	Iris Place	6825 Iris Circle / 6831 Iris Drive	90068	44	B
236	68	Sunset Drive	3626 Sunset Dr / Ac from 1427 Sanborn	90027	43	B
237	126	Lower Cherry Dr	Cherry Alley / 1587 La Loma Road	91105	43	B
238	154	4thLorena west	SW bridge deck / near 404 S. Bernal	90063	42	C
239	164	Jarvis Street	near 628 Park Row / 702 Academy	90012	42	C
240	258	20th Street	429 20th Street / near 502 20th Street	90266	42	B
241	68	Sanborn	1575 Sanborn / Ac from 4001 Clayton	90027	41	B
242	54	Montana Street	Fairbank Stairs / 1396 Echo Park	90026	40	C
243	54	Glend-Sunset	across from 1910 Sunset / 1301 Glendale	90026	40	C
244	60	Manzanita St.	4043 Sunset / 1119 Manzanita	90026	40	B
245	90	Avenue 31	3147 Verdugo Place / 3140 Verdugo Road	90065	40	C
246	248	Elberon	Near 717 Elberon/Gaffey St by overpass	90731	40	B
247	259	Westchester	5915 Abernathy / 5868 W. 76th St.	90045	40	B
248	46	Preston	2051 Preston / across from 1633 Baxter	90026	39	B
249	68	Udell Minor	1982 Mayview / 3870 Udell	90027	39	B
250	82	Hyper-Glendale	top:bridge deck-northbound side	90039	39	C
251	120	Linda Rosa	1507 Linda Rosa / 1531 Linda Rosa	90041	39	B
252	120	Eucalyptus	6035 Eucalyptus Lane / 7149 Figueroa	90041	39	C
253	258	Holmby Hills	10506 Little Sta Monica/10495 Sta Monica	90025	39	C
254	242	Valdez-Zumaya	1325 Via Zumaya / 2640 Via Valdez	90274	38	B
255	68	Hoover Walk	4338 Prospect / 1654 Hoover	90027	37	B
256	126	Grace - Brocadero	95 Grace Terrace / ac fr Brocodero	91105	37	B
257	208	Lower Breve	top: across fr 17711 Porto Marina	90272	37	C
258	40	Alvarado split	1648 Alvarado / 1645 Alvarado	90039	36	C
259	60	Carondelet	107 Carondelet / faces 2417 Beverly Blvd	90057	36	B
260	68	Clayton Avenue	3819 Clayton Ave / 3915 Clayton Ave	90027	36	B
261	248	27th Street	2702 Peck / 674 W. 27th	90731	36	B
262	26	Berkeley sidewlk	2321 Berkeley-corner Berkeley+Mohawk	90026	35	C
263	34	Adelburt	across fr 2100 Roselin / 2566 Lake View	90039	35	B
264	90	Avenue 40	4001 Verdugo View / 3950 Scandia	90065	35	C
265	98	Vista Gloriosa	434 Vista Gloriosa / near 3440 Glenalbyn	90065	35	C
266	238	Arroyo Path	415-445 Palos V Dr W / 440 Via Almar	90274	35	B
267	126	Colorado Bridge	Colorado Bridge / Linda Vista Av	91105	34	C
268	136	Pyrites	2929 Pyrites St / 3033 Pyrites St	90032	34	C
269	242	Via Malona	47 V.Porto Grande / 50 Via Malona	90275	34	B
270	242	Ridgegate	Nr 28223 Covecrest/near 6238 Ridgegate	90275	34	B
271	34	Silver Lk Av(M)	2480 Lake View / Red Car Property	90039	31	B
272	136	Lower Tourmaline	Across from 2929 Pyrites	90032	31	C
273	200	Holly Hill	1970 N. Grace Ave / 2010 Holly Hill Terr.	90068	31	gated
274	242	Via Costa Verde	75 Via Costa Verde / near 28632 Highridge	90275	31	B
275	258	Flores de Oro	884 Flores de Oro / 803 Rollin	91030	31	B
276	34	Silver Lk Av(L)	Red Car Property / 2112 Silver Lake Ave	90039	30	C
277	40	Delta Alvarado	1678 Alvarado / 1677 Alvarado	90039	30	C
278	60	Hoover Bridge	Hoover+Temple / 200 block Silver Lake	90004	30	B
279	112	LaFollette Walk	222 Wayland / 263 Lamont	90042	30	B
280	220	Appleton Way	3428 Beethoven / 12900 Appleton Way	90066	30	B
281	248	Carolina sidewalk	3311 Carolina / 3337 Carolina	90731	30	B
282	46	Little Fargo	2041 Preston / 1630 Fargo	90026	29	B

#	page	stairway	location: top / bottom	zip	steps	grade
283	154	Verde	2400 Verde / 1200 block N. Soto	90033	29	C
284	238	Chico Path	2501 Via Ramon / 2500 Via Pinale	90274	28	B
285	54	Fairbanks	Montana Stairs / 1408 Fairbanks	90026	27	C
286	106	Raphael	5363 Raphael / 5374 Raphael	90042	27	C
287	112	Lwr Monte Vista	281 LaFollette / 246 Livermore	90042	27	gated
288	200	Whitley / Iris	6813 Iris Circle / 6814 Whitley Terrace	90068	27	B
289	248	29th Street	2910 Peck / 670 W. 29th	90731	27	B
290	112	Emerson Walk	Across fr 263 Lamont / 6176 Outlook	90042	26	gated
291	238	Chino Path	549 PV Dr West / 552 Via Almar	90274	26	B
292	46	Donaldson west	2200 Lemoyne / 2167 Vestal	90026	25	B
293	46	Ewing east	1711 Ewing / 1963 Preston	90026	25	B
294	200	Mary Jackson	2044 Grace Ave / near 6687 Whitley Terr	90068	25	B
295	242	Via Porto Grande	48 Via Costa Verde / 46 Via Porto Grande	90275	25	B
296	54	Lilac Terrace	Lilac Terrace / 1266 Lilac Place	90026	24	C
297	106	Avenue 66	near 235 Ave. 66 / Marmion & Avenue 66	90042	24	C
298	136	Hancock-Terry	3033 Terry Place / 2537 Hancock St	90031	24	C
299	18	Tracy Street	2321 Meadow Valley / 2424 Griffith Pk	90039	23	C
300	112	Vista Place	Across fr 6215 Vidette / 6247 Meridian	90042	23	C
301	154	Ramboz	across fr 1265 BonnieBch/3999 Ramboz	90063	23	C
302	200	Los Altos West	2067 Broadview Terr / 2131 High Tower Dr	90068	23	B
303	26	Silverwood N.(L)	near 1623 Occidental / 1618 Silver Lake	90026	22	C
304	98	Glenalbyn Walk	across fr 4555 Glenalbyn / 4547 Marmion	90065	22	B
305	112	Upr Monte Vista	281 Wayland / across from 281 LaFollette	90042	22	B
306	82	Delevan Drive	4035 Avenue 42 / 2872 Delevan Dr	90065	21	C
307	106	Figueroa brick	Top: 4645 Figueroa	90065	21	C
308	112	Avenue 55	5331 Raber / 1847 Avenue 55	90042	21	C
309	146	Huntington	5303 Hunt.Dr N/Huntington+Poplar	90032	21	C
310	164	Solano School	Across fr 617 Academy / 615 Solano	90012	21	B
311	26	Waterloo	2330 Effie Street / 1662 Waterloo	90026	20	C
312	120	Oak Grove	near 1040 Oak Grove in the meridian	90041	20	B
313	146	Carnegie Street	3757 Harriman/Collis+Carnegie	90032	20	C
314	238	Aromitas Path	501 Palos V Dr West / 452 Via Almar	90274	20	C
315	18	Landa sidewalk	in front of 3729 Landa	90039	19	C
316	26	Apex	2130 Apex / corner Glendale Bl & Apex	90039	19	C
317	106	Casa de Adobe	Top: 4605 Figueroa	90065	19	C
318	146	Castalia Ave	across fr 4953 Barstow/3240 Castalia	90032	19	C
319	40	Fargo sidewalk	2142 Fargo / 2146 Fargo	90039	17	C
320	106	Zigler Estate	Top: 4601 Figueroa	90065	16	B
321	120	Tipton	800 block Tipton Terr. / 5811 Tipton Way	90041	15	C
322	112	Mendota Street	4976 Mendota / across from 950 Ave. 50	90042	14	C
323	136	Sierra Sidewalk	2826 Sierra / 3628 Pomona	90031	14	C
324	248	7th & Harbor	150 W. 7th Street	90731	14	C
325	60	Vendome split	on meridian by 914 Vendome	90026	13	C
326	54	Montana-Elys Park	1331 Elysian Park Dr / 1306 Montana	90026	11	C
327	154	Fowler sidewalk	in front of 3233 Whiteside	90063	10	C
328	200	Los Altos East	2164 Rockledge Rd / 2112 High Tower Dr.	90068	10	C
329	220	Wave Crest Ave	Wave Crest pathway / 1101 Main	90291	10	C
330	242	Olivera-Valdez	2633 Via Valdez / 2648 Via Olivera	90274	10	C
331	18	Prkmn-Westerly	1300 Westerly Terr / 1213 Parkman Av	90026	GATED	
332	26	Fargo	2341 Fargo / across from 1965 Rockford	90039	GATED	
333	26	Upper Effie	2305 Effie St / 1661 Mohawk	90026	GATED	
334	60	West 5th Street	side of 626 Coronado / 2416 Bellevue	90057	GATED	
335	82	York Hill Place	2678 Banbury Place / 4051 York Hill Pl	90041	GATED	
336	112	Hosmer walk	243 LaFollette/across fr 6200 MtAng.Dr	90042	GATED	

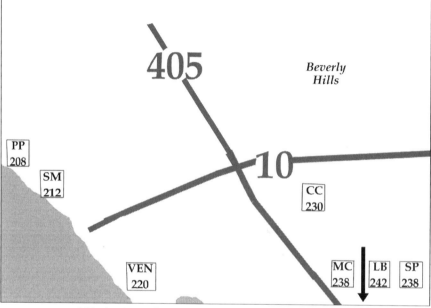

Overview maps of book coverage areas

101

405

Beverly
Hills

PP
208

SM
212

10

CC
230

VEN
220

MC
238

LB
242

SP
238

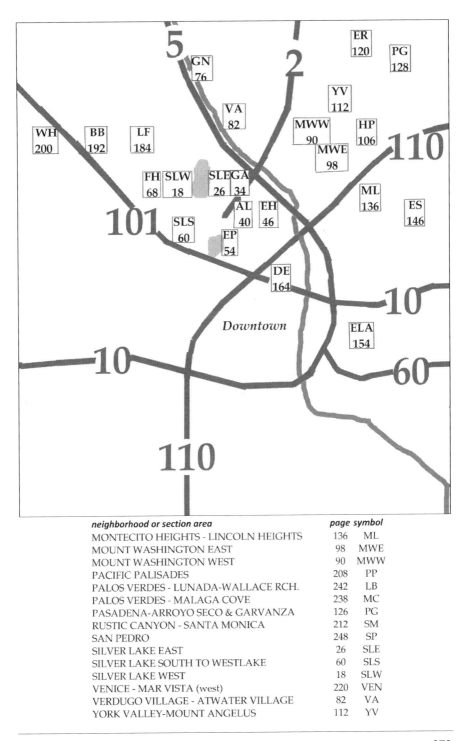

Front cover photo: Woodshire Double stairs – Beachwood Canyon – walk 16

Back cover photos; left to right, top to bottom:
Upper Fire Station trail-Malaga Cove- walk #21
Arroyo Seco Bike path- Highland Park- walk #10
Watts Towers – walk #14
Griffith Observatory – walk #15
Hough Stairs – Garvanza – walk #14 (Steve Matsuda photo)
Venice canal – walk # 19
Red Car Property with *The Big Parade V* – Allesandro valley – walk #1
Breed Street Shul – Boyle Heights – walk #12
Loma Vista-Allesandro stairway – walks #1 & #2

About the author: Bob Inman has lived nearly his entire life in Los Angeles residing in the neighborhoods of Silver Lake, Highland Park and Eagle Rock. His education followed a classic LA city path: Ivanhoe->King->Marshall->Occidental. As this book is published, he is completing a thirty year career in the California fruit and vegetable transportation field, most recently with Sunkist Growers. He is married to Barbara May. Their daughter Leah is a college student majoring in Human Geography. He has enjoyed a lifelong passion for walking, in wilderness as well as in cities. As of the end of 2013, Bob has led over 1800 participants on seven dozen walks in four years. He also assists Dan Koeppel on the Big Parade.

Also self-published by Bob Inman:
Paris 1945: a 120-page portfolio of photographs taken by Clarence Inman during WWII Paris, London, Copenhagen, Nurnberg and L'Orient with the story of John Ford's OSS Field Photo unit. Blurb Books – 2007

A Guide to the public stairways of Los Angeles: an 80 page color photo describer of 280 stairways within Los Angeles. Although slightly incomplete, this remains a compact, colorful and accurate list. Blurb Books – 2nd edition, 2010.

The 300: the way of the stairs across Los Angeles: with Andrew Lichtman and Ying Chen; a 140 page journal with photos and graphs of the first Urban thru-hike. Blurb Books, 2012. The entire content of this book is open to free reading on Blurb.com – search the author and or the title.

Made in the USA
San Bernardino, CA
03 February 2015